THE HUMAN PROSPECT

The Human Prospect

LEWIS MUMFORD

Edited by Harry T. Moore and Karl W. Deutsch

SOUTHERN ILLINOIS UNIVERSITY PRESS

CARBONDALE AND EDWARDSVILLE

COPYRIGHT © 1955 by Lewis Mumford
This edition published by arrangement with Beacon Press
All rights reserved
Arcturus Books Edition October 1965
Second Printing June 1970
This edition printed by offset lithography
in the United States of America
ISBN 0-8093-0172-5

Contents

Introduction

These essays and other writings of Lewis Mumford are taken about equally from his books and previously uncollected magazine articles. One of them has never been published before.

Although most of Lewis Mumford's books have remained in print across these thirty-odd years, and others are reappearing in new editions, the present volume will afford seasoned readers of this American philosopher a chance to renew their acquaintance with old favorites from both books and magazines; and it will give newcomers some appetizing samples which may lead them to the originals. This book is not, however, just a scattered collection of "bests": the editors have tried to present the man and his work as fully as possible, in such a way as to show that work as the development of a singleness of vision.

The idea for this volume was the editors', not Lewis Mumford's. His cordial assistance in occasionally providing copies of difficult-to-obtain articles (including the unpublished essay on "The 'New Man' and the 'New Woman'"), at the editors' request, is gratefully acknowledged; but they have independently chosen and arranged the material. The abundance and many-sidedness of Lewis Mumford's writings kept them in the torment of choosing between richness and richness, with the temptation to go on and on past the frontiers of allotted space. The brief outline of the contents of this book which follows will suggest why the editors selected what they did select. The writings themselves need no comment beyond this outline: they are their own voice.

"The Monastery and the Clock," the opening essay of Part One — The Roots of the Community — is an early chapter of *Technics and Civilization*. It is a keynote passage that shows how time-as-schedule became the dominating ritual of the modern world, and how, like so many of our other important observances, this one had a religious origin. The next selection, " The Origins of the American Mind " (the first chapter of *The Golden Day: A Study in American Literature and Culture*), was written several years before " The Monastery and the Clock," whose thesis it contains in embryo. But " The Origins of the American Mind " carries the story forward through the breakdown of medieval culture and the settlement of the raw continent by bringers of the new European ideas — political democracy, science and invention, Protestantism — which bore new seeds in the American wilderness. In the later chapters of *The Golden Day* (which George Santayana said was " the best book about America, if not the best American book that I have read "), Mumford deals with the great figures who emerged from the American community. For a fuller treatment of one of these, the editors have gone to Mumford's *Herman Melville* and its chapter on " Moby Dick," with its image of Americans in the international community of a whaling ship.

Part Two, Glimpses of the Man, gathers together some autobiographical material. The sketch, " A New York Adolescence," like the three poems which conclude the section, first appeared in the *New Yorker* magazine. The last two poems, " Fantasia on Time " and " The Taste of New England," are from Mumford's unfinished novel in verse, *Victor*. The prose passages on " The Land and the Seasons " and " The Kitchen " are intimate family pictures of the Mumfords' country home at Amenia, New York. They are from the author's biography of his son, *Green Memories: The Story of Geddes Mumford*.

The autobiographical tone continues in the first section of Part Three, Portraits of Persons: the lively James McMaster passages are from Mumford's short novel, *The Little Testament of Bernard Martin Aet. 30*. McMaster is a fictional composite of three men Mumford knew: Victor Branford, Alfred Zimmern, and Patrick Geddes. But McMaster is mostly

Geddes, the biologist and city planner, with whom Mumford deals directly in the essay which follows — a summary of the achievements of this remarkable man who was one of the important influences on the younger Mumford. The next two chapters are memorials to other friends: Joel Elias Spingarn and Henry Wright. They are not so well known as Geddes but, as these essays suggest, they have exerted a quiet influence on modern culture.

"The Imperial Façade," at the beginning of Part Four — Art and Civilization — is a chapter from *Sticks and Stones*. It supplies a full-dimensional backdrop for the following essay, which also has a New York setting. "The Metropolitan Milieu," one of Mumford's best-known essays, first appeared in the volume of tributes to Alfred Stieglitz in 1934. The discussions of Renoir and the surrealists are from the *New Yorker*, for which Lewis Mumford was art critic for five years until a year after moving to the country in 1936. "The America in Europe," which recently appeared in the European review *Comprendre*, reconsiders after a quarter of a century some of the themes of "The Origins of the American Mind." It deepens and expands them and shows the reciprocal influence of America upon Europe as it would not have been possible to show it at the time of *The Golden Day*. Thematically, Part Four goes back to architecture for its conclusion: "Monumentalism, Symbolism and Style," first published in the *Architectural Review* (British) and later in two issues of the *Magazine of Art* (American), is one of Lewis Mumford's fullest statements on the significance of architecture.

The fifth and last part of this book, Notes for a New Age, gives us the prophetic Mumford of the world of wars and rumors of wars. Even the chapter headings in this section bespeak the human and the humanistic values with which his work is always essentially concerned. Part Five begins with a "Program For Survival," from the book *Values For Survival*. Mumford has written later essays on the dangers of the atom bomb, but this 1945 statement is one of the most comprehensive he has made on the subject. It is brought up to date here by the addition of a recent letter he wrote to the editor of the *New York Times* about the hydrogen bomb; this letter, too, contains a program for survival. After it we may turn to a consideration of a " Re-birth of the Family " and a " Culture of the Family," chapters from *Faith For Living*. Next, the problems of individuals — of some individuals — are discussed in " The 'New Man' and the 'New Woman,' " a previously unpublished essay which was originally written as a chapter for *The Condition of Man*. The following two sections, which carry the discussion further — " Individuation and Socialization " and " From a Money-Economy to a Life-Economy " — are from *The Culture of Cities*. The next three related essays — " The New Mutation," " Love and Integration," and " The Renewal of Life " — are from *The Conduct of Life*. The last of them gives its name to the Renewal of Life series, which includes *Technics and Civilization*, *The Culture of Cities*, and *The Condition of Man*, as well as *The Conduct of Life*. For more than twenty years, these books have been Lewis Mumford's principal writing activity, and most of his other productions of the period have been as supplementary chapters to them. The Renewal of Life volumes are all in print, and a revised *Technics and Civilization* is scheduled for issue in a paperback edition.

Then, to conclude, there is a chapter from *The Conduct of Life*, " The Triumph Over Systems " (there called " The Fallacy of Systems "). This is one of Lewis Mumford's most important essays: he has said that it " gives the essence of my philosophy, and is a key to my whole thought and life."

HARRY T. MOORE

Babson Institute

Biographical Sketch

Lewis Mumford grew up in New York City, although he was born (October 19, 1895) in Flushing, Long Island. He was educated at Stuyvesant High School and later at City College, at New York University, at Columbia, and at the New School for Social Research. His writing career began at the age of fourteen, with contributions to popular technical magazines. During the First World War he was a radio operator in the Navy, and afterward became associate editor of the fortnightly *Dial;* in 1920 he was acting editor of the *Sociological Review* (London). In 1921 he married Sophia Wittenberg. Their son Geddes, born in 1925, was killed in Italy in 1944, in the Second World War; their daughter Alison was born in 1935.

The writing career of Lewis Mumford has a broad background of practical activity, which besides editorships includes service on the Board of Higher Education of the City of New York and on the Commission on Teacher Education of the American Council of Education. He was consultant on planning for the City and County Park Board, Honolulu (1938), and at Stanford University (1947), and on the United Nations (1951).

Lewis Mumford belongs to such organizations as: American Philosophical Society; American Academy of Arts and Sciences; National Institute of Arts and Letters; Council on Foreign Relations; Société Européenne de Culture (of which he is vice-president). He is an honorary associate of the Royal Institute of British Architects, an honorary member of the Town Planning Institute, an honorary member of the American Institute of Architects, and since 1947 has been honorary vice-president of the International Housing and Town Planning Federation. He has received the Townsend Harris Medal (for notable achievement), 1939; the Ebenezer Howard Memorial Medal (for services to the Garden City Movement), 1946; and the Medal of Honor, Fairmont Park Art Association, 1953.

His editorships, besides those previously mentioned, include the one he shared with Alfred Kreymborg and Paul Rosenfeld on *The American Caravan* (1927–36), a series of volumes which gave non-commercial writing the encouragement of publication. His teaching has included lectureships and professorships at the Geneva School of International Studies, at Dartmouth College, and at Columbia University, Stanford University, and the University of North Carolina; he is now professor in the School of Fine Arts at the University of Pennsylvania.

Lewis Mumford's work has appeared in magazines throughout the world. His books, which have also had world-wide publication, are: *The Story of Utopias*, 1922; *Sticks and Stones*, 1924; *The Golden Day*, 1926; *Herman Melville*, 1929; *The Brown Decades*, 1931; *Technics and Civilization*, 1934; *The Culture of Cities*, 1938; *Whither Honolulu?*, 1938; *Men Must Act*, 1939; *Faith For Living*, 1940; *The South in Architecture*, 1941; *The Condition of Man*, 1944; *City Development*, 1945; *Values For Survival*, 1946; *Green Memories: The Story of Geddes Mumford*, 1947; *The Conduct of Life*, 1951; *Art and Technics*, 1952; *In the Name of Sanity*, 1954; *The Transformation of Man* (World Perspective Series), 1956; *The City in History*, 1961 (National Book Award Winner, 1962); *The Highway and the City*, 1963. In recent years, Lewis Mumford's public honors have included the Royal Institute of British Architects' Gold Medal for Architecture, 1961, and the Presidency of the American Academy of Arts and Letters, 1962–63. Part six of a six-part film called *Lewis Mumford on the City*, produced by the National Film Board (Canada), won an award at the American Film Festival in 1964. Although he has made it a policy to refuse honorary degrees, he agreed to accept an Hon. LL.D. from the University of Edinburgh in 1965. At present Lewis Mumford is working on two books, one his autobiography and the other a new survey of human development in relation to technology. He expects the latter to do for *Technics and Civilization* what *The City in History* did for *The Culture of Cities;* it goes over quite different ground than the earlier volume, without repeating any of the material; it is a historical supplement rather than a revision or expansion.

In May 1965, the American Academy of Arts and Sciences awarded him the Emerson-Thoreau medal.

Southern Illinois University
February, 1965

Bibliographical Note

The following essays in this volume are taken from books (only the first publication is listed): "The Monastery and the Clock," from *Technics and Civilization* (Harcourt, Brace, 1934). "The Origins of the American Mind," from *The Golden Day* (Boni and Liveright, 1926). "Moby Dick," from *Herman Melville* (Harcourt, Brace, 1929). "The Land and the Seasons" and "The Kitchen," from *Green Memories: The Story of Geddes Mumford* (Harcourt, Brace, 1947). "James McMaster," from *The Little Testament of Bernard Martin Aet. 30,* in *The Second American Caravan,* edited by Alfred Kreymbourg and others (The Macaulay Co., 1928). "The Imperial Façade," from *Sticks and Stones* (Boni and Liveright, 1924). "The Metropolitan Milieu," from *America and Alfred Stieglitz,* edited by Waldo Frank and others (Doubleday, Doran, 1934). "Program For Survival," from *Values For Survival* (Harcourt, Brace, 1946). "Re-birth of the Family" and "Culture of the Family," from *Faith For Living* (Harcourt, Brace, 1940). "Individuation and Socialization" and "From a Money-Economy to a Life-Economy," from *The Culture of Cities* (Harcourt, Brace, 1938). "The New Mutation," "Love and Integration," "The Renewal of Life," and "The Triumph Over Systems," from *The Conduct of Life* (Harcourt, Brace, 1951).

The following material in this volume is taken from periodicals: "A New York Adolescence," from the *New Yorker,* Dec. 7, 1937. "Consolation in Time of War," from the *New Yorker,* Nov. 25, 1944. "Fantasia on Time," from the *New Yorker,* Dec. 30, 1939. "The Taste of New England," from the *New Yorker,* Feb. 27, 1943. "Patrick Geddes," from the *Architectural Review,* August 1950. "J. E. Spingarn," from the *Saturday Review of Literature,* Aug. 5, 1939. "Henry Wright," from the *New Republic,* July 29, 1936. "Pierre-Auguste Renoir," from the *New Yorker,* June 5, 1937. "Surrealism and Civilization," from the *New Yorker,* Dec. 19, 1936. "Monumentalism, Symbolism and Style," from the *Architectural Review,* April 1948. Letter to the Editor, from the *New York Times,* March 28, 1954. "The America in Europe," from *Comprendre* (Société Européenne de Culture), Numbers 10–11, 1954.

I

The Roots of the Community

The Monastery and the Clock

... One is not straining the facts when one suggests that the monasteries ... helped to give human enterprise the regular collective beat and rhythm of the machine; for the clock is not merely a means of keeping track of the hours, but of synchronizing the actions of men.

Where did the machine first take form in modern civilization? There was plainly more than one point of origin. Our mechanical civilization represents the convergence of numerous habits, ideas, and modes of living, as well as technical instruments; and some of these were, in the beginning, directly opposed to the civilization they helped to create. But the first manifestation of the new order took place in the general picture of the world: during the first seven centuries of the machine's existence the categories of time and space underwent an extraordinary change, and no aspect of life was left untouched by this transformation. The application of quantitative methods of thought to the study of nature had its first manifestation in the regular measurement of time; and the new mechanical conception of time arose in part out of the routine of the monastery. Alfred Whitehead has emphasized the importance of the scholastic belief in a universe ordered by God as one of the foundations of modern physics: but behind that belief was the presence of order in the institutions of the Church itself.

The technics of the ancient world were still carried on from Constantinople and Baghdad to Sicily and Cordova: hence the early lead taken by Salerno in the scientific and medical advances of the Middle Age. It was, however, in the monasteries of the West that the desire for order and power, other than that expressed in the military domination of weaker men, first manifested itself after the long uncertainty and bloody confusion that attended the breakdown of the Roman Empire. Within the walls of the monastery was sanctuary: under the rule of the order surprise and doubt and caprice and irregularity were put at bay. Opposed to the erratic fluctuations and pulsations of the worldly life was the iron discipline of the rule. Benedict added a seventh period to the devotions of the day, and in the seventh century, by a bull of Pope Sabinianus, it was decreed that the bells of the monastery be rung seven times in the twenty-four hours. These punctuation marks in the day were known as the canonical hours, and some means of keeping count of them and ensuring their regular repetition became necessary.

According to a now discredited legend, the first modern mechanical clock, worked by falling weights, was invented by the monk named Gerbert who afterwards became Pope Sylvester II, near the close of the tenth century. This clock was probably only a water clock, one of those bequests of the ancient world either left over directly from the days of the Romans, like the water-wheel itself, or coming back again into the West through the Arabs. But the legend, as so often happens, is accurate in its implications if not in its facts. The monastery was the seat of a regular life, and an instrument for striking the hours at intervals or for reminding the bell-ringer that it was time to strike the bells, was an almost inevitable product of this life. If the mechanical clock did not appear until the cities of the thirteenth century demanded an orderly routine, the habit of order itself and the earnest regulation of time-sequences had become almost second nature in the monastery. Coulton agrees with Sombart in looking upon the Benedictines, the great working order, as perhaps the original founders of modern capitalism: their rule certainly took the curse off work and their vigorous engineering enterprises may even have robbed warfare of some of its glamor. So one is not straining the facts when one suggests that the monasteries

— at one time there were 40,000 under the Benedictine rule —
helped to give human enterprise the regular collective beat
and rhythm of the machine; for the clock is not merely a
means of keeping track of the hours, but of synchronizing the
actions of men.

Was it by reason of the collective Christian desire to provide for the welfare of souls in eternity by regular prayers and
devotions that time-keeping and the habits of temporal order
took hold of men's minds: habits that capitalist civilization
presently turned to good account? One must perhaps accept
the irony of this paradox. At all events, by the thirteenth
century there are definite records of mechanical clocks, and
by 1370 a well-designed " modern " clock had been built by
Heinrich von Wyck at Paris. Meanwhile, bell towers had
come into existence, and the new clocks, if they did not have,
till the fourteenth century, a dial and a hand that translated
the movement of time into a movement through space, at all
events struck the hours. The clouds that could paralyze the
sundial, the freezing that could stop the water clock on a
winter night, were no longer obstacles to time-keeping: summer or winter, day or night, one was aware of the measured
clank of the clock. The instrument presently spread outside
the monastery; and the regular striking of the bells brought
a new regularity into the life of the workman and the mer-
chant. The bells of the clock tower almost defined urban
existence. Time-keeping passed into time-serving and time-
accounting and time-rationing. As this took place, Eternity
ceased gradually to serve as the measure and focus of human
actions.

The clock, not the steam-engine, is the key-machine of the
modern industrial age. For every phase of its development
the clock is both the outstanding fact and the typical symbol
of the machine: even today no other machine is so ubiquitous.
Here, at the very beginning of modern technics, appeared
prophetically the accurate automatic machine which, only

after centuries of further effort, was also to prove the final consummation of this technics in every department of industrial activity. There had been power-machines, such as the water-mill, before the clock; and there had also been various kinds of automata, to awaken the wonder of the populace in the temple, or to please the idle fancy of some Moslem caliph: machines one finds illustrated in Hero and Al-Jazari. But here was a new kind of power-machine, in which the source of power and the transmission were of such a nature as to ensure the even flow of energy throughout the works and to make possible regular production and a standardized product. In its relationship to determinable quantities of energy, to standardization, to automatic action, and finally to its own special product, accurate timing, the clock has been the foremost machine in modern technics: and at each period it has remained in the lead: it marks a perfection toward which other machines aspire. The clock, moreover, served as a model for many other kinds of mechanical works, and the analysis of motion that accompanied the perfection of the clock, with the various types of gearing and transmission that were elaborated, contributed to the success of quite different kinds of machine. Smiths could have hammered thousands of suits of armor or thousands of iron cannon, wheelwrights could have shaped thousands of great water-wheels or crude gears, without inventing any of the special types of movement developed in clockwork, and without any of the accuracy of measurement and fineness of articulation that finally produced the accurate eighteenth-century chronometer.

The clock, moreover, is a piece of power-machinery whose "product" is seconds and minutes: by its essential nature it dissociated time from human events and helped to create the belief in an independent world of mathematically measurable sequences: the special world of science. There is relatively little foundation for this belief in common human experience: throughout the year the days are of uneven duration, and not merely does the relation between day and night steadily change, but a slight journey from East to West alters astronomical time by a certain number of minutes. In terms of the human organism itself, mechanical time is even more foreign: while human life has regularities of its own, the beat of the pulse, the breathing of the lungs, these change from hour to hour with mood and action, and in the longer span of days, time is measured not by the calendar but by the events that occupy it. The shepherd measures from the time the ewes lambed; the farmer measures back to the day of sowing or forward to the harvest: if growth has its own duration and regularities, behind it are not simply matter and motion but the facts of development: in short, history. And while mechanical time is strung out in a succession of mathematically isolated instants, organic time — what Bergson calls duration — is cumulative in its effects. Though mechanical time can, in a sense, be speeded up or run backward, like the hands of a clock or the images of a moving picture, organic time moves in only one direction — through the cycle of birth, growth, development, decay, and death — and the past that is already dead remains present in the future that has still to be born.

Around 1345, according to Thorndike, the division of hours into sixty minutes and of minutes into sixty seconds became common: it was this abstract framework of divided time that became more and more the point of reference for both action and thought, and in the effort to arrive at accuracy in this department, the astronomical exploration of the sky focused attention further upon the regular, implacable movements of the heavenly bodies through space. Early in the sixteenth century a young Nuremberg mechanic, Peter Henlein, is supposed to have created " many-wheeled watches out of small bits of iron " and by the end of the century the small domestic clock had been introduced in England and Holland. As with the motor car and the airplane, the richer classes first took over the new mechanism and popularized it: partly be-

cause they alone could afford it, partly because the new bourgeoisie were the first to discover that, as Franklin later put it,
" time is money." To become " as regular as clockwork "
was the bourgeois ideal, and to own a watch was for long a
definite symbol of success. The increasing tempo of civilization led to a demand for greater power: and in turn power
quickened the tempo.

Now, the orderly punctual life that first took shape in the
monasteries is not native to mankind, although by now Western peoples are so thoroughly regimented by the clock that it
is " second nature " and they look upon its observance as a
fact of nature. Many Eastern civilizations have flourished on
a loose basis in time: the Hindus have in fact been so indifferent to time that they lack even an authentic chronology of
the years. Only yesterday, in the midst of the industrializa-
tions of Soviet Russia, did a society come into existence to
further the carrying of watches there and to propagandize
the benefits of punctuality. The popularization of time-keeping, which followed the production of the cheap standardized
watch, first in Geneva, then in America around the middle of
the last century, was essential to a well-articulated system of
transportation and production.

To keep time was once a peculiar attribute of music: it gave
industrial value to the workshop song or the tattoo or the
chantey of the sailors tugging at a rope. But the effect of the
mechanical clock is more pervasive and strict: it presides over
the day from the hour of rising to the hour of rest. When one
thinks of the day as an abstract span of time, one does not go
to bed with the chickens on a winter's night: one invents
wicks, chimneys, lamps, gaslights, electric lamps, so as to use
all the hours belonging to the day. When one thinks of time,
not as a sequence of experiences, but as a collection of hours,
minutes, and seconds, the habits of adding time and saving
time come into existence. Time took on the character of an
enclosed space: it could be divided, it could be filled up, it

could even be expanded by the invention of labor-saving in-struments.

Abstract time became the new medium of existence. Organic functions themselves were regulated by it: one ate, not upon feeling hungry, but when prompted by the clock: one slept, not when one was tired, but when the clock sanctioned it. A generalized time-consciousness accompanied the wider use of clocks: dissociating time from organic sequences, it became easier for the men of the Renaissance to indulge the fantasy of reviving the classic past or of reliving the splendors of antique Roman civilization: the cult of history, appearing first in daily ritual, finally abstracted itself as a special discipline. In the seventeenth century journalism and periodic literature made their appearance: even in dress, following the lead of Venice as fashion-center, people altered styles every year rather than every generation.

The gain in mechanical efficiency through co-ordination and through the closer articulation of the day's events cannot be overestimated: while this increase cannot be measured in mere horsepower, one has only to imagine its absence today to foresee the speedy disruption and eventual collapse of our entire society. The modern industrial régime could do without coal and iron and steam more easily than it could do without the clock.

The Origins of the American Mind

> . . . It is for the beginnings of a genuine culture, rather than
> for its relentless exploitation of materials, that the American ad-
> venture has been significant.

The settlement of America had its origins in the unsettle-
ment of Europe. America came into existence when the
European was already so distant in mind from the ancient
ideas and ways of his birthplace, that the whole span of the
Atlantic did not materially widen the gulf. The dissociation,
the displacement, and finally, the disintegration of European
culture became most apparent in the New World: but the
process itself began in Europe, and the interests that eventually
dominated the American scene all had their origin in the Old
World.

The Protestant, the inventor, the politician, the explorer,
the restless delocalized man — all these types appeared in Europe before they rallied together to form the composite American. If we can understand the forces that produced them,
we shall fathom the origins of the American mind. The
settlement of the Atlantic seaboard was the culmination of one
process, the breakup of medieval culture, and the beginning
of another. If the disintegration went farthest in America,
the processes of renewal have, at intervals, been most active
in the new country; and it is for the beginnings of a genuine
culture, rather than for its relentless exploitation of materials,
that the American adventure has been significant. To mark
the points at which the culture of the Old World broke down,
and to discover in what places a new one has arisen are the
two poles of this study. Something of value disappeared with

the colonization of America. Why did it disappear? Something of value was created. How did that come about? If I do not fully answer these questions, I purpose, at least, to put them a little more sharply, by tracing them to their historic beginnings, and by putting them in their social context.

II

In the thirteenth century the European heritage of medieval culture was still intact. By the end of the seventeenth it had become only a heap of fragments, and men showed, in their actions if not by their professions, that it no longer had a hold over their minds. What had happened?

If one tries to sum up the world as it appeared to the contemporaries of Thomas Aquinas or Dante one is conscious of two main facts. The physical earth was bounded by a narrow strip of seas: it was limited: while above and beyond it stretched the golden canopy of heaven, infinite in all its invitations and promises. The medieval culture lived in the dream of eternity: within that dream, the visible world of cities and castles and caravans was little more than the forestage on which the prologue was spoken. The drama itself did not properly open until the curtains of Death rang down, to destroy the illusion of life and to introduce the main scene of the drama, in heaven itself. During the Middle Ages the visible world was definite and secure. The occupations of men were defined, their degree of excellence described, and their privileges and duties, though not without struggle, were set down. Over the daily life lay a whole tissue of meanings, derived from the Christian belief in eternity: the notion that existence was not a biological activity but a period of moral probation, the notion of an intermediate hierarchy of human beings that connected the lowest sinner with the august Ruler of Heaven, the idea that life was significant only on condition that it was prolonged, in beatitude or in despair, into the next world. The beliefs and symbols of the Christian Church had guided men, and partly modified their activities, for roughly a thousand years. Then, one by one, they began to crack; one by one they ceased to be " real " or interesting; and gradually the dream that held them all together started to dissolve. When the process ceased, the united order of Christendom had become an array of independent and sovereign states, and the Church itself had divided up into a host of repellent sects.

At what point did medieval culture begin to break down? The current answer to this, " With the Renaissance," is merely an evasion. When did it finally cease to exist? The answer is that a good part of it is still operative and has mingled with the customs and ideas that have succeeded it. But one can, perhaps, give an arbitrary beginning and an arbitrary end to the whole process. One may say that the first hint of change came in the thirteenth century, with the ringing of the bells, and that medieval culture ceased to dominate and direct the European community when it turned its back upon contemporary experience and failed at last to absorb the meanings of that experience, or to modify its nature. The Church's inability to control usury; her failure to reckon in time with the Protestant criticism of her internal administration; the unreadiness of the scholastics to adapt their methods to the new interests and criteria of science; the failure to prevent the absorption of the free cities, the feudal estates, and the monasteries by the central government — these are some of the stigmata of the decline. It is impossible to give a date to all of them; but it is pretty clear that by the end of the seventeenth century one or another had come to pass in every part of Europe. In countries like England, which were therefore " advanced," all of them had come to pass.

It is fairly easy to follow the general succession of events. First, the bells tolled, and the idea of time, or rather, temporality, resumed its hold over men's minds. All over Europe, beginning in the thirteenth century, the townsman erected campaniles and belfries, to record the passing hour. Immersed in traffic or handicraft, proud of his city or his guild, the citizen began to forget his awful fate in eternity; instead, he noted the succession of the minutes, and planned to make what he could of them. It was an innocent enjoyment, this regular tolling of the hour, but it had important consequences. Ingenious workmen in Italy and Southern Germany invented clocks, rigorous mechanical clocks: they adapted the principle of the woodman's lathe and applied it to metal. Here was the beginning of the exact arts. The craftsman began by measuring time; presently he could measure millimeters, too, and with the knowledge and technique introduced by the clockmaker, he was ready to make the telescope, the microscope, the theodolite — all of them instruments of a new order of spatial exploration and measurement.

The interests in time and space advanced side by side. In the fifteenth century the mapmakers devised new means of measuring and charting the earth's surface, and scarcely a generation before Columbus' voyages they began to cover their maps with imaginary lines of latitude and longitude. As soon as the mariner could calculate his position in time and space, the whole ocean was open to him; and henceforward even ordinary men, without the special skill and courage of a Marco Polo or a Leif Ericsson, could travel to distant lands. So time and space took possession of the European's mind. Why dream of heaven or eternity, while the world was still so wide, and each new tract that was opened up promised, if not riches, novelty, and if not novelty, well, a new place to breathe in? So the bells tolled, and the ships set sail. Secure in his newly acquired knowledge, the European traveled outward in space, and, losing that sense of the immediate present which went with his old belief in eternity, he traveled backward and forward in time. An interest in archæology and in utopias characterized the Renaissance. They provided images of purely earthly realizations in past and future: ancient Syracuse and The City of the Sun were equally credible.

The fall of Constantinople and the diffusion of Greek litera-ture had not, perhaps, such a formative influence on this change as the historian once thought. But they accompanied it, and the image of historic Greece and Rome gave the mind a temporary dwelling-place. Plainly, the knowledge which once held it so firmly, the convictions that the good Christian once bought so cheaply and cheerfully, no longer sufficed: if they were not altogether thrown aside, the humanists began, with the aid of classic literature, to fill up the spaces they had left open. The European turned aside from his traditional cathedrals and began to build according to Vitruvius. He took a pagan interest in the human body, too, and Leonardo's St. John was so lost to Christianity that he became Bacchus without changing a feature. The Virgin herself lost her old sanctity. Presto! the Child disappeared, the responsibilities of motherhood were gone, and she was now Venus. What had St. Thomas Aquinas to say about theology? One could read the Phædo. What had Aristotle to say about natural history? Leonardo, unaided, discovered fossils in the Tuscan hills and inferred that the ocean was once there. Simple peasants might cling to the Virgin, ask for the intercession of the saints, and kneel before the cross; but these images and ideas had lost their hold upon the more acute minds of Europe. They had broken, these intellectual adventurers, outside the tight little world of Here and Eternity: they were interested in Yonder and Yesterday; and since eternity was a long way off and and we'll " be damnably moldy a hundred years hence," they accepted tomorrow as a substitute.

There were some who found it hard to shake off the medieval dream in its entirety; so they retained the dream and aban-doned all the gracious practices that enthroned it in the daily life. As Protestants, they rejected the outcome of historic Christianity, but not its inception. They believed in the Eucharist, but they did not enjoy paintings of the Last Supper. They believed in the Virgin Mary, but they were not softened by the humanity of her motherhood. They read, voraciously, the literature of the Ancient Jews, and the legends of that sect which grew up by the shores of Galilee, but, using their private judgment and taking the bare words as the sum and substance of their religion, they forgot the interpretations from the early Fathers to St. Thomas which refined that literature and melted it into a comprehensible whole. When the Protestant renounced justification by works, he included under works all the arts which had flourished in the medieval church and created an independent realm of beauty and magnificence. What remained of the faith was perhaps intensified during the first few generations of the Protestant espousal — one cannot doubt the original intensity and vitality of the protest — but alas! so little remained.

In the bareness of the Protestant cathedral of Geneva one has the beginnings of that hard barracks architecture which formed the stone tenements of seventeenth century Edinburgh, set a pattern for the austere meetinghouses of New England, and finally deteriorated into the miserable shanties that line Main Street. The meagerness of the Protestant ritual began that general starvation of the spirit which finally breaks out, after long repression, in the absurd jamborees of Odd Fellows, Elks, Woodmen, and kindred fraternities. In short, all that was once made manifest in a Chartres, a Strasbourg, or a Durham minster, and in the mass, the pageant, the art gallery, the theater — all this the Protestant bleached out into the bare abstraction of the printed word. Did he suffer any hardship in moving to the New World? None at all. All that he wanted of the Old World he carried within the covers of a book. Fortunately for the original Protestants, that book was a whole literature; in this, at least, it differed from the later protestant canons, perpetrated by Joseph Smith or Mrs. Mary Baker Eddy. Unfortunately, however, the practices of a civilized society cannot be put between two black covers. So, in many respects, Protestant society ceased to be civilized.

III

Our critical eyes are usually a little dimmed by the great release of energy during the early Renaissance: we forget that it quickly spent itself. For a little while the great humanists, such as More, Erasmus, Scaliger, and Rabelais, created a new home for the spirit out of the fragments of the past, and the new thoughts were cemented together by the old habits of medieval civilization, which persisted, among the peasants and the craftsmen, long after they had been undermined in the Church and the palace.

The revival of classic culture, however, did not give men any new power of command over the workaday routine of life, for the very ability to re-enter the past and have commerce with its great minds implied leisure and scholarship. Thus the great bulk of the community had no direct part in the revival, and if the tailor or the tinker abandoned the established church, it was only to espouse that segment called Protestantism. Tailors and tinkers, almost by definition, could *not* be humanists. Moreover, beyond a certain point, humanism did not make connections with the new experience of the Columbuses and the Newtons any better than did the medieval culture. If the criticism of the pagan scholars released a good many minds from Catholic theology, it did not orient them toward what was " new " and " practical " and " coming." The Renaissance was not, therefore, the launching out of a new epoch: it simply witnessed the breakdown and disruption of the existing science, myth, and fable. When the Royal Society was founded in London in the middle of the seventeenth century the humanities were deliberately excluded. " Science " was indifferent to them.

Once the European, indeed, had abandoned the dream of medieval theology, he could not live very long on the memory of a classic culture: that, too, lost its meaning; that, too, failed to make connections with his new experiences in time and space. Leaving both behind him, he turned to what seemed to him a hard and patent reality: the external world. The old symbols, the old ways of living, had become a blank. Instead of them, he took refuge in abstractions, and reduced the rich actuality of things to a bare description of matter and motion. Along this path went the early scientists, or natural philosophers. By mathematical analysis and experiment, they extracted from the complicated totality of everyday experience just those phenomena which could be observed, measured, generalized, and, if necessary, repeated. Applying this exact methodology, they learned to predict more accurately the movements of the heavenly bodies, to describe more precisely the fall of a stone and the flight of a bullet, to determine the carrying load of a bridge, or the composition of a fragment of " matter." Rule, authority, precedent, general consent — these things were all subordinate in scientific procedure to the methods of observation and mathematical analysis: weighing, measuring, timing, decomposing, isolating — all operations that led to results.

At last knowledge could be tested and practice reformed; and if the scientists themselves were usually too busy to see the upshot of their investigations, one who stood on the sidelines, Francis Bacon, was quick to announce their conclusion: science tended to the relief of man's estate.

With the aid of this new procedure, the external world was quickly reduced to a semblance of order. But the meanings created by science did not lead into the core of human life: they applied only to " matter," and if they touched upon life at all, it was through a post-mortem analysis, or by following Descartes and arbitrarily treating the human organism as if it were automatic and externally determined under all conditions. For the scientists, these new abstractions were full of meaning and very helpful; they tunneled through whole continents of knowledge. For the great run of men, however, science had no meaning for itself; it transferred meaning from the creature proper to his estate, considered as an independent and external realm. In short, except to the scientist, the only consequences of science were practical ones. A new view of the universe developed, naturally, but it was accepted less because of any innate credibility than because it was accompanied by so many cogent proofs of science's power. Philosophy, religion, art — none of these activities had ever baked any bread: science was ready, not merely to bake the bread, but to increase the yield of the wheat, grind the flour, and eliminate the baker. Even the plain man could appreciate consequences of this order. Seeing was believing. By the middle of the seventeenth century all the implications of the process had been imaginatively grasped. In 1661 Glanvill wrote:

I doubt not posterity will find many things that are now but rumors, verified into practical realities. It may be that, some ages hence, a voyage to the Southern tracts, yea, possibly to the moon, will not be more strange than one to America. To them that come after us, it may be as ordinary to buy a pair of wings to fly to remotest regions, as now a pair of boots to ride a journey; and to confer at the distance of the Indies by sympathetic conveyances may be as usual in future times as by literary correspondence. The restoration of gray hairs to juvenility, and renewing the exhausted marrow, may at length be effected without a miracle; and the turning of the now comparatively desert world into a Paradise may not improbably be effected from late agriculture.

IV

The process of abstraction began in the theology of Protestantism as an attempt to isolate, deform, and remove historic connections; it became habitual in the mental operations of the physical scientist; and it was carried over into other departments.

The extended use of money, to replace barter and service, likewise began during this same period of disintegration. Need I emphasize that in their origin Protestantism, physical science, and finance were all liberating influences? They took the place of habits and institutions which, plainly, were moribund, being incapable of renewal from within. Need I also emphasize the close historic interconnection of the three things? We must not raise our eyebrows when we discover that a scientist like Newton in seventeenth century England, or Rittenhouse in eighteenth century America, became master of the mint, nor must we pass by, as a quaint coincidence, the fact that Geneva is celebrated both as the home of John Calvin and as the great center of watches and clocks. These connections are not mystical nor factitious. The new financial order was a direct outgrowth of the new theological and scientific views. First came a mechanical method of measuring time: then a method of measuring space: finally, in money, men began more widely to apply an abstract way of measuring power, and in money they achieved a calculus of all human activity.

This financial system of measurement released the European from his old sense of social and economic limitations. No glutton can eat a hundred pheasants; no drunkard can drink a hundred bottles of wine at a sitting; and if any one schemed to have so much food and wine brought to his table daily, he would be mad. Once he could exchange the potential pheasants and Burgundy for marks or thalers, he could direct the labor of his neighbors, and achieve the place of an aristocrat without being to the manner born. Economic activity ceased to deal with the tangible realities of the medieval world — land and corn and houses and universities and cities. It was transformed into the pursuit of an abstraction — money. Tangible goods were only a means to this supreme end. When some incipient Rotarian finally coined the phrase, " Time is money," he expressed philosophically the equivalence of two ideas which could not possibly be combined, even in thought, so long as money meant houses, food, pictures, and time meant only what it does in Bergson's *durée*, that is, the succession of organic experiences.

Does all this seem very remote from the common life? On the contrary, it goes to the roots of every activity. The difference between historical periods, as the late T. E. Hulme pointed out, is a difference between the categories of their thought. If we have got on the trail of their essential categories, we have a thread which will lead outward into even remote departments of life. The fact is that from the seventeenth century onward, almost every field was invaded by this process of abstraction. The people not affected were either survivals from an older epoch, like the orthodox Jews and Roman Catholics in theology, or the humanists in literature, or they were initiators, working through to a new order — men like Lamarck, Wordsworth, Goethe, Comte.

Last and most plainly of all, the disintegration of medieval culture became apparent in politics. Just as " matter," when examined by the physicist, is abstracted from the esthetic matrix of our experience, so the " individual " was abstracted by the political philosopher of the new order from the bosom of human society. He ceased, this individual, to maintain his omnipresent relations with city, family, household, club, college, guild, and office: he became the new unit of political society. Having abstracted this purely conceptual person in thought — he had, of course, no more actual existence than an angel or a cherub — the great problem of political thinking in the eighteenth century became: How shall we restore him to society? — for somehow we always find man, as Rousseau grimly said, in chains, that is, in relations with other human beings. The solution that Rousseau and the dominant schools of the time offered was ingenious: each individual is endowed with natural rights, and he votes these political rights into society, as the shareholder votes his economic rights into a trading corporation. This principle of consent was necessary to the well-being of a civil society; and assent was achieved, in free political states, through the operation of the ballot, and the delivery of the general will by a parliament.

The doctrine broke the weakening chain of historical continuity in Europe. It challenged the vested interests; it was ready to declare the existing corporations bankrupt; it was prepared to wipe away the traditional associations and nets of privileges which maintained the clergy, the nobility, the guilds. On its destructive side, the movement for political liberty, like that for free contract, free association, and free investigation, was sane and reasonable; for the abuses of the past were genuine and the grievances usually had more than a small touch of justice. We must not, however, be blind to the consequences of all these displacements and dissociations. Perhaps the briefest way of characterizing them is to say that they made America inevitable. To those who were engaged in political criticism, it seemed that a genuine political order had been created in the setting up of free institutions; but we can see now that the process was an inevitable bit of surgery, rather than the beginning of a more organic form of political association. By 1852 Henry James, Sr., was keen enough to see what had happened. He observed:

Democracy is not so much a new form of political life as a dissolution and disorganization of the old forms. It is simply a resolution of government into the hands of the people, a taking down of that which has before existed, and a recommitment of it to its original sources, but it is by no means the substitution of anything else in its place.

V

Now we begin to see a little more clearly the state of mind out of which the great migrations to the New World became possible. The physical causes have been dwelt on often enough; it is important to recognize that a cultural necessity was at work at the same time. The old culture of the Middle Ages had broken down; the old heritage lingered on only in the "backward" and "unprogressive" countries like Italy and Spain, which drifted outside the main currents of the European mind. Men's interests became externalized — externalized and abstract. They fixed their attention on some narrow aspect of experience, and they pushed that to the limit. Intelligent people were forced to choose between the fossilized shell of an old and complete culture, and the new culture, which in origin was thin, partial, abstract, and deliberately indifferent to man's proper interests. Choosing the second, our Europeans already had one foot in America. Let them suffer persecution, let the times get hard, let them fall out with their governments, let them dream of worldly success — and they will come swarming over the ocean. The groups that had most completely shaken off the old symbolisms were those that were most ready for the American adventure: they turned themselves easily to the mastery of the external environment. To them matter alone mattered.

The ultimate results of this disintegration of European culture did not come out, in America, until the nineteenth century. But its immediate consequence became visible, step by step, in the first hundred and fifty years or so of the American settlement. Between the landing of the first colonists in Massachusetts, the New Netherlands, Virginia, and Maryland, and the first thin trickle of hunters that passed over the Alleghenies, beginning figuratively with Daniel Boone in 1775, the communities of the Atlantic seaboard were outposts of Europe: they carried their own moral and intellectual climate with them.

During this period, the limitations in the thought of the intellectual classes had not yet wrought themselves out into defects and malformations in the community itself: the house, the town, the farm were still modeled after patterns formed in Europe. It was not a great age, perhaps, but it had found its form. Walking through the lanes of Boston, or passing over the wide lawns to a manor house in Maryland, one would have had no sense of a great wilderness beckoning in the beyond. To tell the truth, the wilderness did not beckon: these solid townsmen, these freeholders, these planters, were content with their civil habits; and if they thought of expansion, it was only over the ocean, in search of Palladian designs for their houses, or of tea and sperm-oil for their personal comfort. On the surface, people lived as they had lived in Europe for many a year.

In the first century of colonization, this life left scarcely any deposit in the mind. There was no literature but a handful of verses, no music except the hymn or some surviving Elizabethan ballad, no ideas except those that circled around the dogmas of Protestantism. But, with the eighteenth century, these American communities stepped fully into the sphere of European ideas, and there was an American equivalent for every new European type. It is amusing to follow the leading biographies of the time. Distinguished American figures step onto the stage, in turn, as if the Muse of History had prepared their entrances and exits. Their arrangement is almost diagrammatic: they form a résumé of the European mind. In fact, these Edwardses and Franklins seem scarcely living characters: they were Protestantism, Science, Finance, Politics.

The first on the stage was Jonathan Edwards: he figured in American thought as the last great expositor of Calvinism. Edwards wrote like a man in a trance, who at bottom is aware that he is talking nonsense; for he was in love with beauty of the soul, like Plato before him, and it was only because he was caught in the premises of determinism that, with a heavy conscience, he followed his dire train of thought to its destination. After Edwards, Protestantism lost its intellectual backbone. It developed into the bloodless Unitarianism of the early nineteenth century, which is a sort of humanism without courage, or it got caught in orgies of revivalism, and, under the name of evangelical Christianity, threw itself under the hoofs of more than one muddy satyr. There were great Protestant preachers after Edwards, no doubt: but the triumph of a Channing or a Beecher rested upon personal qualities; and they no longer drew their thoughts from any deep well of conviction.

All the habits that Protestantism developed, its emphasis upon industry, upon self-help, upon thrift, upon the evils of "idleness" and "pleasure," upon the worldliness and wicked-ness of the arts, were so many gratuitous contributions to the industrial revolution. When Professor Morse, the inventor of the telegraph, was still a painter, traveling in Italy, he re-corded in one of his letters the animus that pervaded his re-ligious creed: the testimony loses nothing by being a little be-lated. He wrote:

> I looked around the church to ascertain what was the effect upon the multitude assembled. . . . Everything around them, instead of aiding devotion, was entirely calculated to destroy it. The imagina-tion was addressed by every avenue; music and painting pressed into the service of — not religion but the contrary — led the mind away from the contemplation of all that is practical in religion to the charms of mere sense. No instruction was imparted; none ever seems to be intended.

It is but a short step from this attitude to hiring revivalist mountebanks to promote factory morale; nor are these thoughts far from that fine combination of commercial zeal and pious effort which characterize such auxiliaries as the YMCA. The fictions of poetry and the delusions of feeling were the bugbears of Gradgrind, Bounderby, and M'Choak-umchild in Dickens's classic picture of industrialism: for the shapes and images they called forth made those which were familiar to the Protestant mind a little dreary and futile. It was not merely that Protestantism and science had killed the old symbols: they must prevent new ones from developing: they must abolish the contemplative attitude in which art and myth grow up, and create new forms for man's activities. Hence the fury of effort by which the leaders of the new day diverted energies to quantitative production. The capacity to do work, which the new methods in industry had so enormously increased, gave utilitarian objects an importance they had not hitherto possessed. Did not God's Word say: " Increase and multiply "? If babies, why not goods: if goods, why not dollars? Success was the Protestant miracle that justified man's ways to God.

The next figure that dominated the American scene stood even more completely for these new forces. He was, according to the pale lights of his time, a thoroughly cultivated man, and in his maturity he was welcomed in London and Paris as the equal of scientists like Priestley and Erasmus Darwin, and of scholars like D'Alembert and D'Holbach. As a citizen, by choice, of Philadelphia, Benjamin Franklin adopted the plain manners and simple thrifty ways of the Quakers. He went into business as a publisher, and with a sort of sweet acuteness in the pursuit of money, he imparted the secrets of his success in the collection of timely saws for which he became famous. The line from Franklin through Samuel Smiles to the latest advertisements for improving one's position and doubling one's income, in the paper that dates back to Franklin's ownership, is a pretty direct one. If one prefers Franklin's bourgeois qualities to those of his successors, it is only perhaps because his life was more fully rounded. If he was not without the usurious habits of the financier, he had also the dignity and freedom of the true scientist.

For Franklin was equally the money-maker, the scientist, the inventor, and the politician, and in science his fair boast was that he had not gained a penny by any of his discoveries. He experimented with electricity; he invented the lightning rod; he improved the draft of chimneys; in fact, on his last voyage home to America, shortly before his death, he was still improving the draft of chimneys. Finally he was a Deist: he had gotten rid of all the " gothick phantoms " that seemed so puerile and unworthy to the quick minds of the eighteenth century — which meant that he was completely absorbed in the dominant abstractions and myths of his own time, namely, matter, money, and political rights. He accepted the mechanical concept of time: time is money; the importance of space: space must be conquered; the desirability of money: money must be made; and he did not see that these, too, are phantoms, in preoccupation with which a man may lose most of the advantages of a civilized life. As a young man, Franklin even invented an elaborate system of moral-bookkeeping: utilitarianism can go no further.

Although Franklin's sagacity as a statesman can hardly be overrated, for he had both patience and principle, the political side of the American thought of his time is best summed up in the doctrines of a new immigrant, that excellent friend of humanity, Thomas Paine. Paine's name has served so many purposes in polemics that scarcely anyone seems to take the trouble to read his books: and so more than one shallow judgment has found its way into our histories of literature, written by worthy men who were incapable of enjoying a sound English style, or of following, with any pleasure, an honest system of thought, clearly expressed. *The Rights of Man* is as simple as a geometrical theorem; it contains, I think, most of what is valid in political libertarianism. I know of no other thinker who saw more clearly through the moral humbug that surrounds a good many theories of government. Said Paine:

Almost everything appertaining to the circumstances of a nation has been absorbed and confounded under the general and mysterious word government. Though it avoids taking to its account the errors it commits and the mischiefs it occasions, it fails not to arrogate to itself whatever has the appearance of prosperity. It robs industry of its honors by pedantically making itself the cause of its effects; and purloins from the general character of man the merits that appertain to him as a social being.

Passage after passage in *The Rights of Man* and *The Age of Reason* is written with the same pithiness. Paine came to America as an adult, and saw the advantages of a fresh start. He believed that if first principles could be enunciated, here, and here alone, was a genuine opportunity to apply them. He summed up the hope in reason and in human contrivance that swelled through the eighteenth century. Without love for any particular country, and without that living sense of history which makes one accept the community's past, as one accepts the totality of one's own life, with all its lapses and mistakes, he was the vocal immigrant, justifying in his political and religious philosophy the complete break he had made with old ties, affections, allegiances.

Unfortunately, a man without a background is not more truly a man: he has merely lost the scenes and institutions which gave him his proper shape. If one studies him closely, one will find that he has secretly arranged another background, made up of shadows that linger in the memory, or he is uneasy and restless, settles down, moves on, comes home again, lives on hopeless tomorrows, or sinks back into mournful yesterdays. The immigrants who came to America after the War of Independence gave up their fatherland in exchange for a Constitution and a Bill of Rights: they forfeited all the habits and institutions which had made them men without getting anything in exchange except freedom from arbitrary misrule. That they made the exchange willingly proves that the conditions behind them were intolerable; but that the balance was entirely in favor of the new country is something that we may well doubt. When the new settlers migrated in bodies, like the Moravians, they sometimes managed to maintain an effective cultural life; when they came alone, as " free individuals," they gained little more than cheap land and the privileges of the ballot box. The land itself was all to the good; and no one minded the change, or felt any lack, so long as he did not stop to compare the platitudes of Fourth of July orations with the actualities of the Slave Trade, the Constitutional Conventions, Alien and Sedition Acts, and Fugitive Slave Laws.

It was possible for Paine, in the eighteenth century, to believe that culture was served merely by the absence of a church, a state, a social order such as those under which Europe labored. That was the error of his school, for the absence of these harmful or obsolete institutions left a vacancy in society, and that vacancy was filled by work, or more accurately speaking, by busywork, which fatigued the body and diverted the mind from the things which should have enriched it. Republican politics aided this externalism. People sought to live by politics alone; the national state became their religion. The flag, as Professor Carleton Hayes has shown, supplanted the cross, and the Fathers of the Constitution the Fathers of the Church.

The interaction of the dominant interests of industry and politics is illustrated in Paine's life as well as Franklin's. Paine was the inventor of the take-down iron bridge. Indeed, politics and invention recurred rhythmically in his life, and he turned aside from his experiments on the iron bridge to answer Edmund Burke's attack on the French Revolution. As he himself said:

> The War of Independence energized invention and lessened the catalogue of impossibilities. . . . As one among thousands who had borne a share in that memorable revolution, I returned with them to the enjoyment of a quiet life, and, that I might not be idle, undertook to construct a bridge of a single arch for this river [the Schuylkill].

That I might not be idle! What a tale those words tell! While the aristocracy was in the ascendant, patient hirelings used to apply their knowledge of hydraulics to the working of fountains, as in Versailles, or they devised automatic chess-players, or they contrived elaborate clocks which struck the hour, jetted water, caused little birds to sing and wag their tails, and played selections from the operas. It was to such inane and harmless performances that the new skills in the exact arts were first put. The bored patron was amused, life plodded on; nothing was altered. But in the freedom of the new day, the common man, as indifferent to the symbols of the older culture as the great lords and ladies, innocent of anything to occupy his mind, except the notion of controlling matter and mastering the external world — the common man turned to inventions. Stupid folk drank heavily, ate gluttonously, and became libertines; intelligent, industrious men like Franklin and Paine turned their minds to increasing the comforts and conveniences of existence. Justification by faith: that was politics — the belief in a new heaven and a new earth to be established by regular elections and parliamentary debate. Justification by works: that was invention. No frivolities entered this new religion. The new devices all saved labor, decreased distances, and in one way or another multiplied riches.

With these inventors, the American, like his contemporary in Europe, began the utilitarian conquest of his environment. From this time on, men with an imaginative bias like Morse, the pupil of Benjamin West, men like Whitney, the schoolteacher, like Fulton, the miniature painter, turned to invention or at least the commercial exploitation of inventions without a qualm of distrust: to abandon the imaginative arts seemed natural and inevitable, and they no longer faced the situation, as the painters of the Renaissance had done, with a divided mind. Not that America began or monopolized the developments of the Industrial Revolution: the great outbreak of technical patents began, in fact, in England about 1760, and the first inklings of the movement were already jotted down in Leonardo da Vinci's notebooks. The point is that in Europe heavy layers of the old culture kept large sections of the directing classes in the old ways. Scholars, literary men, historians, artists still felt no need of justifying themselves by exclusive devotion to practical activities. In America, however, the old culture had worn thin, and in the rougher parts of the country it did not exist. No one in America was unaffected by the progress of invention; each improvement was quickly cashed in. When Stendhal wrote *De l'Amour*, the

American love of comfort had already become a by-word: he refers to it with contempt.

Given an old culture in ruins, and a new culture *in vacuo*, this externalizing of interest, this ruthless exploitation of the physical environment was, it would seem, inevitable. Protestantism, science, invention, political democracy, all of these institutions denied the old values; all of them, by denial or by precept or by actual absorption, furthered the new activities. Thus in America the new order of Europe came quickly into being. If the nineteenth century found us more raw and rude, it was not because we had settled in a new territory; it was rather because our minds were not buoyed up by all those memorials of a great past that floated over the surface of Europe. The American was thus a stripped European; and the colonization of America can, with justice, be called the dispersion of Europe — a movement carried on by people incapable of sharing or continuing its past. It was to America that the outcast Europeans turned, without a Moses to guide them, to wander in the wilderness; and here they have remained in exile, not without an occasional glimpse, perhaps, of the promised land.

Moby Dick

Moby Dick . . . brings together the two dissevered halves of the modern world and the modern self — its positive, practical, scientific, externalized self, bent on conquest and knowledge, and its imaginative, ideal half, bent on the transposition of conflict into art, and power into humanity.

I

Before we can take the measure of *Moby Dick* we must throw aside our ordinary measuring sticks: one does not measure Saturn with the aid of an opera glass and a dress-maker's tape. The conventional critic has dismissed *Moby Dick* because it is " not a novel," or if it is a novel, its story is marred by all sorts of extraneous material, history, natural history, philosophy, mythological excursions, what-not. This sort of criticism would belittle *Moby Dick* by showing that it does not respect canons of a much pettier nature than the work itself, or because its colossal bulk cannot be caught in the herring-net of the commonplace story or romance. Even Mr. John Freeman, one of the most sympathetic interpreters of Melville, falls into this error; for, while acknowledging the great qualities of *Moby Dick*, he refers to its " digressions and delays " as if they were in fact digressions and delays; that is, as if the " action " in the common novelist's development of plot carried the thread of the story.

The matter is very easily put to rights if we simply abandon these false categories altogether. *Moby Dick* stands by itself as complete as the *Divine Comedy* or the *Odyssey* stands by itself. Benedetto Croce has correctly taught us that every work of art is indeed in this same position: that it is uniquely what it is, and cannot be understood except in terms of its own purpose. If, for purely practical reasons, we ignore this in dealing with the ruck of novels and stories, because their inner purpose is so insignificant, we must respect it strictly when we confront a work that does not conspicuously conform to the established canons; for, needless to say, an imaginative work of the first rank will disclose itself through its differences and its departures, by what it originates, rather than by what it is derived from or akin to. Had Melville seriously sought in *Moby Dick* to rival the work of Trollope or Reade or Dickens, had he simply desired to amuse and edify the great bourgeois public that consumed its three-decker novels as it consumed its ten-course public dinners, and wanted no delay in the service, no hitch in the round of food, drink, toasts, speeches, and above all, no unaccustomed victuals on such occasions, then *Moby Dick* would have been a mistake and failure. But one cannot count as a failure what was never an attempt. *Moby Dick* does not belong to this comfortable bourgeois world, any more than horsehair shirts or long fasts; it neither aids digestion nor increases the sense of warm drowsy good nature that leads finally to bed: and that is all there is to it.

The same criticism that disposes of the notion that *Moby Dick* is a bad novel, by admitting freely that it is not a novel at all, equally disposes of its lack of verisimilitude. Although Melville was at first challenged on his facts, such as the ramming of the *Pequod* by Moby Dick, events were just as kind to his reputation here as they were in the case of *Typee:* for while *Moby Dick* was on the press, news came of the sinking of the whaler *Ann Alexander* by the ferocious attack of a whale. No one of authority has attempted to quarrel with Melville's descriptions of the life and habits of whalemen and the whale: the testimony of every observer is that Melville left very little for any one else to say about the subject. This does not, however, dispose of the charge; for those who are wisely captious of Melville here will confine themselves to saying that no such crew ever existed, no such words ever passed human mouth, and no such thoughts could enter the mind of a Nantucketer as entered Ahab's.

Again, one is tempted to grant the objection; for it makes no difference in the value of *Moby Dick* as a work of art. In the realistic convention, *Moby Dick* would be a bad book: it happens that the story is projected on more than one plane, and a good part of it belongs to another, and equally valid, convention. Melville himself was aware of the difference, and early in the book he calls upon the Spirit of Equality, which has spread its royal mantle of humanity over all his kind, to defend him against all mortal critics " if, then, to the meanest mariners, and renegades, and castaways, I shall here-after ascribe high qualities, though dark; weave round them tragic graces; if even the most mournful, perchance the most abased among them all shall at times lift himself to the exalted mounts; if I shall touch that workman's arm with some ethereal light; if I shall spread the rainbow over his disastrous set of sun." Now, the convention in which Melville cast this part of *Moby Dick* was foreign to the nineteenth century; obscure people, like Beddoes, alone essayed it: to create these ideal-ized figures called for such reserves of power that only minor poets, for the most part, unconscious of their weaknesses, attempted the task.

The objections to Melville's use of this convention would be fair enough if, like the minor poets, he failed; but, through his success, one sees that the limitations of naturalism are no closer to reality than the limitations of poetic tragedy; and, on the contrary, Melville's valiant use of this convention en-abled him to present a much fuller picture of reality than the purely external suggestions of current realism would have per-mitted him to show. What we call realism is a method of approaching reality: an external picture of a Cowperwood or a Gantry may have as little human truth in it as a purely fanciful description of an elf: and the artist who can draw upon more than one convention is, at all events, free from the curious illusion, so common in the nineteenth century, alike in philosophy, with its pragmatism, in science, with its dogmatic materialism, and in imaginative writing, with its realism, that this convention is not limited, and so far arbitrary, but the very stuff and vitals of existence. The question to settle is not: Did an Ahab ever sail from Nantucket? The question is: Do Ahab and Stubb and Starbuck and Tashtego live within the sphere where we find them? The answer is that they are tremendously alive; for they are aspects of the spirit of man. At each utterance, one feels more keenly their imaginative embodiment; so that by the time Ahab breaks into his loftiest Titanisms, one accepts his language, as one accepts his pride: they belong to the fiber and essence of the man. Ahab is a reality in relation to *Moby Dick*; and when Melville projects him, he ceases to be incredible, because he is alive.

We need not concern ourselves particularly with those who look upon *Moby Dick* solely as a sort of World's Almanac or Gazetteer of the Whaling Industry, unhappily marred by the highly seasoned enticements of the narrative. This criticism is, indeed, but the other side of the sort of objection I have disposed of; and it tells more about the limitations of the reader than it does about the quality of *Moby Dick*. For the fact is that this book is a challenge and affront to all the habits of mind that typically prevailed in the nineteenth century, and still remain, almost unabated, among us: it comes out of a different world, and presupposes, for its acceptance, a more integrated life and consciousness than we have known or experienced, for the most part, these last three centuries. *Moby Dick* is not Victorian; it is not Elizabethan; it is, rather, prophetic of another quality of life which Melville had experienced and had a fuller vision of in his own time — a quality that may again come into the world, when we seek to pass beyond the harassed specialisms which still hold and pre-occupy so many of us. To fathom this quality of Melville's experience and imagination, we must look a little deeper into his myth and his manner of projecting it. What is its meaning? And first, in what manner is that meaning conveyed to us?

II

Moby Dick is a poetic epic. Typographically, *Moby Dick* conforms to prose, and there are long passages, whole chapters, which are wholly in the mood of prose: but in spirit and in actual rhythm, *Moby Dick* again and again rises to polyphonic verse which resembles passages of Webster's in that it can either be considered as broken blank verse, or as cadenced prose. Mr. Percy Boynton has performed the interesting experiment of transposing a paragraph in *Pierre* into excellent free verse, so strong and subtle are Melville's rhythms; and one might garner a whole book of verse from *Moby Dick*. Melville, in *Moby Dick*, unconsciously respects Poe's canon that all true poetry must be short in length, since the mood cannot be retained, unbroken or undiminished, over lengthy passages, and if the form itself is preserved, the content nevertheless is prose. But while Poe himself used this dictum as an excuse for writing only short lyrics, Melville sustained the poetic mood through a long narrative by dropping frankly into prose in the intervening while. As a result, he was under no necessity of clipping the emotions or of bleaching the imaginative colors of *Moby Dick*: like a flying-boat, he rises from the water to the air and returns to the water again without losing control over either medium. His prose is prose: hard, sinewy, compact; and his poetry is poetry: vivid, surging, volcanic, creating its own form in the very pattern of the emotional state itself, soaring, towering, losing all respect for the smaller conventions of veracity, when the inner triumph itself must be announced. It is in the very rhythm of his language that Ahab's mood and all the devious symbols of *Moby Dick* are sustained and made credible: by no other method could the deeper half of the tale have been written. In these poetic passages, the phrases are intensified, stylicized, stripped of their habitual associations. If occasionally, as with Shakespeare, the thought itself is borne down by the weight of the gold that decorates it, this is only a similar proof of Melville's immense power of expression.

Both Poe and Hawthorne share some of Melville's power, and both of them, with varying success, wrought ideality and actuality into the same figure: but one has only to compare the best of their work with *Moby Dick* to see wherein Melville's great distinction lies. *The Scarlet Letter, The House of the Seven Gables,* " William Wilson," like most other works of fiction, are melodic: a single instrument is sufficient to carry the whole theme; whereas *Moby Dick* is a symphony: every resource of language and thought, fantasy, description, philosophy, natural history, drama, broken rhythms, blank verse, imagery, symbol, are utilized to sustain and expand the great theme. The conception of *Moby Dick* organically demands the expressive interrelation, for a single total effect, of a hundred different pieces: even in accessory matters, like the association of the Parsee, the fire-worshipper, with the death of Ahab, the fire-defier, or in the makeup of the crew, the officers white men, the harpooneers the savage races, red, black, brown, and the crew a mixed lot from the separate islands of the earth, not a stroke is introduced that has not a meaning for the myth as a whole. Although the savage harpooneers get nearest the whale, the savage universe, it is Ahab and the Parsee, the European and the Asiatic, who carry the pursuit to its ultimate end — while a single American survives to tell the tale.

Melville's instrumentation is unsurpassed in the writing of the last century: one must go to a Beethoven or a Wagner for an exhibition of similar powers; one will not find it among the works of literature. Here are Webster's wild violin, Marlowe's cymbals, Browne's sonorous bass viol, Swift's brass,

Smollett's castanets, Shelley's flute, brought together in a single orchestra complementing each other in a grand symphony. Melville achieved a similar synthesis in thought; and that work has proved all the more credible because he achieved it in language, too. Small wonder that those who were used to elegant pianoforte solos or barrel-organ instrumentation, were deafened and surprised and repulsed.

What is the meaning of *Moby Dick?* There is not one meaning; there are many; but in its simplest terms, *Moby Dick* is, necessarily, a story of the sea and its ways, as the *Odyssey* is a story of strange adventure, and *War and Peace* a story of battles and domestic life. The characters are heightened and slightly distorted: Melville's quizzical comic sense is steadily at work on them, and only Ahab escapes; but they all have their recognizable counterparts in the actual world. Without any prolonged investigation one could still find a Starbuck on Nantucket or a Flask on Martha's Vineyard — indeed, as Mr. Thomas Benton's portraits properly indicate, queerer fish than they.

On this level, *Moby Dick* brings together and focuses in a single picture the long line of sketches and preliminary portraits Melville had assembled in *Typee, Omoo, Redburn,* and *White-Jacket.* As a story of the sea, *Moby Dick* will always have a call for those who wish to recapture the magic and terror and stress and calm delight of the sea and its ships; and not less so because it seizes on a particular kind of ship, the whaler, and a special occupation, whaling, at the moment when they were about to pass out of existence, or rather, were being transformed from a brutal but glorious battle into a methodical, slightly banal industry. Melville had the singular fortune to pronounce a valedictory on many ways of life and scenes that were becoming extinct. He lived among the South Sea Islanders when they were still pretty much as Captain Cook found them, just before their perversion and decimation by our exotic Western civilization. He recorded life on a man-of-war half a generation before the sail gave place to steam, wood to armor-plate, and grappling irons to long-range guns. He described life on a sailing-packet before steam had increased the speed, the safety, and the pleasant monotony of trans-Atlantic travel: and finally, he recorded the last heroic days of whaling. *Moby Dick* would have value as firsthand testimony, even if it were negligible as literature. If this were all, the book would still be important.

But *Moby Dick*, admirable as it is as a narrative of maritime adventure, is far more than that: it is, fundamentally, a parable on the mystery of evil and the accidental malice of the universe. The white whale stands for the brute energies of existence, blind, fatal, overpowering, while Ahab is the spirit of man, small and feeble, but purposive, that pits its puniness against this might, and its purpose against the blank senselessness of power. The evil arises with the good: the white whale grows up among the milder whales which are caught and cut up and used: one hunts for the one — for a happy marriage, livelihood, offspring, social companionship and cheer — and suddenly heaving its white bulk out of the calm sea, one comes upon the other: illness, accident, treachery, jealousy, vengefulness, dull frustration. The South Sea savage did not know of the white whale: at least, like death, it played but a casual part in his consciousness. It is different with the European; his life is a torment of white whales: the Jobs, the Aeschyluses, the Dantes, the Shakespeares, pursue him and grapple with him, as Ahab pursues his antagonist.

All our lesser literature — all our tales of Avalon or heaven or ultimate redemption, or, in a later day, the future — is an evasion of the white whale: it is a quest of that boyish beginning which we call a happy ending. But the old Norse myth told that Asgard itself would be consumed at last, and the very gods would be destroyed: the white whale is the symbol of that persistent force of destruction, that meaningless force, which now figures as the outpouring of a volcano or the atmospheric disruption of a tornado or again as the mere aimless dissipation of unused energy into an unavailable void — that spectacle which so disheartened the learned Henry Adams. The whole tale of the West, in mind and action, in the philosophy and art of the Greeks, in the organization and technique of the Romans, in the precise skills and unceasing spiritual quests of the modern man, is a tale of this effort to combat the whale — to ward off his blows, to counteract his aimless thrusts, to create a purpose that will offset the empty malice of Moby Dick. Without such a purpose, without the belief in such a purpose, life is neither bearable nor significant: unless one is polarized by these central human energies and aims, one tends to become absorbed in Moby Dick himself, and, becoming a part of his being, can only maim, slay, butcher, like the shark or the white whale or Alexander or Napoleon. If there is no God, exclaims Dostoyevsky's hero, then we may commit murder: and in the sense that God represents the totality of human purpose and meaning, the conclusion is inevitable.

It is useless to derive man's purposes from those of the external universe; he is a figure in the web of life. Except for such kindness and loyalty as the creatures man has domesticated show, there is, as far as one can now see, no concern except in man himself over the ceaseless motions and accidents that take place in nature. Love and chance, said Charles Peirce, rule the universe: but the love is man's love, and although in the very concept of chance, as both Peirce and Captain Ahab declare, there is some rough notion of fair play, of fifty-fifty, of an even break, that is small immediate consolation for the creature that may lose not the game, but his life, by an unlucky throw of the dice. Ahab has more humanity than the gods he defies: indeed, he has more power, because he is conscious of the power he wields, and applies it deliberately, whereas Moby Dick's power only seems deliberate because it cuts across the directed aims of Ahab himself. And in one sense, Ahab achieves victory: he vanquishes in himself that which would retreat from Moby Dick and acquiesce in his insensate energies and his brutal sway. His end is tragic: evil engulfs him. But in battling against evil, with power instead of love, Ahab himself, in A. E.'s phrase, becomes the image of the thing he hates: he has lost his humanity in the very act of vindicating it. By physical defiance, by physical combat, Ahab cannot rout and capture Moby Dick: the odds are against him; and if his defiance is noble, his methods are ill chosen. Growth, cultivation, order, art — these are the proper means by which man displaces accident and subdues the vacant external powers in the universe: the way of growth is not to become more powerful but to become more human. Here is a hard lesson to learn: it is easier to wage war than to conquer in oneself the tendency to be partial, vindictive, and unjust: it is easier to demolish one's enemy than to pit oneself against him in an intellectual combat which will disclose one's weaknesses and provincialities. And that evil Ahab seeks to strike is the sum of one's enemies. He does not bow down to it and accept it: therein lies his heroism and virtue: but he fights it with its own weapons and therein lies his madness. All the things that Ahab despises when he is about to attack the whale, the love and loyalty of Pip, the memory of his wife and child, the sextant of science, the inner sense of calm, which makes all external struggle futile, are the very things that would redeem him and make him victorious.

Man's ultimate defence against the universe, against evil and accident and malice, is not by any fictitious resolution of these things into an absolute which justifies them and utilizes them for its own ends: this is specious comfort, and Voltaire's answer to Leibniz in *Candide* seems to me a final one. Man's defence lies within himself, not within the narrow, isolated ego, which may be overwhelmed, but in that self which we share with our fellows and which assures us that, whatever happens to our own carcasses and hides, good men will remain to carry on the work, to foster and protect the things we have recognized as excellent. To make that self more solid, one must advance positive science, produce formative ideas, and embody ideal forms in which all men may, to a greater or less degree, participate: in short, one must create a realm which is independent of the hostile forces in the universe — and cannot be lightly shaken by their onslaught. Melville's method, that of writing *Moby Dick*, was correct: as correct as Ahab's method, taken literally, that of fighting Moby Dick, was fallacious. In *Moby Dick*, Melville conquered the white whale in his own consciousness: instead of blankness there was significance, instead of aimless energy there was purpose, and instead of random living there was life. The universe *is* inscrutable, unfathomable, malicious, *so* — like the white whale and his element. Art, in the broad sense of all humanizing effort, is man's answer to this condition: for it is the means by which he circumvents or postpones his doom, and bravely meets his tragic destiny. Not tame and gentle bliss, but disaster, heroically encountered, is man's true happy ending.

III

Here, it seems to me, is the plainest interpretation of Melville's fable, and the one he was partly conscious of in the writing of it. But a great book is more a part of its milieu than either the writer or his public knows; and there is more in *Moby Dick* than the figure of man's heroic defiance of brute energy, and evil, and the high gods.

In another sense, the whale stands for the practical life. Mankind needs food and light and shelter, and, with a little daring and a little patience, it gains these things from its environment: the whale that we cut up, dissect, analyze, melt down, pour into casks, and distribute in cities and households is the whale of industry and science. The era of whaling which opened only in the late seventeenth century is timed with the era of modern industry; and in the very year Mel-

ville wrote *Moby Dick*, 1851, industry and science were an-
nouncing their triumphs in that great cockcrow of the Crystal
Palace Exhibition in London. Side by side with this purpose,
which secures man's material existence, is another set of purposes which, though they sometimes take advantage of the
means offered by the practical life, as Ahab takes advantage
of his sordid crew and ordinary whaling to carry out his private revenge, run counter to the usual flow of our daily efforts.
The white whale cannot be met and captured by the usual
means; more than that: to fulfill man's own deeper purposes,
the captains of the spirit must oppose the prudence of Starbuck and the common sense of Stubb. Material sustenance,
home, comfort, though their pursuit occupy the greater part
of the daily round of humanity, are sometimes best forgotten
and set at naught: indeed, when nobler human purposes are
uppermost, they must be set at naught. He who steadily seeks
to preserve life and fortify it must be ready to give up his life
at a moment's notice when a fellow creature is in danger: he
who would provide others with daily bread must be prepared
to go hungry if the wheat that would nourish him is needed
for the planting. All the more does this hold in the affairs of
the spirit. When the human spirit expands itself to the uttermost, to confront the white whale and hew meaning and form
from the blank stone of experience, one must reverse all the
practical maxims: earth's folly, as Melville says, is heaven's
wisdom, and earth's wisdom is heaven's greatest disaster.

The crew of the vessel seek the ordinary whale: they are
after comfort and contentment and a greater share of the
" lay "; but the Ahabs seek danger and hardships and a lay that
has no value in terms of material sustenance and magnificence.
And the paradox, the hard paradox, is this: both purposes are
essential; Ahab could not set out at all without the aid of Peleg
and Bildad and Charity and his harpooners and sailors, and
they, for their part, would never know anything except sluggish routine were they not at times stirred up to great efforts

by purposes they do not easily understand or consciously accept. Yet: there is an Ahab in every man, and the meanest member of the crew can be awakened to the values that Ahab prizes: given a storm and a stove boat, and the worst rascal on shipboard may be as magnificent as Odysseus. All men live most intensely when they are moulded by such a purpose — or even, wanting that, by an enterprise that counterfeits it. Art, religion, culture in general, all those intangible triumphs of the spirit that are embodied in forms and symbols, all that spells purpose as opposed to senseless energy, and significance as opposed to routine — these efforts develop human life to its fullest, even when they work contrary to the ordinary standards of the world.

There is, it seems to me, another meaning in Ahab's struggle with Moby Dick. He represents, not as in the first parable, an heroic power that misconceives its mission and misapplies itself: here he rather stands for human purpose in its highest expression. His pursuit is " futile " because it wrecks the boat and brings home no oil and causes material loss and extinguishes many human lives; but in another sense, it is not futile at all, but is the only significant part of the voyage, since oil is burned and ships eventually break up and men die and even the towers of proud cities crumble away as the buildings sink beneath the sand or the jungle, while all that remains, all that perpetuates the life and the struggle, are their forms and symbols, their art, their literature, their science, as they have been incorporated in the social heritage of man. That which is useful for the moment eventually becomes useless; the mummy's food and drink shrivel away or evaporate: but that which is " useless," the graven image or the tomb itself, continues to nourish the spirit of man. Life, Life purposive, Life formative, Life expressive, is more than living, as living itself is more than the finding of a livelihood. There is no triumph so petty and evanescent as that involved in capturing the ordinary whale: the nineteenth century made this triumph the end and object of all endeavor; and it put the spirit in chains of comfort and material satisfaction, which were heavier than fetters and harder to bear than the stake. By the same token, there is no struggle so permanent and so humanly satisfactory as Ahab's struggle with the white whale. In that defeat, in that succession of defeats, is the only pledge of man's ultimate victory, and the only final preventive of emptiness, boredom, and suicide. Battles are lost, as Whitman cried, in the same spirit that they are won. Some day the physical powers of man may be commensurate with his utmost spirit, and he will meet Leviathan on even terms.

IV

The epic and mythic quality of *Moby Dick* has been misunderstood because those who examined the book have thought of the epic in terms of Homer, and the myth itself in relation to some obvious hero of antiquity, or some modern folk-hero, a Washington, a Boone, raised to enormous dimensions. As Melville said in his essay on Hawthorne:

The great mistake seems to be that even with those Americans who look forward to the coming of a great literary genius among us, they somehow fancy he will come in the costume of Queen Elizabeth's day; be a writer of dramas founded upon old English history or the tales of Boccaccio. Whereas, great geniuses are parts of the times, they themselves are the times and possess a corresponding colouring.

Now, *Moby Dick* was written in the best spirit of the nineteenth century, and though it escaped most of the limitations of that period, it escaped with its finest qualities intact. Heroes and gods in the old sense, as Walt Whitman plainly saw, had had their day: they fitted into a simpler scheme of life and thought, and a more credulous sort of attitude; so far from representing the ultimate triumph of the human imagination, from which the scientific mode of thought was not merely a departure but a falling off, the old myths were but the product of a juvenile fantasy. One might still use these figures, as Milton used an Arcadian image to express the corruptions of the Established Church; but they stood for a mode of consciousness and feeling remote from our modern experience. Science did not, as has been foolishly believed, destroy the myth-making power of man, or reduce all his inner strivings to bleak impotence: this has been the accidental, temporary effect of a one-sided science, serving, consciously or not, a limited number of practical activities. What the scientific spirit has actually done has been to exercise the imagination in finer ways than the autistic wish — the wish of the infant possessed of the illusion of power and domination — was able to express. Faraday's ability to conceive the lines of force in a magnetic field was quite as great a triumph as the ability to conceive fairies dancing in a ring: and, as Mr. A. N. Whitehead has shown, the poets who sympathized with this new sort of imagination, poets like Shelley, Wordsworth, Whitman, Melville, did not feel themselves robbed of their specific powers, but rather found them enlarged and refreshed.

One of the finest love poems of the nineteenth century, Whitman's " Out of the Cradle Endlessly Rocking," is expressed in such an image as Darwin or Audubon might have used, were the scientist as capable of expressing his inner feelings as of noting " external " events: the poet haunting the seashore and observing the mating of the birds, day after day following their life, could scarcely have existed before the nineteenth century. In the seventeenth century, such a poet would have remained in the garden and written about a literary ghost, Philomel, and not about an actual pair of birds; in Pope's time, the poet would have remained in the library and written about the birds on a lady's fan. Almost all the important works of the nineteenth century were cast in this mode and expressed this new imaginative range: they respect the fact: they are replete with observation: they project an ideal realm in and through, not over, the landscape of actuality. *Notre Dame* might have been written by an historian,

War and Peace by a sociologist, *The Idiot* might have been created by a psychiatrist, and *Salammbô* might have been the work of an archaeologist. I do not say that these books were scientific by intention, or that they might be replaced by a work of science without grave loss; far from it. I merely point out that they are conceived in the same spirit; that they belong to a similar plane of consciousness. Much as Melville was enriched by the Elizabethan writers, there is that in *Moby Dick* which separates him completely from the poets of that day — and if one wants a word to describe the element that makes the difference, one must call it briefly science.

Now, this respect for fact, as opposed to irresponsible fantasy, did not of course exist for the first time in the nineteenth century: Defoe had this habit of mind in quite as great a measure as Melville: what is important is that in the nineteenth century it was for the first time completely wedded to the imagination. It no longer means a restriction, a dried-up quality, an incompleteness; it no longer deifies the empirical and the practical at the expense of the ideal and the aesthetic: on the contrary, these qualities are now completely fused together, as an expression of life's integrated totality. The symbolism again becomes equal to the reality. Hercules no longer serves in this way, although originally he was doubtless as full of immediate relationships as whaling; and a more complex and diffuse symbol — like Kutuzov's army in *War and Peace* — is necessary. Had Milton sought to tell this parable of Melville's, he would probably have recast the story of Jonah and the whale, making Jonah the hero; but in doing so he could not help losing all the great imaginative parallels Melville is able to work out, through using material hitherto untouched by previous myth or history. For Ahab's hate and the pursuit of the whale is only one part of the total symbol: the physiological character of the whale, its feeding, its mating, its whole life, from whatever sources Melville drew the data, is equally a part of it. Indeed, the symbol of Moby Dick is complete and rounded, expressive of our present relations to the universe, only through the passages that orthodox criticism, exercised on lesser works and more meagre traditions, regards as extraneous or unimportant.

Moby Dick, then, is one of the first great mythologies to be created in the modern world, created, that is, out of the stuff of that world, its science, its exploration, its terrestrial daring, its concentration upon power and dominion over nature, and not out of ancient symbols, Prometheus, Endymion, Orestes, or mediaeval folk-legends, like Dr. Faustus. *Moby Dick* lives imaginatively in the newly broken soil of our own life: its symbols, unlike Blake's original but mysterious figures, are direct and explicit: if the story is bedded in facts, the facts themselves are not lost in the further interpretation. *Moby Dick* thus brings together the two dissevered halves of the modern world and the modern self — its positive, practical, scientific, externalized self, bent on conquest and knowledge, and its imaginative, ideal half, bent on the transposition of conflict into art, and power into humanity. This resolution is achieved in *Moby Dick* itself: it is as if a Shakespeare and a Bacon, or, to use a more local metaphor, as if an Eakins and a Ryder, had collaborated on a single work of art, with a heightening of their several powers. The best handbook on whaling is also — I say this scrupulously — the best tragic epic of modern times and one of the fine poetic works of all time.

That is an achivement; and it is also a promise. Whitman went as far in his best poems, particularly in the " Song of Myself "; and, with quite another method, Tolstoy went as far in *War and Peace*, Dostoyevsky in the *Brothers Karamazov*; Hardy, less perfectly, approximated it perhaps in *The Dynasts*; but no one went further. It is one of the great peaks of the modern vision of life. " May God keep us," wrote Blake, " from single vision and Newton's sleep." We now perhaps see a little more clearly what Blake's enigmatic words mean. In *Moby Dick* Melville achieved the deep integrity of that double vision which sees with both eyes — the scientific eye of actuality, and the illumined eye of imagination and dream.

v

I have dwelt for a little on some of the meanings of *Moby Dick;* but this does not exhaust the matter. Each man will read into *Moby Dick* the drama of his own experience and that of his contemporaries: Mr. D. H. Lawrence sees in the conflict a battle between the blood-consciousness of the white race and its own abstract intellect, which attempts to hunt and slay it; Mr. Percy Boynton sees in the whale all property and vested privilege, laming the spirit of man; Mr. Van Wyck Brooks has found in the white whale an image like that of Grendel in *Beowulf,* expressing the Northern consciousness of the hard fight against the elements; while for the disciple of Jung, the white whale is the symbol of the Unconscious, which torments man, and yet is the source of all his proudest efforts.

Each age, one may predict, will find its own symbols in *Moby Dick.* Over that ocean the clouds will pass and change, and the ocean itself will mirror back those changes from its own depths. All these conscious interpretations, however, though they serve the book by approaching its deeper purpose, do not, cannot, quite penetrate the core of its reality. *Moby Dick* has a meaning which cannot be derived or dissociated from the work itself. Like every great work of art, it summons up thoughts and feelings profounder than those to which it gives overt expression. It introduces one, sometimes by simple, bald means, to the depths of one's own experience. The book is not an answer, but a clue that must be carried further and worked out. The Sermon on the Mount has this quality. It does not answer all the difficult problems of morality, but it suggests a new point of view in facing them: it leads one who is sufficiently moved to follow through

all the recesses of conduct which can be influenced by mild-
ness, understanding, and love, but not otherwise. So with
Moby Dick: the book itself is greater than the fable it embodies, it foreshadows more than it actually reflects; as a work
of art, *Moby Dick* is part of a new integration of thought, a
widening of the fringe of consciousness, a deepening of insight, through which the modern vision of life will finally be
embodied.

The shadow cast by *Moby Dick* throws into obscurity not
merely the sandhills, but likewise some of the mountains, of
the last three centuries. Noting the extent of that shadow,
one begins to suspect how high the mountain itself is, and how
great its bulk, how durable its rock.

2

Glimpses of the Man

A New York Adolescence

By the time we had visited foundries on the East River, practiced tennis on courts in Staten Island, traveling two hours for the
sake of playing one, cheered baseball games in the Bronx, and
dickered with one-horse job printers on John Street, we knew our
way about the city and we knew a lot about what life had to offer
ourselves and our fellows.

Toward the end of the first decade of the century, the hori-
zons of New York visibly widened for me. My main activities ceased to be bounded by my neighborhood. Up to that
time, one could be identified by the block one lived on. West
Ninety-fourth Street boys were quite different in manner and
social outlook and the ability to play one-old-cat from West
Ninety-first Street boys, who were sissies, and we all would
shrink into areaways or dive behind the portals of our apartment houses when the Ninety-eighth Street gang, tough,
dirty, brutal, appeared on the scene. Occasionally friendships
would break across block lines, but only rarely did they span
a distance of more than a couple of blocks. It was like living
in a walled town.

Adolescence and high school advanced together, although
I don't think my voice broke or my legs became gangly till at
least a year after I had left grammar school. When I was
graduated from grammar school, we had sung a song at com-
mencement about our eternal loyalty to dear old 166, but in
our hearts we knew that in our part of the West Side one
school was practically identical with another, whereas the
high schools we had to choose from had names, not numbers,
and each one had a collective character. Townsend Harris
was almost collegiate in its standards, but, despite its playing
fields on Convent Avenue, was terrible in sports. Commerce,

at Sixty-fifth Street near Broadway, had a fine baseball team, and it turned out fellows who became bookkeepers, accountants, and male secretaries. De Witt Clinton, at Fifty-ninth Street near Tenth Avenue, was just literary, while Stuyvesant, which had a good basketball team and a new building, prepared people for engineering.

At the time the choice came to me, I was making clumsy models of airplanes on the lines of the Wright plane — models that would never fly in the air and would hardly even stay glued together in repose on my bedroom table. With the help of an old instrument-maker to whom Dr. Phillips, our family doctor, had introduced me, I had begun to rig up feeble little wireless sets with which I purposed to communicate with another ingenious lad in the next block, if either of us ever had the patience to master the Morse code. So I chose Stuyvesant. I think the good basketball team erased any lingering doubts I may have had about it.

Emerson used to say that the essence of a college education was having a room of one's own, with a fire, in a strange city. Going to high school on East Fifteenth Street, between Stuyvesant Square and First Avenue, gave me essentially the same sort of shock. In those days, the upper West Side had a fairly homogeneous population; there was the typical New York mixture of German and Irish stocks, interspersed with older branches of the American. Our fathers and mothers, at least, had usually been born in the United States, and in a class of forty boys, only eight or ten would be even identifiably Jewish, while the newer Russo-Polish migration was so sparsely represented that I can still remember the name of Malatzky, the bright, beady-eyed son of a glazier on Columbus Avenue.

Except for Broadway, which was very spottily built up until the opening of the subway in 1904 defined its new character, this part of the West Side had taken shape in the late eighties and nineties. The poorer classes lived on Amsterdam and Columbus Avenues: the cabmen and the clerks and the mechanics and the minor city employees. The rich lived in the big apartments on Central Park West or in the heavy, stone-encrusted mansions on Riverside Drive; between them, on the cross streets, and more sumptuously on West End Avenue, was the connecting tissue of the bourgeoisie, in brownstone rows whose dinginess was sometimes graced by some of the lighter-yellow, brick-and-limestone houses designed by Stanford White and his imitators. A boy growing up in such a neighborhood took middle-class comfort to be the dominant pattern of life, and except for an occasional twist of Irish, everyone spoke plain Manhattanese.

Suddenly I was thrown into a remote quarter of the city, and surrounded by a group of boys with foreign faces and uncouth, almost undecipherable accents and grubby, pushing manners: boys who ate strange food whose flavors pervaded their breath and seemed to hang about their clothes; boys whose aggressive vitality left me feeling like a sick goldfinch among a flock of greedy sparrows. One had to fend for oneself among people who had learned the art of survival in a far more difficult environment than I had come from, and in the lunch hour I would inevitably find myself near the tag end of the line that filed past the cafeteria counter, never capable of making decisions fast enough to get what I wanted before I was pushed beyond reach.

My school comrades were mostly the second generation of the great Russian and Polish Jewish immigration that had swept into the East Side after the assassination of Czar Alexander II. They had names like Moscowitz and Lefkowitz and Pinsky, and they had not merely learned in the settlement houses how to play circles round most of us in basketball or track sports, but they had an equally strenuous grip on the academic subjects. Indeed, most of them also excelled in the use of their hands, not having had so many of their manual opportunities shorn from them by solicitous parents and nursemaids. All in all, these boys were good stuff, but for one who had lived a more pallid existence, they were, during the first year, a little overwhelming.

My new schoolfellows brought the raw facts of life home to me with a rush. My own family knew the pinch of genteel poverty, but here was poverty on a grand scale, massive, extensive, blighting vast neighborhoods, altering the whole character of life, a poverty that, instead of shrinking submissively behind a false front, reached out into the city, creating its own forms, demanding, arguing, asserting, claiming its own, now busy with schemes for making money, now whispering the strange word Socialism as a key that would open the door. My political views were extremely conservative in those days; the rights of property seemed axiomatic; and I remember how shocked I was when I found out that one of my pals named Stamer, whose father was a Greenpoint cigarmaker of the old '48 German stock, was a Socialist. Stamer jarred my middle-class complacency with his scornful descriptions of what had hitherto seemed a reasonable and well-balanced world, and I was gradually unsettled in all my views, not so much through the strength of his arguments as through the obvious feebleness of my replies. Even a couple of teachers, quiet, upright men, were Socialists and would occasionally explain their views in class. I might have lived and died in my part of the upper West Side without realizing that neither the Democratic nor the Republican party had ever recognized the class struggle.

Fourteenth Street, too, was something of an education for a provincial West Side boy. Tammany Hall still reigned in its dingy building near Third Avenue, embracing the old Tony Pastor's theatre, and almost across the way was Tom Sharkey's saloon, with a wide glass front, and the Dewey Theatre, painted white, where lurid posters of obese beauties, who did the belly dances that preceded strip tease, were spread before our gaze. "Don't do that dance I tell you Sadie, that ain't no business for a lady" was one of the popular songs.

of the period, and all of us knew, at least at second hand, how much farther Fourteenth Street went than Broadway's Sadie. My usual route to school was through Irving Place and along Fifteenth Street, because I discovered in my second year that a beautiful girl with austere white cheeks and black hair would pass me almost every morning on her way to the Quaker school at the corner of Stuyvesant Square. I can still see her graceful figure, in a blue serge dress, topped by a black hat with a jaunty feather, her poised, unhurried walk, and her slightly archaic inward smile, which was at once impenetrable and yet not indifferent, and I wonder now if I played anything of the part in her secret dream life that she did in mine.

When school was out, one would encounter in the same street, nearer Third Avenue, white-faced and heavily rouged prostitutes, no longer young, already on patrol. We knew what these ladies were, in a vague way; some of the boys, who lived on Forsythe or Chrystie Street, had even encountered them closer at hand in the halls of their own tenements; and we held a certain resentment against them because they were mainly responsible for the fact that we were not permitted to go out on the streets for lunch, but had to remain cooped in our building. The year after I was graduated, however, a new social ferment began to work in school. A group of boys rushed the teacher who was guarding the main door and broke for liberty during the lunch hour; this precipitated a school strike, and when the matter was settled the boys had won the right to eat outdoors. The squirrels in Stuyvesant Square benefited more by this arrangement, I am sure, than the painted ladies.

Often I preferred to spend my carfare on candy and walked home, usually with a couple of other lads. The path led diagonally across the city, sometimes up Broadway, sometimes around the open New York Central yards and across to Central Park. I watched the Public Library and the Grand Central Terminal during their building, and remember parts of

Fifth Avenue below Fifty-ninth that were still lined with brownstone dwellings and plushy-looking mansions before which victorias and hansoms would stop, and the stages — as my mother still calls the buses — would roll by. Yet visually these walks remain dim, because so much of them, particularly when a sallow, evangelical boy named George Lush was along, was spent in talks about God and immortality and True Christianity. The openness of the midtown district then, its low buildings and the vast unbuilt spaces on Park Avenue, of course remain with me, for they were still visible when the Shelton was erected as late as 1924, but I dearly wish some heavenly stenographer would transcribe one of those theological debates for me. Both Lush and I were still pious lads. Could it be that we spent all those hours comparing the practices of the Baptists and the Episcopalians? Or were we battling with Higher Criticism? I can't remember.

In grammar school, most of the male teachers were aged men, who had grown old in a profession they conducted with dignity untouched by inspiration — men who could remember the draft riots, or the black-walled city that celebrated Lincoln's funeral. In high school, there were a lot of young teachers who brought into the place the contemporary flavor of Cornell, Chicago, or Wisconsin, as well as nearer universities, people who were stirred up over their subjects and who would break into their routine demonstrations in physics with hints of exciting scientific news that would not for a decade or more penetrate the textbooks — Einstein's first theory of relativity, or the electronic theory of matter, which made the old-fashioned doctrine of the indivisible atom look silly except as a convenience in writing chemical equations. Our principal, a sweet, portly man with a gray Vandyke beard and a bald head, was excited about science, too; he kept a class in physics for himself all through his principalship, and he would beam on us when he had made a good demonstration. Some of the more menial subjects in engineering, like mechanical drawing, seemed to attract routineers, but to make up for it, there were teachers in pattern-making or metal-turning who had worked with the Yale & Towne lock company or in the Baldwin Locomotive Works, and who were not tethered to the profession of teaching out of mere ineptitude for worldly tasks or for the sake of premature repose. As for the man who taught us forging, he was a German blacksmith of the old school, and his iron roses and scrolly leaves were our envy.

That a school so strenuously dedicated to science and the mechanical arts should have had a good English department was extremely fortunate for a lad whose mathematical aptitude waned shortly after he wrote his first love letter. The English teachers worked against odds, too, because the Board of Regents had chosen a lot of pretty stale literature for our edification, and it didn't help matters that, by some oversight, we had already gone through *The Lady of the Lake* and *Julius Caesar* in grammar school. But my teacher in freshman English, Thomas Bates, a rapt, brooding young man with a freckled face and a huge mop of carroty hair, encouraged a group of us to write a play, and from his lips I first heard the name of Bernard Shaw. That was what was important, as one looks back on it, in all the classes. Not the lesson itself, but the overflow — a hint, a pat on the shoulder, the confession of a secret ambition, a fragment of unposed life as someone had actually lived it.

I hated quadratic equations and I wasn't overly fond of geometry, but high school had none of the close-packed boredom that remains the chief impress of my earlier education. It was a big chunk of life to swallow, and maybe we were stretched a little too hard at study during a period when our bodies demanded a larger share of idleness and relaxation than we gave them. But there was no lack of intellectual stimulus in this new milieu. By the time we had visited foundries on the East River, practiced tennis on courts in Staten Island, traveling two hours for the sake of playing one, cheered baseball games in the Bronx, and dickered with one-horse job printers on John Street, we knew our way about the city and we knew a lot about what life had to offer ourselves and our fellows.

When I left high school, however, my ambitions had changed. I wanted to be a newspaperman as a first step toward becoming a novelist. Shep Friedman was then the city editor of the *Morning Telegraph,* and since he was a friend of the family, I kept on politely nagging him for a job for the next year or two. I would usually drop in around 6 P.M., before he had started the heavy business or the heavy drinking of the day, and although I was palpably a callow and ratty adolescent, he was always decent enough to drag me down to the corner bar for a friendly beer. After this he would give me a note of introduction to the most recent occupant of the *Evening Journal's* city desk. Being idiotic as well as honorable, I never examined these notes. I suspect now that they said, "For God's sake dump this kid somewhere or drown him." At the end of six months I compromised with my ambitions and went on the *Evening Telegram* as copyboy for the lobster trick. My feelings were a little like those of a broken-down gentleman I once knew who was finally reduced to taking a job as dishwasher in a big hotel. But, he proudly explained to his friends, he was not an ordinary dishwasher; he washed only the dishes of the guests who were served privately in their rooms. It was understood that I was to become a cub reporter the first time someone moved up or out.

The job forced me to get up at 2:50 A.M., make my own breakfast, and catch a Sixth Avenue "L" to Herald Square. The back of our flat faced Columbus Avenue, and I could tell by leaning out the kitchen window and noting whether the passing train had green or white lights how much time I had left for finishing my cocoa. It made one feel slightly superior to be abroad in the city at that hour, before the milkman started on his rounds. The cold white flare of the arc lights intensified one's feeling of aloofness, and an occasional light in the bedroom of an otherwise darkened tenement house might even add a touch of mystery, hinting of someone in pain, someone quarreling, someone dying or being born. But often I would be oblivious of the sleeping city because I was reading, with an indescribable priggish elation, a few pages in Plato or William James. Reading *A Pluralistic Universe* at 3:25 in the morning almost wiped away the humiliation of sweeping the floor and setting out the flimsy in the stale air of the city room half an hour later. If I happened to catch a train ten minutes earlier, I would encounter the last of the reporters, winding up their poker game in a corner of our common city room.

The *Telegram* was even in 1913 a pretty seedy sheet, but James Gordon Bennett was still alive, and some faint, ridiculous spark of his vindictive energy would cause an editor or a reporter suddenly to jump out of his skin. (Bennett was the same insolent devil who offered Stanley his old job on the *Herald* after he had found Livingstone and made himself famous.) At this time, the name Roosevelt was taboo; he could be referred to only as the Third Termer. Among other examples of Bennett's crotchets, there was an ice chest in one corner of the city room, which was duly filled with ice every day, supposedly because the Old Boy himself might suddenly appear and want ice for his champagne. Bennett's alpaca coat, too, hung on a hook in his private office, waiting. I rushed the beer and sandwiches and coffee while the night city editor was marking up the morning papers for the rewrite men. Even at that hour, the saloon on the northeast corner of Thirty-fifth Street would have a few stragglers in it. The rewrite men, who averaged around thirty-five dollars a week then — the night city editor got only fifty — used to tip me, too, even if I did read William James and sometimes do a stick or two of rewrite myself when one of the men got in late. If any small story broke in the neighborhood, I would be sent out to cover it, but a sewer explosion and a burning mattress were about all that came my way, and my pride suffered as my boredom grew, so I chucked the job after a couple of months. It was a cheap and harmless inoculation. I never looked for Life in newspaper offices any more, and thenceforward I read newspapers with a scorn and a skepticism born of intimacy. Had I not, when a freighter without a wireless sank near Halifax, seen a big front-page story manufactured in three-quarters of an hour out of a rewrite man's stinking clay pipe and his otherwise unaided imagination?

All this time, and for the next few years, I was studying at City College at night, from 7:30 to 10:20. In every way that was a remarkable experience, and one that only New York could have offered. Even New York could offer it only once, for the college I knew, with some five hundred students and a close, intimate life, disappeared — under mere pressure of congestion — within half a dozen years after its inception. It was one of those important experiments that the City College began before it went the way of other metropolitan institutions by succumbing to giantism. Dr. Stephen Duggan was the director and Dr. Frederick B. Robinson (he of umbrella memory) was then his assistant, an affable, clever man who was yet to disclose his remarkable talent for disingenuously setting a whole institution by the ears.

The students were mostly mature men, and they spoiled me for any other kind of undergraduate. One of them was a well-established maritime lawyer, with an argumentative Scotch tongue; another was a South American consul; and there were doctors, brokers, accountants, engineers, as well as people almost as infirmly established as myself. Being under no obligations to regularity, I took my college education backward, skipping most of the freshman subjects and plunging into junior and senior courses in politics, philosophy, and English. In all the new plans for revising curricula that I have examined, not even Dr. Hutchins seems to have hit on this particular dodge, but perhaps it would work no worse for others than it did for me.

There is something amoeboid about the ordinary under-graduate, but we night students had a shape and a backbone and a definite point of view. Our discussions were battles, and though we often lived to change sides, there was nothing tentative or hesitating in our espousals; we did not suffer from the academic disease of evasive " open-mindedness." Our professors were men of character — men like Morris Cohen, who thought and taught out of a passion for things of the mind as pure as that of a Socrates or a Spinoza. There was Alfred Compton, a slim, sardonic gentleman with a touch of Robert Louis Stevenson about him. There was John Pickett Turner, a handsome man with a massive dark head, a wart on his cheek, and shoulders of Platonic dimensions; he spoke with a Southern deliberation and enlivened his course on psychol-ogy with case histories drawn undisguised from his own life and marital experience. Even-handed and tolerant, he didn't quiver a hairbreadth when a sharp little Rumanian, Jallyer, in the ethics class, declared that the *summum bonum* would be to die at the height of an orgasm in the arms of a beautiful woman. There was J. Salwyn Schapiro, one of J. H. Robin-son's brilliant disciples, who filled the air with epigrams and paradoxes, one of which seems even more startling today than it did in 1913 — " The Constitution might be overthrown, but it could not be amended." And then there was Earle Palmer, a little man with a drawn white face, hunched shoulders, and dark eyes that smoldered behind his glasses. He took us through Pancoast's anthology of poetry, living and enacting the poems, with an acrid humor in commentary that sprang out of passion rather than bitterness — a frail but ageless fig-ure, half pixie, half demon, with the sudden dark touch of one who had not lightly triumphed over terror and wrath and pain. My Harvard friends have overfilled me with tales about their famous Copey, but none of them has ever made me feel the least regretful that I missed the histrionic Harvard professor. One touch of Palmer's ruthless sincerity was at least half a college education.

The trustees of City College had chosen a grand site for their new buildings when the college moved up from Twenty-third Street, and the architecture had a powerful effect when one climbed the hill past the Hebrew Orphan Asylum through the deepening October twilight and saw the college buildings, in their dark stone masses and white terra-cotta quoins and moldings, rising like a collection of crystals out of the formless rocks on the crest. Below, the plain of Harlem spread, a vapor of light beneath the twinkle and flood of a large beer sign. In the afterglow, or on a dark night, these buildings could awaken nostalgic memory as easily as those of Brasenose or Magdalen. Often we would accompany one of our professors to his home, along Convent Avenue or Broadway, or sometimes a group of us, heady with the discussions started in the classroom, would stalk down Riverside Drive, matching outrageous puns, arguing about free will and determinism, bursting into irrelevant song. It had the intimacy that only a small college can give, plus the variety and intensity of stimulus that come in a great city.

The other part of my adolescence, particularly in the earlier years, centered chiefly around the old tennis courts in Central Park on the south side of the transverse at Ninety-sixth Street. The courts were then covered with grass, and the most popular court, half-denuded by constant playing, was called the dirt court. An aged keeper, with a gray beard spattered with tobacco juice, had charge of the markings of the courts and the stowing away of the nets. He was probably one of those Civil War pensioners who were still favored on the public payrolls, and we called him " Captain," but he had a vile temper and carried on an uncivil war of his own with most of the people who played there. He was often drunk, and the white lines he marked with his sprinkler showed no disposition to follow the straight and narrow path, but this crusty character gave the place a certain flavor which contrasts with the colorless, antiseptic courtesy of today. We couldn't start playing till the Captain raised the flag on the flagpole.

It was a queer gang that hung around the courts in those days — a few newspaper reporters on the *American* and the *Press;* a theatrical agent whom we called Ted; a little hunchback with no visible occupation, whom we called Dirty Ferdie; a few semi-professional loafers who used to play for stakes; and a handful of young women who were usually attached to the older men, ancients who might be at least thirty years old, as well as a few boys of my own age who took tennis very seriously. Day after day through the muggy summer we would lounge around on the hill behind the dirt court, and play, and lounge, and play again till we could scarcely drag our feet around the court. This was a complete, self-contained world; even on a rainy day, we would come over to the courts with our racquets, sprawling on benches beneath the trees toward the reservoir, speculating on the weather. When the males were alone, the conversation would often descend to basement level, and I would go home with new words I couldn't find in the ten-volume Century Dictionary, sometimes with lickerish hints about aspects of life I hadn't the faintest clue to till I studied abnormal psychology. On the whole, perhaps it was a good thing we played so much tennis.

I don't know if I can convey the precise flavor of the city that one inhaled on those Central Park courts in my day. It was perhaps closest to what one feels on a clean, sunny beach onto which the ocean periodically washes stale watermelon rinds, mildewed oranges, and discarded paper boxes. There was nothing particular in my immediate life to make me look naturally for meanness or sordidness or dishonesty, but constant hints of these things seeped in from the world around me. By the time I was fifteen, I had acquired a layer of protective cynicism that would have honored the proverbial cub reporter, and my tennis coach in high school, an excellent English teacher named Quimby, once said in perfectly justifiable horror, " You talk like a disillusioned man of sixty." Yet with all my early knowingness, I went through the first experience of being in love at fifteen — with Sybil, a girl I met at the tennis courts — as if all my life had been spent among the innocents of Arcadia. The other day I attended a singing festival given by the girls in one of our municipal colleges, a charming mass of hussies whose dance routines would have done credit to Broadway. In the very alluring performance they put on, in the songs they had made up, I detected the same combination of virginity and cynicism, of chastity and shamelessness — the curious patina of hardness that forms over youth in the big city. They were exquisitely young and fresh, yet already they were a little cheapened, a little soiled.

My own girl was one of those ruthless beauties who are never at ease unless they put five or six men simultaneously in a state of torture. With one, she danced for tango prizes in the footsteps of Irene Castle; with another, she swam; with another, she went to football games. She had us all, in fact, pretty well specialized and subordinated and it was usually for one of the older lads that she reserved her emotional complications. If I began earlier and remained on the scene longer than any of her other young admirers, it was because I served as a sort of fixed spar to mark the height of the incoming or the ebbing tide. Every once in a while she would cling to me to get her bearings. My specialty was playing tennis on the courts near Morningside Park, a few blocks from her apartment, at six in the morning, before she started her day as artist's model. It was perhaps the only time in my life, except in the Navy, that I visibly profited by my gift of waking up easily.

I can't pretend that there was anything very typical of New York in this relationship. The closest it came to taking on the color of the city was one hot summer night, on a street swarming with children and inundated by a hurdy-gurdy thumping out "Cavalleria Rusticana," when I told her I wanted to marry her. She was very self-possessed about that. She sent me round the corner for some ice cream, which the dealers then used to heap up in flimsy paper boxes, and then she took me up to the roof of her apartment house, a flight higher than the elevator went, so that we could talk matters over while we dipped, turn and turn, into the ice cream box. The thick summer sky flared to the east with the lights of Harlem, and on this high roof one had a sense of separation from the rest of the world one usually doesn't achieve in nature at a level lower than five thousand feet. But nobody ever succeeded in making love convincingly when his hands were all sticky from ice cream. Perhaps Sybil knew that when she complained about the heat. On her telling me what good friends we would always be — pals, in fact — I abruptly left her, and went down onto the steamy pavement, on which big raindrops were beginning to spatter, feeling dramatically solemn. The same tune — probably from the same hand organ — was still clanging in the distance. And I was already sketching in my mind the first act of a play to be called *Love on Morningside Heights*.

The Land and the Seasons

> . . . One of the reasons he hated living in the city, why in fact
> he regarded it as a prison, was that it gave him so little inkling of
> nature's ways and purposes from day to day.

To us who live in the northeastern countryside, the rhythm
of the seasons is strongly defined, and Geddes delighted to
follow that rhythm. He felt it unnatural, almost perverse,
when we lived in California, that the flowers should be bloom-
ing almost all through the winter and that "spring fever"
should threaten to be only a literary expression. (He was
delighted to find, a few months later, that his fears had been
unfounded: he carried spring within him.)

The seasons changed the aspect of the landscape and the
landscape, in rain and snow, in mist and moonlight, in drought
and heat, changed one's occupations, one's interests, one's responses, and so altered the inner man, too. As in the city, our
clothes varied in character from season to season, but far more
markedly, more fragrantly, as it were, in rime with nature.
I am not sure which season moved Geddes's heart to leap
highest; but there is no doubt about the character of his response; and one of the reasons he hated living in the city, why
in fact he regarded it as a prison, was that it gave him so little
inkling of nature's ways and purposes from day to day.

For all of us, the year-round span of country life was a new
experience. We would walk through the woods above the
lake, early in spring, to find the first hepatica or bloodroot,
while there were still crusts of ice over the leafy floor the sun
had not yet reached; we would watch for the first red-winged

NOTE: This and the following section, "The Kitchen," are family sketches
from *Green Memories*, Lewis Mumford's biography of his son Geddes, who
was killed in World War II.

blackbird to rise from the swamp on the way to the river, or hold our breaths the first mild night when the frogs would burst forth in spring. Day by day we would visit our buck-eye tree, at a corner of our home acre, to watch the great candles unfolding, and would almost dance around it when the solemn drone of the bees told us, what our eyes already knew, that the flowers were out in all their fullness: it was Geddes who suggested taking a picture of that tree in full bloom. We would sniff the air in June for the first honeyed scent of the locust trees; and we knew to a day, thanks to Geddes's vigilance, when the wild wood strawberries would be ripe.

There wasn't a wild apple tree within a mile whose apples we had not sampled and whose week of ripening we could not predict in advance. Like Thoreau, we thought they had a special savor, if you weren't after the more domestic virtues. We knew the pastures where, after July, we could usually expect to find field mushrooms, and we knew where, if we were willing to eat them in an unripened state, we might find the hazelnuts before the squirrels were ready to garner them: as for the hickory and butternuts, they were so plentiful that we and the squirrels shared and shared alike.

Our games and sports, of course, would vary with the seasons, too. But I don't think Geddes ever found a sport that seemed to him the equivalent of the realities of living in the country. He played baseball in his early high-school years, yes; and he played water polo with much gusto later, when he got the chance. But I find on the report of his prep school that although he was set down as a good soccer player, the team was forced to dispense with him as soon as the hunting season opened, and that thereafter the only sport he indulged in, apart from skiing, was " walking." That is all of a piece. Though Geddes quickly surpassed his parents at skiing and disdained, on such occasions, to be seen in their company, it was as a family that we used to go tobogganing on the hill beside the Farley house, or, when the lake froze over, go skating.

But the land offered pleasures that were too spontaneous and too brightly evanescent to be catalogued under sport: my notes tell of a day when he was fourteen and Geddes and I trudged to the lake, breaking through the crust of snow. A fox track, made when the top layer was soft, was still visible. The ice at the lake, rough and knobbly, was almost at the level of the dock. We clambered over the ridges between the lake and the river, hoping to make our way back across the stream; but we found the Webutuck open. Geddes, who had on rubber boots, ventured across on a log to visit a trap. Climbing back up the sandbank, he discovered swordlike icicles hanging from the undercut edge, and each of us seized one for a duel, literally breaking swords together. When we had only a fist of ice left, we'd reach for another cold sword. That duel must stand for a hundred unrecorded, rollicking moments.

The meaning of the seasons was not exhausted for us by any one thing we did or saw or felt. Autumn was squirrel hunting and pheasant shooting; but it was also wearing a leather jacket and a peaked hunting cap, even sporting a red kerchief; it was returning home in the dark indigo shadow of the mountain, at four-thirty, when the sinking sun made the white birches gleam against the cedars on the opposite slope. Autumn was helping to put up the storm windows and coming back in the afternoon after school to the doughnuts that Sophy might be frying in the kitchen, the smell of hot fat mingling with the spice of nutmeg, and a cold gallon of sweet cider, fresh from the cider mill, waiting in the pantry. Autumn was eating the well-ripened Mackintoshes and sampling, every few days, the ripening Spies or Baldwins; it was eating Nellie Honour's sausage meat and Sophy's currant jelly for breakfast, with bread fried golden brown in bacon fat, on a cold morning. Autumn was doping the boots with waterproofing when the heavy rains of November started to come down; it was burning the old stems of the asparagus right on the bed, or lighting greater bonfires of autumn leaves in the midst of the bare vegetable garden, with all of us raking the leaves together, and Geddes tumbling around in the great piles — often the other children of the village joining in the smoky fun. Autumn was picking the last fringed gentian in some sheltered spot, or bringing in great festoons of bitter-sweet, whose berries the first frost had broken open, and whose orange husks and crimson heart would splash color on the gray walls of the dining room through the darkest days of winter. Autumn was the smell of wood fires as one passed down the Leedsville road, or the not less pungent smell of freshly baked bread coming from the Duffys' kitchen, often followed for Geddes by generous slices of the bread itself, when he'd join John or Francis or Joe inside.

" Life is now! " In that nowness, as Geddes touched it and tasted it in the country, he had the keenest delight. In this vein his mother wrote: " Each moment is the only time in all of his life that has reality." If Geddes rarely looked before and after, he had no need, during this period, to pine for what was not; for between the ages of eleven and seventeen the country met his most exorbitant demands.

Do not fancy that I am reading into Geddes's heart our own special feelings toward the seasons and the landscape. On such matters he was always articulate. He openly scorned us as slugabeds because we would not join him at five-thirty on a winter morning, when he went down to the river to visit his trap-lines. When his mother marveled at his fortitude in going forth when the sky was still darkling and the earth cold and damp, shivering at the very thought, he exclaimed passion-ately: " You don't know what beauty is, if you've never been down to the river when the sun is just peeping over the hill and the alders are bright red against the snowbanks." He had no use for people who valued comfort above beauty; we seemed old and dismal to him then. So, too, he counted it a mark of good fortune, he wrote from Africa in 1944, that he had at least had a glimpse of spring at the port of embarkation, before his division sailed overseas.

In these feelings of his there was nothing exceptional; he was just a true countryman. I have heard Henry Duffy marvel at the freshness of a May morning when he went to milk the cows. " That's the time to be up," Henry said. " The day is never so grand as when the dew is still on the grass and the sun is catching it. It has a different smell, and I wouldn't miss it if you paid me." So, too, another neighbor, Johnny Green, remarked when Sam went to live on a fine old rundown farm in the hills: " If I were a rich man I'd get aholt of that place, just so's I could have the right to walk around it and look at it." Geddes's love for the rural scene was as direct and as unsophisticated as theirs. One Saturday morning when Geddes was twelve, Sophy records, Geddes and she went for a walk along the ridge in front of our house. It was fall; the colors were just turning; the dew glistened on grass and leaf, on wild aster, wilted bergamot and red sumach; the air was still and the sun brilliant. Geddes was enraptured by the scene and talked freely of it. After a while he turned to her with a slightly self-conscious smile and said: " You know, Mom, I can talk to you this way, but it'd never do to try it on the fellows. They'd think I was soft." He went on to say that he understood how they felt, because their backgrounds had given them no reason for feeling otherwise; but he was glad he could see beauty and appreciate it out loud. What Geddes got from his domestic background was only a heightened consciousness of what he felt, first of all, with passionate directness.

Often I had planned to photograph our familiar haunts in the country at various seasons of the year, just for the family record. But it actually remained for Geddes, when he was twelve, and had begun to take pictures and to print them — he was in partnership with John and they used a bricked-in part of the cellar for their dark room — it remained for him to leave behind a series of snapshots of the scenes he loved. There is our cornbrake blind, where we would lie in wait for a passing duck, till the cold numbed the trigger finger; there are the calves and horses in the pasture; there are teasing snaps of our cocker, Sol, a minute speck, ranging at impossible distances from the camera; there is the Webutuck in winter, half-covered with ice; yes, there is the countryside he knew, with its cows, its horses, its children, mute witness of his pursuits and his interests.

In all this, Geddes was renewing the spirit Thoreau had brought to the American landscape; the connection was not altogether an inappropriate one, either; for over these same pastures and hills had walked Myron Benton, the farmer and poet who had originally owned Troutbeck; the very Benton who had read Whitman and corresponded with Thoreau, the man to whom, indeed, Thoreau's last letter was written. Geddes responded in every fiber to Thoreau's question: " Who would not rise to meet the expectation of the land? " In another Benton of the same original line, the Benton MacKaye who conceived the Appalachian Trail, Geddes came within listening distance of a Yankee of the same breed as Thoreau. But he needed no one else to lead him to what these men had, each for himself, found; for nature's call came to him directly in the beat of his pulse, the breath of his lungs, the gleam of his eyes.

The Kitchen — What Went On There

... The kitchen was the great common family domain, and it could not have served its purposes if it had been planned for cooking alone. Mark that, you economical architects and you close calculators of costs per cubic foot!

Perhaps the best thing about our farmhouse was that it had a large old-fashioned kitchen, with a pantry that served as a secondary workroom for messier jobs. Its low crumbled ceiling was patched with puddles of ancient plaster; near the two windows facing south was a large deal table, painted daffodil yellow; and the walls were a lighter yellow that stood out against the gray woodwork.

The fittings of the kitchen changed from time to time; but the main thing about it was that it was spacious and many activities besides cooking went on there; for here is where the loot of Geddes's trapping and hunting would be piled; here is where, in winter at all events, he might — especially before his room was enlarged — play dominoes or chess with John; here is where he tested his traps, wound his fishing lines, greased his boots, or just lounged about and chatted with his mother. To some of the houseworkers who came and went during the next few years, Geddes's affairs seemed an intrusion; but, at least till he was fourteen, the kitchen was the great common family domain, and it could not have served its purposes if it had been planned for cooking alone. Mark that, you economical architects and you close calculators of costs per cubic foot!

Geddes had scope in this kitchen. His traps and gear hung on the hooks by the door; his guns nestled in the corner; his school books would be tossed on the window sill while he dashed out, with his shotgun, to " paste " some derisive crows.

Sophy gave him plenty of leeway in puttering around: my desk still has a paperweight, now precious and venerable, consisting of a little wooden boat carved by Geddes in the kitchen, its interior being a lead weight he had melted down on the stove from old foil and sinkers and poured into it. Much that Geddes and his mother had in common, apart from temperament, was bred of the intimacy that grew up out of this working relationship, with her baking or cooking while Geddes painstakingly cleaned his gun, or scraped the stretched skin of a muskrat. Naturally, cooking did not make the room less attractive to a growing boy. The aroma of pies, cakes, icings, cookies, hung over the house; on baking days, there would be bowls to lick, too.

It may well have been homesickness as well as appetite, that would lead Geddes, when he was at boarding school, to write Sophy: " I am thanking you in advance for those lovely brownies, *brownies,* and those supercolossal, stupendously good kookies with chocolate bits in them. And I do so like those cookies, especially when they are shipped by the hogshead the way you do." Yes: the kitchen and its products played no small part in Geddes's growing years. We used to broil steaks and chops over the open fire in the dining room, for Geddes and I both held, against Sophy, that they needed to be charred; but the kitchen remained the center of our actions and our affections: indeed, one could not pass from one part of the house to the other without going through it. No good architect could have planned the place so badly; but from a family point of view, no good architect would have had imagination enough to make such a happy, sociability-provoking blunder.

The best moments of life are usually unplanned for, indeed unplannable. The most one can do in designing a house to further intimacy and family living is to allow enough space to have one occupation take place beside another, so that people will meet spontaneously even when they are not drawn together by a common job. What is wrong with too sedulous a division of labor is simply the fact that it divides people. If the room is large enough, a family won't get into one another's way. Geddes's gear sometimes piled up too heavily and overflowed too copiously into the kitchen; but Sophy, wiser by instinct than I am, was always ready to sacrifice neatness and order to spontaneity and good fellowship, at least this side of sheer chaos. It is not an accident that shortly after news of Geddes's death came, while Sophy was lying in bed one night, midway between waking and sleeping, she saw him appear by the table in the kitchen. He said nothing; but he broke open his shotgun and squinted down the barrel: then he looked at her gravely. Many a time before that figure had stood in the doorway and ejected a cartridge or a shell before putting his gun away in the corner. This image was hardly even an hallucination. It stayed with her for days.

The kitchen was one of the best places for spontaneous confidences; and in the years before we had any sort of regular maid, that is, before Geddes was eleven, he used to take his turn at drying the dishes; and he and Sophy would talk together of school, of the outdoors, of tempting items in the Sears, Roebuck catalogue; in fact, about almost everything under the sun except guns, where a mere woman was no use. More than a few of these talks stand out in his mother's memory, though they occurred so often that the total effect is naturally blurred. Discussions of his future career were, however, perennial; and at twelve or so she remembers a very intent and serious one. One condition he laid down about a career then and never abandoned: he did not want to get into anything that would keep him indoors. That was the prime condition. He might be a doctor, for that would be of some service; but he wasn't sure he would make a good doctor, because his temper was short and he knew a doctor needed patience. Biological research then? Well, that would be interesting; but it might keep him indoors too much; so he didn't know. An old-fashioned naturalist? Maybe that or maybe a forester. He wasn't sure. It was a hard decision to make. He wanted to be of some use to other people.

Except at night, the kitchen was our living room, the very center of our indoor life as a family; but the whole house was very much to our taste, from the somber introverted living room to the bright extroverted sun room which faced the west. Compared with this Leedsville house, shabby, splintered, dented, battered though it is, and patched in a hundred places, the other houses we've lived in have seemed unbearably prim and formal. We couldn't from any fresh specifications have made a house that better conformed to our ideals of life than this homely structure, so lovable even in its faults, so warm in its feeling, so " matey " as the British say, even when the wind whistled through the clapboards and the none-too-tight joining of plaster and window. Geddes took pride in every fresh touch that added to its livability; when we finally put down a carpet in the living room in 1937, he exclaimed proudly, after helping unroll it: " Now we have a *house!* " The young roughneck liked the extra touch of elegance. There weren't too many.

Poems

CONSOLATION IN TIME OF WAR

Happy the dead!
If we do ill,
They will not know we lied.
Happy the dead!
If we do well,
Their death is justified.

FANTASIA ON TIME

Slip the reel into the rack, wind up the played-out film!
  Let beginnings be endings; let skeletons be
    enigmatic eggs.
Reverse the irreversible; let age deflate to youth and youth
  look forward to nonentity.

Mark how gray stubble darkens, how the flesh fills out
  the languid calf, the pain-dulled eyes awaken
    to expectancy;
Watch how easily the adolescents unlearn their letters,
  sheathe defiant frowns,
    recover their bloated infanthood
Until, leaving a stifled shout behind, they retreat
  into the womb: to disappear forever nine months earlier
With the orgasm that fades out into an early tremor of flesh
Beneath a lover's hand.

Dead men now levitate in coffins and return to sweaty beds
  whose creases unrumple before the sick arise to cautious
    health.

Thunders of war become the fainter thud of marching men;
Wild shot returns, unerring, to the cannon's mouth; trenches
     refill
With earth made innocent again; cathedrals geyser upward
From powdered stone to permanence; unknown soldiers re-
     cover dog tags of identification
And achieve the final anonymity of a name
Before they lose it for a second time at the baptismal font.

The daily bread, uneaten, vivifies into green shoots
     that down-pierce the earth and so retreat to seed.
An airplane, winging rearward for a landing place, hits the
     runway,
          dismantles into sticks and wires, becomes once more a
          sketchy
     mind thing, part hunch, part hope, part blueprint,
Part fanatic leer that vexes sleep with billowing motions
     in unfettered space.

And so it goes: the coal, consumed as heat, dispersed as gas, and
     dumped about as ashes, funnels downward
Into black clumps beneath the crannied earth,
While newspapers rise up again from libraries and moldy
     cupboard shelves,
          from scrapbooks, from rubbish heaps, from walls
          in mountain cabins, from the muck of cesspools,
To resume once more their pitiless serenity as trees.

The parted reunite; the dwindling friends recover intimacy;
     the wanton wife relapses into faithfulness, the husband
     reflates from boredom to unpunctured adoration:
And so the years diminish — diminish and recover clarity.

Slip the reel into the rack and wind it back again: let the past
     return upon itself: reverse the years!
Then youth's at hand once more
And all that worked toward our undoing is undone.

The cone of light sharpens the blackness that enfolds our
         images:
The sound track, returning to gibberish
     our pompous affirmations,
     the plot itself, unravelling to threadlike ends,
     unite to send us hurtling back
Through shrinking minutes, hours, days, lifetimes till we reach
     the point where credits are assigned and origins
     obliquely cited —
Whereat the celluloid will rip
     and leave cold silver light to shine embarrassment upon
     our certainty as to the authorship.

Wind up the paid-out reel no more!   This is the limit of our
         resurrection
And as much as we can bear of immortality.

THE TASTE OF NEW ENGLAND

On winter days alone one finds New England.
Brown slush creeps from South Station toward the India
         Wharf,
The bromine State House dome blends with the fog;
Upon the sullen muck, the powder-sprinkled newness
     of the snow, like sugar on burned hot cross buns,
Dissolves again.   The taste of brown grits in the mouth.

Brown is New England's color: the brown of sunburnt barns
     on Vermont hills,
The reddish brown beneath kelp-tangled rocks that thrust
     against the sea;
Umbers, cedars, bistres, coffees, chocolates, cinnamons;
The brown of sandalwood from India, Cuba's mahogany, and
     milo from Hawaii;

The brown of rotting wharves at Newburyport and Glouces-
         ter;
Brewed tea, tarred hemp, brown kegs and bean pots,
    smoked fish and tarpaulin;
Brown coils of rope, the spider brown of fishing nets;
    froth brown of turbid rivers in spring flood;
Brown tastes, acrid with spice or smoke; the tanner's brown
    at Lynn; butternut smears upon the hand;
Brown bacon rind, brown cider, plowed meadows, brown rus-
         sets
    that outstay the fall;
The moss-brown velvet of the tidal flats; brown oak leaves
    that scrape against a sodden sky.

Pull off New England's shroud!   White is for surfaces alone —
    white is for coverlets and icing.
Dissolve the genteel paint; scour the wood until you find the
         grain!
Beneath the mask you'll come upon the dark New England,
Dark as a face that's sailed around the Horn and blistered
    under the equator.
That's it: the sumac brown; the Fairbanks House and Haw-
         thorne's Seven Gables;
Richardson's Sever Hall, his shingled house on Brattle Street,
    his earth-brown libraries;
The smoke-charred soul of Melville standing alone,
    grim as a chimney when the house is gone.

Here is a proper home and, what is more, a destination;
This is what makes one hunger for the walnut-bitter hills
And poke around the tunnelled root cellars of old farmhouses,
         Where, at winter dawn, a pin of light between the rocks
         Shines like a sun.

3

Portraits of Persons

" James McMaster "

The perpetual energy of McMaster's mind bulges the brain itself into a forehead that becomes him like a crown.

Letters come from Hong-kong: letters come from Calcutta: they come from Jerusalem: Cairo: Marseilles: Paris: Brussels: Amsterdam: London, the New Forest: the letters are scraps of James McMaster: when Bernard reads them he partakes of the sacrament of discipleship: one of McMaster's ideas thrills Bernard like the touch of Eunice's arm: an invitation to collaborate on a book with McMaster causes shivers of frightened delight to run up and down Bernard's spine: to be a spoke in McMaster's wheel would be a short way of traveling far: Jerusalem and Hong-kong and the Sea of Japan are but suburban boroughs in James McMaster's realm: letters are dated there but the thoughts they bear edge slantwise toward infinity: a counter-love to Eunice plays in Bernard: if she is a warm sun, McMaster is the whole vault of sky: letters come from Aberdeen: letters come from Bergen: a letter from Pimlico invites Bernard to become a fellow in Comte House: a letter from Pimlico is a very hard letter to resist.

When Bernard and Eunice trudge through a soft mist of snow on Park Avenue, he tells her: I am going to London for a year. If I were not going away so long — the snowmist becomes a fuzzy carpet — the flakes cling to red wisps of Eunice's hair, unmelted, and flicker on her lashes — if I were not going to be away so long, says Bernard . . . if and if and if, mocks Eunice. If time in buckets, and gallons and gallons of ocean

NOTE: This selection, with its fictional portrait of Patrick Geddes, is from Lewis Mumford's novel *The Little Testament of Bernard Martin Aet. 30.*

85

were not to part us, says Bernard firmly, I'd say I love you. That is very sweet says Eunice: did it take a visit to the passport office to find this out? I love you, says Bernard stubbornly: if you will marry me I'll not go off to join McMaster. If I loved you, says Eunice, I'd have to bid you go *because* I loved you: it makes no difference: I bid you go because I don't. Don't shake me so: I am not mocking now. I don't love you, but gee oh gee: I wish I did. I'll paint your picture and keep it near to me: if I say yes to it, there's hope for you. There's something deep between us: I don't think we're going to part: but Bernard, you are very young, and I am twice as old as you already: so hurry up. My wild oats are nearly ready to be gathered: but yours are scarcely planted yet. Let's sow and reap together, cries Bernard. That's marriage, says Eunice: but marriage needs more love than I can muster for anyone: so let's be friends. I am not the girl you dream about: one never is: and you are what I want a friend to be, but nothing more. That night Bernard kisses Eunice: his warmth is far too courteous: it jeers at his illusion. The Sunday before Bernard sails is icy blank with jealous despair. Eunice's kisses have a mocking reserve, and Bernard's passion is too dispersed and fretful to convince anyone, even a virgin of eighteen. Virgins of eighteen know what love is without previous demonstration.

A hundred pounds a year in London is better than nothing at all a year in New York. Butter and sugar require ration cards in 1920 but Pimlico recovers from the effects of invalid soldiers by the application of paint to the gentlemanly grayness of houses that might have been friends with Colonel Newcome. Sociology was made by Comte the mistress of the sciences: but the concubines of science refuse to recognize the first wife of the Prophet. Comte House in Pimlico preaches the mistresship of sociology to spinsters who are looking for something useful to do as well as to the passionate souls who have watched the dawn of James McMaster's thought upon a gray world solemn with wheels, six per cent, and tick-tock.

Alighting from a donkey cart by a brick farmhouse whose thatched roof brightens to the gorse-gold moor at the edge of the New Forest Bernard beholds the man he has begun to call his master. Age has achieved the victory of a red beard beneath a spreading crown of silver hair. Gray eyes leap to Bernard with a friendly kiss: a knotted hand that seems a tough old root holds Bernard's hand and claps him on the shoulder: and through the beard a trickle of impatient questions runs off without an answer. The cuckoo calls across the moor. Bernard puts down his handbag. So this is he!

We do not dress for dinner says McMaster: but note the gorse Linnæus worshiped when first he trod upon these shores: ticker fools with country estates hoard their gold in banks and turn their backs to the gorse; of course you ride? New Forest ponies are perhaps too small for your six feet: my five-foot-six still finds them helpful: do you want to wash? or shall we climb that little rise and look the country over: don't bother about toilets: Cockneys pollute the rivers and deplete the land in the interest of sanitation while China keeps her civilization and her health by watching her stools: I hope you got your sea-legs quickly? a thermometer dropt into the water as Franklin did is a good way to study oceanography: did you remember? This is the common that keeps the widow's cow and some of Hampshire's yeomen independence: black days for England when enclosures broke up old folkways and prosperity: poor moles in London libraries now laugh at Goldsmith for picturing deserted villages they might find for themselves by leaving London for a day. You found Comte House and Mrs. Long? The place is a little bleak perhaps but tidy: a fine figure of a woman: they breed well in Inverness: but ay de mi! gray London will take away her scarlet cheeks: the

clear thought of us Scots has all it can to penetrate the beer and
fog that cover London from dawn to closing time: our bodies
suffer: Henry the first —

Bernard's head bobs like a groggy bottle in a mountain torrent. The perpetual energy of McMaster's mind bulges the
brain itself into a forehead that becomes him like a crown.
Bernard longs for the slow digestion of solitude but is relieved
to find a master looking like a master. . . . Stuffed furniture
and stuffy coals hem in the night. McMaster says abruptly:
What have your days been like? What have you done and
seen? What have you thought? What have you got for me?
What can I give you? Begin at your beginning not later than
your grandfather. When Bernard puts himself and all he's
been before the kindly sternness of those eyes he feels like
children who in manhood still take their dolls to be the proof
of their fecundity. The days have been crowded with emptiness; the days are the black embers of a letter with an irretrievable message.

A stew of paper! is McMaster's epithet. The brief diurnal
flickers of your journalism have neither light nor heat enough
to shame a candle. The worming through of books experience does not season is scarcely worth a worm's life, still less
yours: the poor preservative of abstention is all that's kept
your life from rotting utterly. You live like clerks and academic dunces who, wound in paper cocoons, prepare to met-
amorphose into dead butterflies. Soldiers, though stupid, have
the discipline of drill: but you have neither discipline nor the
strength that can forego it. Brace up, my lad, you're twenty-
four and you have scarce as yet begun to live. Now look you
here —

A panic sobs in Bernard's bosom. It is true. His days bear
the imprint of tick-tock: they bear the imprint of escaping

tick-tock: but little else is there. In the forest of Bernard's bewilderment McMaster spreads a map that diminishes the impenetrable confusion of the landscape: each contour is a shrunken reproduction of life's explored terrain. Life active and passive, now dominating circumstances by dreams, thoughts, and inventions, now submitting like soft wax to circumstance's mold: sea-shell and house, antheap and city, tropism and full-fledged idea march into an organic unity: nothing exists as by itself, but always reacting and being reacted upon as Life's pendulum swings from not-being into being and back again. Priapic beasts and the seven gods and goddesses of Greece reveal man's biological aspiration: at every stage the ideal is but the hidden uttermost of life's own reality.

The natural history of life and life's environment, portrayed by Kepler, Newton, Boyle and Kelvin, by Chambers, Lyell, Darwin, Pasteur, Faraday, reveals a truncated panorama in which the foreground is forgotten — which is man. Upon the empty destiny of things man flings the challenge of himself: Pythagoras married mathematics and music to make the stars dance: Plato, Buddha, the Nine Muses and Shakespeare brought forms into existence that Nature, unfulfilled by man, did not suspect. Jesus Christ is just as real as Plato's Socrates: dead, each achieved a new life in the mind more powerful than any Alexander knew on earth. How many men have followed Christ who would not recognize divinity in flesh? By idea, image, and ideal man makes new bestiaries: he dreamed himself out of some blinder shape: his thought imposes destinies and ends upon a formless world that chases its own tail. Man is the chimera and the centaur and all the devils in hell and all the gods above!

The donkeys from whose backs young Bernard had painfully unloaded their damaged wares had made of science something hostile and averse to life; and all that smelt of life became a wanton idleness and imbecility. Truth and beauty were at war among the donkeys: dead science was the counterfeit of endless externalities which might be turned to the practical account of tick-tock: literature and art were phantom faces dancing in non-existent fires. Good-truth is gospel! Truth beautiful is life's highest symmetry! But donkeys purposely kept truth in calico and curl-papers lest she be raped by ambushed admirers, whilst esthetic donkeys emptied out beauty's brains, because sawdust had been found more satisfactory for dolls. Among the tough and tender donkeys the real and the ideal could never meet: they gave each other the cold shoulder and the cut direct: the grounds for their divorce were science's frigidity, slightly aggravated by imagination's impotence.

Science and art were separate loads upon the backs of donkeys: but in James McMaster's thought Life had begot them both: they were the modes in which Life's rhythm, now turning ego-ward for sustenance, now turning toward the world for mastery, achieved that harmony of acts and facts and dreams and deeds without which life does not dance or leap at all but moves in palsy or droops in a paralysis, now overwhelmed by facts it cannot master or by acts it can't direct, now breaking out in wishful dreams that come from nowhere, lead to nothing, now galloping in vain achievements like the conquests of Napoleon or the misplaced ingenuity of printing presses whose precise and utmost excellence makes yellow journals spawn more easily each hour. Euclid and Plato are not at war: the reality of conic sections or electrons cannot deny the other life-reality of Goethe, Michelangelo, or Blake. Life spans all categories in its movement and reconciles all verbal contradictions: we move in spite of Zeno! Our being is what makes the difference to an indifferent universe!

Living, men break through all the husks that keep them safe but undeveloped: the husk of status and profession: the husk of empty creed: the husks of brainless actions and inactive brains: the husk of fixed environments and habits: the husk of righteousness that clings to well-established evils lest it meet greater ones: the husk of comfort and security. Donkeys live on husks: they gorge themselves to sleep and balkiness. Their daily diet is a bag of husks, the husk of politics and mediocre letters, the husk of invention, business, scientific inquiry directed to the greater glory of card-indexes and tick-tock: the husk of acting, moving, thinking, planning, feeling with a minimum of discomfort and disarrangement: the husk of preparing for eventualities that never arrive and discoursing at length about unimportant contingencies so that stuffed donkeys may earn glass cases in museums. . . . *Vivendo discimus!* If appetites are ready, food will follow. To be alive means clear eyes and a good digestion: a readiness to risk one's neck or lose one's sleep: a willingness to work at anything one needs for bread or knowledge from catching fish to measuring an atom's dance: the will to be incorporated with others in a family, union, shop or city, and yet to keep one's proper self intact. A life well-keyed will find its way with equal ease about a landscape or a library. To be a man at all means sharing in the modes of life that men have found a help to sheer existence or to ecstasy.

These were McMaster's thoughts. They broke through many husks young Bernard had built up and labeled Education, Wisdom, Culture. They robbed his idols of their forehead's jewels: Bernard Shaw became a cockney limping on a crutch whose shape denied his limb's deformity: he proclaimed the Life-Force but forgot its main activities. Old Berkeley's ego-begotten world was the mooniness of lonely nights. Dear William James seemed but a half-philosopher whose appetite for life was what alone gave life to his philosophy. Dewey kept close to acts and facts but dared not embrace dreams and deeds, lest he be smothered: his better world was generated in an experimental vacuum. The socialists were cockneys, too, who took machines to be prime-movers, and forgot the sun, and what the sun does to the leaf, and how the leaf spreads through man's life. Science used Cartesian dialectics to despise philosophy: philosophy was cowed into forgetting it had forged the weapon for its defeat. Whitman, Emerson, Wordsworth, and Plato kept their seats in Bernard's pantheon: Tolstoy and Goethe joined them: most of the rest were called upon for kitchen duty or for music at vacant intervals. Rabelais and Dickens were the chief factotums in this refurbished household; but there were others. Bernard began to worship trees, because he found in them the vital harmony McMaster sought. If men were sycamores or beeches they'd know less movement and more growth.

Temples are built of solid stones: idols do not fall at once. The night McMaster talks till dawn with Bernard finds Bernard shrinking into a chaos of complicated resistances, half paralyzed by worship, weariness, and fear. He shrinks chamberwise with a trickling taper and cannot find the outer door of sleep, aghast at that great pride and energy of mind which takes life for its province and falters at nothing between the astronomy of distant stars and the aspirations of religion or the physiology of our inmost cells, but has a place for all, and an appetite to master more. The furious iteration of McMaster's voice, the gray eyes that look past sorrow and love into the core of the Whirlwind, become the image of the dreadful God that Gustave Doré had set up in Bernard's skies at five or seven. Eventually Bernard sleeps. Eventually Bernard awakes. Eventually the reality of his own sapless days is mixed with the memory of a conversational dream that ended in an intangible triumph. India rubber tubs chill the spine: Americans are not used to bathing in a can of hot water.

In London dreams evaporate and intellectual discourse is difficult after a breakfast at nine that includes oatmeal, kippers,

eggs, marmalade, and toast. Men worship Mammon: but Mc-
Master plays with him and Moloch: thrice each month he
meets with financiers who build railways in remote provinces
of India in order to bring the curse of Manchester's dirt to a
civilization that has long enjoyed its own ordure. On the
other days, McMaster plans museums and cities, plows through
the muck of learned discourses to seize jettisoned diamonds,
exhibits ideas like specimens in cases to the willing few who
make Comte House their intellectual home, throws pearls to
swine and goldpieces to beggars who achieve academic re-
spectability and a modicum of fame out of the remains of
McMaster's breakfast cogitations. Bernard does not rise at
five. New Yorkers bred with perpetual janitors and steam
do not like to arise in a cold room at five. Bernard's day with
McMaster begins when the stuff of McMaster's thinking has
already shaped itself in many folded wads of paper, each teasing symbol leading to a book perhaps that's still unwritten.
Sanderson shares their quarters: a grizzled cherub whose pink
skin is like his own translucent thought: whose blue eyes burst
in merriment over entertaining ideas. When Bernard talks
with Sanderson and McMaster all ideas are entertaining.
Even Bernard learns to spend a whole day in discussion without feeling that breakfast dinner supper are more important.
It is a great victory for an American to forget breakfast, lunch,
and dinner — but even Sanderson and McMaster remember
tea!

Twilight hours on the Chelsea Embankment: twilight mist:
the snaily creep of smoke from distant chimneys: the words of
Eunice's letters that never deepen beyond the twilight of scattered friendship into firm and starry night. Red Chelsea pensioners blotted against the green twilight of remote gardens:
red Chelsea houses against the purple twilight of the afterglow. Human twilight! The white twilight of Carlyle's
pain: the blue twilight of Whistler's sentimental cynicism:

the dusky mottled twilight of the stones that whisper ancient titles to Henry James: the greasy twilight that swims around a Crosby Hall no nearer to Eutopia than Thomas More himself was!   To strain for Eunice's words through the twilight of a summer's night: to find the words no warmer and no brighter than the evening: to drop one's hopes in the muddy slime of the receding Thames: to find no rest in the creaky twilight of a deserted house. . . .

Verhaeren and Van Gogh went mad in London: who would not?   Miles of dull streets are miles of dull streets.   Where does Whitechapel Road end and has anybody ever found Tooting or tried to walk through Clapham Junction or get a drink at the Elephant and Castle?   To survive a beef stew in a yellow-greasy Lyons is to earn the Order of the Iron Stomach with bars: the sound of a coster hawking fresh filberts or white heather would make harsh the faint murmur of distant winds: but the English of Oxford is worse than the French of Strat-ford-atte-Bowe.   Unsuspecting foreigners have been killed at the heart by an icy Euooh? aimed at the indecency of their candor.   But a bus-conductor may be a friend in need: a weaver from Nottingham may turn a weekend labor confer-ence at Morley College into an assembly of dignified and help-ful men.   Snout, Bottom, and Starveling have more humanity than the prigs, false-faces, uniforms, and worldly wisemen — and the crowd always feeds the pigeons in front of St. Paul's.

The red fog of a September morning by Green Park suc-cessfully counterfeits Joseph Mallord William Turner.   When the barges slide past the Doulton potteries on a dank afternoon, they are better than almost anything in the Tate Galleries. Saturday night market on Churton Street has a levity that finds only feeble echoes in colossal music halls — and God never

made a June day for anything but a walk up the tow path from
Kew Gardens to Richmond.   The shade of William Morris
saunters under the willows to Richmond meditating news from
nowhere; Bernard and Charlotte follow the shade, two
friendly people drawn into the friendly world that Morris
pictured, under willow, over stile, past a grass bank, by a lock,
till Richmond Bridge and many punts and picnickers close up
the vista.

Charlotte came from Aberdeen to help fallen women before
she knew exactly what fallen women were.   That was seven
years before she found a post in Comte House and left a posey
of tulips over the fireplace in Bernard's room when he arrived.
Charlotte plumbed the depths of other people's tragedies so
successfully she made them forget her own was deeper: but
love, despair, suicide, jealousy had singed the hem of every
garment that she wore.   She had watched her youngest friends
go bitterly and unconvinced to death in France: she had
worked with labor men and conscientious objectors in the
face of a family that took comfort in the editorial certitudes
of the *Morning Post:* her sweetness tartened as one side of her
clutched loyalty, the other love. . . .   She says: Oh dear: I
thought so! when Bernard tells her about Eunice.   She says:
Remember to wear your evening clothes, when he almost goes
to a dinner in Notting Hill Gate without a dinner coat.   She
says: They have Maids of Honor tarts some people call nice
at Richmond: and there is an old tree in the park that was
meant to shelter lovers or conversation.   We have plenty to
talk about she adds firmly.   Charlotte dresses with the am-
biguous primness of a private secretary.   Her tweeds are a
little too heavy and her shirtwaists not less serviceable than
ugly.   Her voice is a clear Northern voice.   Her face and her
body are a fine landscape, shorn by a November storm: her
mind is a lake in the midst of the landscape, agitated but deep.

When one sees her mind gleaming through a copse of hazel eyes one finds that her face is beautiful. Like a blindman, poor young Bernard plucks at the heavy tweeds and the assertiveness of metallic dress supporters, and takes a long time to discover that her face is beautiful.

Charlotte gently wipes clear the foggy patches in Bernard's mind. Charlotte smiles at Bernard's rages against old England: she finds the southern English funny, too, and likes the gaunt dank air of Edinburgh, drinking terror in black closes, more than the slatternly complacence of London. A Sunday spent discussing Eunice in the greenwet silence of the Chiltern beeches almost removes the thought of Eunice from Bernard's heart. When Charlotte recites patches of Chaucer from a northern Down-top near the grassy Pilgrim's Way, Bernard swoops with her to Canterbury, quite forgetting ties of Franco-German-American ancestry. The smell of marjoram and mignonette: the blush of Charlotte's prim-dancing face: almost make England a possibility if ten years and many customs did not come between their pairing. In complementary qualities, Bernard and Charlotte are well-married: but the parish register does not recognize marriages made in Heaven unless they come down to earth. Charlotte feels too tender towards Bernard to let him come down to earth. She has an uncle who was a general in Afghanistan, and her father retired from the Hong-kong Customs Service with honors: Oxford, Cambridge, Eton, or Cheltenham are the prerequisites for marriage in her family. Charlotte has five equally maiden sisters.

The days are wrung by the dry torture of desire: the days crawl with the slow crawl of a thirsty man over a desert. . . . The days do not bring Eunice and the days do not bring peace. Ideas are gadflies that add to the sting of unslaked thirst. When Bernard proposes to Eunice again by letter she answers tardily that she prefers to keep her pastels fresh without such fixatives. She is a little diverted by the snorting raptures of a Spanish sculptor who has asked her to be his mistress: she disdains the fetters of such minor titles, too, but likes the bulky power that would impose them. She hopes that Bernard will remain her friend in any case: she does not love Bernard yet: his portrait made her brush go mushy: she's turned it to the wall: and she is rather overpowered by the Spanish bull.

Five boats go back and forth across the Atlantic before Bernard is reasonably sure that the bull has not immediately succeeded. When McMaster says: Come to Palestine to plan the New Jerusalem this fall, Bernard replies: I am going back to America: I want a terrestrial girl more than I want the City of God itself. McMaster says: Ask her to join you there! Bernard fuzzes a mournful and despairing reply. Ideas and sweethearts do not mix: marriage comes first or never. McMaster says: But girls are everywhere: so why turn back? And Bernard says: Such rootlets as Americans have they must preserve. Eunice was born in Brooklyn, I in Staten Island: we both know what a walk along the Palisades is like. Having no deeper roots, I keep those that I have: I'm going back: sometimes I think that Eunice is only America: I need America too. Tough French and Scottish roots are French and Scotch wherever they may be: but what is an American but a hope that has not taken root? Old stocks may rove: we pioneers must settle down. If you would understand it, read *The Ordeal of Mark Twain*. You have given me all that I can take — a thousand thoughts still wait to be digested. I'll give them a sea-change and set them out in an American garden. Bear with me! And McMaster says: Marriage sometimes wrecks philosophy: but a married philosopher thinks with a double mind: one such in Athens stirred up Plato — all hail Xantippe! My thoughts must stand the biological test: if marriage brings oblivion to philosophy the fault's not marriage's. An old angler never blames the fish. Good luck! my lad. When you come back, bring Eunice with you. Don't mind if there's a bairn or two: we'll find a bit for all. Unless young folks live dangerously they'll only have skeletons for thoughts and rabbits for progeny.

Patrick Geddes

Geddes is primarily the philosopher of life in its fullness and unity: his doctrine rests on the perpetual capacity of life to renew itself and transcend itself.

Patrick Geddes was born in 1854, two years before Bernard Shaw. One of Shaw's biographers rated Geddes the only contemporary whose conversation equaled Shaw's in brilliance and range; but apart from that, the life and work of the two men stand in striking contrast: so much so that the qualities of one bring into relief those of the other. Shaw was a man of letters who sought to startle his contemporaries by a new formula for originality: common sense disguised as perversity and perversity parading as common sense. Geddes was primarily a scientist, shy of committing his thoughts to writing, lest the provisional and dynamic and tentative become static and absolute. Since his was a truly original mind he was more ready to embrace a healthy truism than a meretricious originality: he valued truth itself rather than the vanity of its authorship. From the first, Shaw fell in love with his own image and spent the greater part of his life erecting a pedestal for it and laying wreaths around it. Geddes, on the other hand, had no concern with his own advancement and no skill in the Shavian art of publicity: his last pathetic bid for influence, his acceptance of a knighthood, an honor he had spurned in middle life, was indirectly responsible for his death.

For all Shaw's verbal audacity he was by nature a Fabian: a prudent man, with an essentially middle-class mind, concealing his inability to come to grips with the ultimate matters of human existence, birth or death, love or marriage or man's destiny, by contriving witty arguments, with a legalistic turn, about the more peripheral aspects of these subjects. Geddes was by instinct and intention the opposite type of personality: a Scipian, if I may coin the term, as different from Shaw as the bold Scipio Africanus was from Fabius. Geddes was committed to the frontal attack and to direct action, not because he loved power, but because he put the needs of life first. Even when Shaw was most verbally revolutionary, he usually played the game and sought the rewards of the game; while even when Geddes was most loyal to tradition he would not play the game. Though Geddes sought to become a teacher, he refused to qualify for a degree; though he held a professorship in botany he taught only for three months in summer term; though he helped to found the Sociological Society and though the Martin White chair of Sociology at the University of London was founded for his occupancy, he did so little in his probationary lecture to win the approval of the University Committee that they turned him down. Once Shaw was well started as dramatist his career was engulfed by success; whereas Geddes' life was, superficially, a long succession of failures: crowned by the final failure of his last decade, the heap of stone buildings and exotic gardens at Montpellier which he called the Collège des Ecossais: an attempt, in defiance of his own philosophy, to transmit ideas through buildings instead of through other personalities.

Yet these contrasts and antagonisms between Shaw and Geddes need not wipe out all the essential qualities they had in common, little though that brought them together: they shared high spirits, a gift for satiric criticism, and a savage contempt for sham; and if any single philosophy threads through Shaw's work it is that of evolutionary vitalism: a doctrine of the primacy of life both men derived from a scientific source, Darwin, and a humanistic source, John Ruskin. The preface to *Man and Superman*, and the " Metabiological Penta-teuch " of *Back to Methuselah*, even parts of *Major Barbara*, float on the same stream of ideas that carried Geddes along:

both men were vitalists, rather than mechanists; and both were ultimately "Lamarckians" as well, in that they gave to the organism an active role that the purely negative theory of natural selection erroneously overlooked. In an ideal world Geddes and Shaw, who encountered each other from time to time, at least in the meetings of the Sociological Society, in the first decade of this century, should have been allies and co-partners, lending each to the other his own special strength; but, as so often happens with contemporaries, they were hardly close enough to graze each other as rivals, to say nothing of becoming friends. So each lost what the other might have given him: if Geddes had studied the arts of winning an audience as carefully as Shaw, and if Shaw had acquired any of Geddes' gift for detachment and impersonality, they both might have left a deeper mark on their age.

If Geddes died a little prematurely, Shaw alas! outlived himself by almost a generation: after *St. Joan* little but hollow echoes and shallow cackles remain even in his dramas, while his judgment of men and events revealed progressively the weakness of the mind that had hailed Houston Chamberlain's rubbishy *Foundations of the Nineteenth Century* as one of the great books of our age; so his words spelled confusion, and his admiration went forth to tyrants and dictators. As a result, Shaw has become an anachronism, and, one grieves to say of a youthful idol, a figure of folly, even during his lifetime; whereas Patrick Geddes, though dead these eighteen years, is fast becoming a rallying center for the best minds of this generation: his thought, like that of his old associate and friend, Kropotkin, will probably guide the future, since the mechanists and the Marxists, in the present hour of their triumph, demonstrate the failure of their philosophies to do justice to either life or the human spirit.

Geddes is primarily the philosopher of life in its fullness and unity: his doctrine rests on the perpetual capacity of life to renew itself and transcend itself, a capacity first interpreted in the sequence of evolutionary forms, and now in the extra-organic transformations brought about by man in his personality and culture. Other biologists have described life in terms of assimilation and responsiveness, of sensitiveness and growth, but Geddes added to the usual list of organic traits a quality he himself exhibited to the utmost degree: insurgence — a capacity to overcome, by power or cunning, by plan or dream, the forces that threaten the organism. Above all, he exemplified a robust wholeness of personality, ready to meet life at every level and to make the most of every occasion; he was against the pseudo-efficiency of specialization, which creates efficient machines and ruins good men. He himself refused to be pigeonholed in any single compartment, as botanist, sociologist, educator, artist, or townplanner, and he paid a heavy penalty for this refusal. Though Geddes had a high professional competence in every field he entered, his colleagues tended to accord him a lower status than he was entitled to. Instead of perceiving that Geddes' capacity for coordinated and interrelated thinking was a far more exacting discipline than any single specialism demanded, Geddes' conventional contemporaries saved their own pride by treating this special capacity as inferior to their smaller gifts.

Fortunately for those who came after him, Geddes took all knowledge as his province and all life as his field of action; and by his example he has made it easier to introduce organic methods of thought and action into aspects of life hitherto severed, amputated, discrete. But Geddes' immediate influence was mainly a direct personal one; his books, even when supplemented by his manuscripts and notes, were only a small part of his total productivity. For that reason, as year by year the people who were acquainted with Geddes diminish, his written work — meagre and ineffectual though it is — takes on greater importance than it did in his lifetime. Hence one's special welcome for the new edition of *Cities in Evolution*.

Cities in Evolution came out in 1915: apart from his com-

prehensive study of the parks and civic institutes of Dun-
fermline, this was Geddes' first book on the subject of civics
and urban development; and if one sets aside his town planning reports, it was also his last. The 1950 edition, edited by
Arthur Geddes and Jaqueline Tyrwhitt, is both greater and
less than the original text. The book was not a closely woven
treatise, but a series of papers; and because some of these papers
have long since become dated, the editors have omitted five
chapters. These deletions are well justified, and Geddes himself would have been the last to insist on pious adherence to
the letter of the original text. In only one respect does the
editing seem to me a little ruthless: namely, in the omission of
Geddes' characteristic story of what happened to Cinderella's
kitchen, when the proud sisters dismantled her abode and her
working utensils to bedeck other parts of the house. That
parable still seems to me in Geddes' best vein, condensing centuries of history into a few memorable images; so I regret the
loss.

But if the editors have eliminated some of the vitamins with
the chaff, they have also fortified the loaf with ingredients
that were not contained in the original book; and for a generation that hardly knows Geddes, except at second hand, these
additions more than make up for the losses. First, they have
added part of a lecture on the Valley Section given by Geddes
at the New School for Social Research in New York in 1923.
Though the editors have also left out Geddes' original illustrations for the book, they have again more than made up for this
by utilizing illustrations from the second Town Planning Exhibition, accompanied by a text by Geddes himself, drawn
from the first exhibition's catalogue of 1910. Finally, the editors have published in the generous appendix Geddes' " Nota-
tion of Life " on 36 squares, an appreciative essay on his
graphic presentation of interrelated phenomena by two keen,
modern students, John Turner and W. P. Keating Clay, along
with Amelia Defries's description of his final Dundee lecture,

an essay from Geddes' "Sunday Talks With My Children," and a synopsis of Geddes' life, based on Boardman's biography.

With the help of this supplementary fare, a representative part of Geddes' essential thought on cities and civilizations is now for the first time at hand. Before I attempt to estimate Geddes' message, I should like to forfend any possible disappointment, on the part of the reader who may feel a certain letdown on first encountering Geddes, by saying a more personal word about the book's original impact on the American reader thirty-five years ago.

Cities in Evolution was first published in the second year of the First World War; and not a small part of my initial pleasure in its contents came from the way in which Geddes referred, without a word of rancor, to the sinking of his first Town Planning Exhibition en route to India by (to use his words) the "vigilant and enterprising *Emden*." There was something Olympian about Geddes' magnanimity in the face of this grievous loss of a lifetime's collecting. And it was the more striking because Geddes was a forthright critic of Prussianism in all its phases and had no doubts about the justice or the necessity of resisting with arms the military rule it sought to impose on the rest of the world. Geddes had greatness of soul as well as of mind; and though I never achieved any real degree of intimacy with him, that first sense of his greatness was not dulled by successive contacts. He could be willful; he could be self-absorbed; he could even be tyrannical, with the ruthlessness of a man wholly intent on his own ideas, to the exclusion of any other human considerations that stood in their way. But behind such petty phenomena was a noble understanding. Perhaps what makes his writing so pregnant with thoughts beyond anything he actually expressed are the perpetual hints he gave of that magnanimity and amplitude of spirit.

Cities in Evolution opened a wider vista on a world I had first explored in reading his earlier volume on *City Develop-*

ment. No member of the present generation, with normal opportunities for study and reading, can fancy how exciting any book on cities was before 1920 — to say nothing of one like Geddes', which related the transformation of cities to the social, economic, and cultural situation of our time. Except for a few tracts on housing and municipal reform, a series of anecdotal histories, a handful of town planning treatises mainly retrospective in outlook, whether they went back to Versailles or Rothenburg, and finally Ebenezer Howard's brave utopian proposal for garden cities, the literature of cities was singularly barren: indeed, in English, almost non-existent. Though the nineteenth century was certainly, in a quantitative way, the greatest era of city building the world had ever known, it created its new urban environment without benefit of art or science. Neither the methods nor the goals of urban planning were understood: for the city itself, as an artifact of culture, had hardly been described; and without knowledge the last century lacked the power to create.

During the first decade of the present century, Geddes' life-long survey of cities began to take fruit in a series of papers on the sociology of cities, first presented as lectures at the Sociological Society, founded by him and his colleague Victor Branford. These were, I believe, the first systematic contribution to the sociology of cities. Though the Germans had done much important work on the historic origin of cities, and in France a new school of urban geographers were dealing with the geographic determinants of urban structure, few students had Geddes' grasp of both the geographic and the historical factors in the evolution of cities.

Cities in Evolution, however, was not a contribution to scholarship; its essential subject was the education of the citizen toward his understanding of urban processes and his active assistance in urban development. Using his own self-education, through study and practical activity as a basis, Geddes sketched out the background the citizen needed in history and geography and travel, in economics, politics, architecture, sociology. Thus at that juncture in urban history, *Cities in Evolution* performed the most valuable service that any single book could have performed: it taught the reader, in simple terms, how to look at cities and how to evaluate their development. See for yourself; understand for yourself; act on your own initiative on behalf of the community of which you are a part. That summarized Geddes' message. From the moment I gathered the import of Geddes' words, I began walking through the streets of New York and planning excursions into its hinterland with a new purpose: looking into its past, understanding its present, replanning its future became indissoluble parts of a single process, a task for all citizens, not merely for professionals.

Peering forth alone, the first green shoot in a garden that had hardly been spaded, *Cities in Evolution* had an effect that the much richer and fuller literature now available can scarcely produce. Like Wordsworth's Lucy, Geddes' book was as a star when only one is shining in the sky. The uniqueness of that moment cannot be recalled by the present republication of the book; but if Geddes' words seem as familiar as lines from *Hamlet*, it is only because by now they have successfully taken possession of us. Directly or indirectly, a large part of the essential thought of Geddes has been happily absorbed by both the theorists and practitioners of town planning and regional reconstruction. For all that, *Cities in Evolution* is no mere monument. Though time has disclosed certain weaknesses in Geddes' approach, we have hardly yet done justice to his merits; and for a long time to come Geddes' own personality will remain as a preservative of the text: a perpetual challenge to the academic, a threat to routineers, a curse upon the bureaucrats, and a blessing to re-enforce the self-respect and the humanity of the plain citizen.

Patrick Geddes' approach to cities was colored by his training as a biologist: he was a student of Huxley and in the direct line of descent from the great Victorian thinkers who gave an adequate interpretation, for the first time, to the impact of nature on man. Just as he was vividly aware of the persistence of primitive occupational types in the more complex social order of the city, so he was equally interested in the effect of geographic and economic factors on the higher life of the city: the effect of jute manufacture on Dundee, of silk manufacture on Lyons, of cotton on Manchester. As a naturalist, his first approach to cities, in *Cities in Evolution*, was by way of the population map, by whose shadings and colorings he showed that the cities of the twentieth century had ceased to be self-contained units, as in the Middle Ages, but were spreading and thickening along the lines of transportation into urban coagulations, "man-reefs" as he called them: areas on which he bestowed the name of conurbation, a coinage that waited a generation before it found acceptance in England.

This new situation called for direct adaptations: first formulated by the Webbs from their quite different point of view in their New Heptarchy series. "The old Borough Councils and County Councils," Geddes pointed out, "can no longer separately cope with what are becoming so plainly yet larger Regional and Inter-Regional tasks, like those of water supply and sanitation for choice. . . ." That perception was a timely one; but Geddes, trusting to the slow processes of social interaction and growth, was reluctant to push on with the Webbs' program of "municipalization by provinces." Instinctively he disliked the Webbs and all they stood for: their arid utilitarian outlook, their wooden formulae, their wily managerial efforts; and that disagreement was a deep and vital one. But he himself seemed to feel that science, once sufficiently diffused, would take the place of active political pressure: that once people looked at the same map together and recognized the same facts, they would find that they had no substantial differences of opinion or policy. Even when Geddes recognized the conflicts in interests and ideals that were currently expressed in politics, he believed that these would be nullified by the further advances in technology. In this disregard for non-rational factors, both attitudes were a little naïve.

Geddes' hopes here were supported — somewhat mistakenly — by his brilliant analysis of the industrial revolution: he was the first to see that, so far from being a uniform transformation, due to a succession of related inventions, there were substantial technical differences between the first stage (paleotechnic), based on coal and iron and steam, and the second phase (neotechnic), based on the water turbine, electricity, and the lighter metals. The essays defining these stages form the fourth and fifth chapters of *Cities in Evolution*. In this original contribution, both Geddes' observations and his intuitions were excellent, though, characteristically, he was more inclined to repeat his first discoveries than to work them out in any detail. Unfortunately, like most of the great thinkers of his period from Karl Marx to Henri Bergson, he was disposed to overestimate the direct effect of technics upon social life and to overlook the way in which surviving social institutions and customs can subvert both science and technology to their own purposes: the neotechnic city, based on the use of hydroelectric energy, which Tony Garnier had outlined with such startling clarity and beauty in his plans for the Rhone valley, did not automatically come into existence; rather, our new technical facilities, steel construction, electric lifts, electric railways, and motor cars, were all utilized to augment the congestion of the paleotechnic city and prepare further costly palliatives of its disorder. The hope that progress was immanent and inherent in the application of science and technics to the social order was one that Geddes shared with his age; he died, indeed, before he had a chance to confront the ultimate contradiction between science and human intentions: the fact that the most triumphant application of human thought to the understanding of nature, which has led to the release of atomic energy, has also, because of our social

delinquency and moral depravity, endangered the very existence of the human race.

Both temperament and conviction led Geddes to center his
attention on education rather than on politics, though political
activity is itself a powerful instrument of education. In *Cities
in Evolution*, he was concerned with the preparation of the
citizen for active citizenship, first of all by travel. Geddes
believed that the way to overcome the current disparagement
of the " politics of the parish pump " was to first drink, as it
were, from many different pumps. By traveling the student
observes cities in the context of their regions and their cultures — all the better if he travels on foot part of the way and
takes his sightseeing slowly. This outdoor education was an
essential part of Geddes' civic philosophy, indeed, of his professional preparation as townplanner: a corrective for the
limitations of one-sided views, second-hand knowledge, third-
hand statistics. Moreover, the eye unifies what the practical
mind breaks up and analyzes: without the synoptic view, one
cannot take in the complex interrelationships of urban life,
even though one utilizes Geddes' squared paper diagrams.

But travel must be not merely wide but intensive: applying
the same methods to one's home one produces the regional
and the civic survey — both in their modern form inventions
of Geddes, though Mayhew and Booth had partly anticipated
him. Geddes' slogan, " Diagnosis before Treatment," has now
been so generally accepted that it is in danger of being perverted into an end in itself: as with the physicians of Park
Avenue and Harley Street, the mechanical technique of diagnosis, by sheer elaboration, may almost divert effort from the
need for curative measures or the possibility of taking short
cuts to health. Here the example of Geddes' *Civic Survey of
Edinburgh* should serve as both encouragement and warning
to the planner. Though Geddes knew that city in more intimate detail than any other, his survey was but a pamphlet.
In all creative thought, there is perhaps as great a danger in

knowing too much as in knowing too little. Geddes, despite his insatiable curiosity and his capacious scholarship, always valued an ounce of direct " acquaintance with " more than a pound of " knowledge about."

Since only a small fraction of the population travels widely, Geddes sought to make up for the lack of personal acquaintance with other cities, among the mass of citizens, by organizing Cities Exhibitions. In his day the film was still undeveloped and the documentary was almost non-existent: even the lantern slide projector was a clumsy machine to use. So Geddes chose to use pictures and photographs, hung on walls and screens, as the main means of a comparative study of cities. Perhaps Geddes overrated the Exhibition as such, for these pictures and their captions did not do the work by themselves: when first used, Geddes himself, or his son Alasdair, was usually on hand, to provide, as it were, the sound track; and it seems doubtful to me if the pictorial presentation in a general survey is capable of doing by itself all that Geddes hoped. But Geddes was right in holding that a certain richness of visual background is a minimum requirement for making creative decisions in town planning: most people, as Mass Observation has demonstrated, are satisfied with their existing quarters, however mean, because they have no conception of a better alternative. Except in a few films, all of them inadequate, Geddes' successors have been backward in developing this powerful educational device.

Geddes made a further proposal toward civic education that is even more important: he proposed that city surveys should have a permanent place of exhibition in a civic museum, thus lifting the dead hand of the archæologist and the garret-looter from the city museums that many places now boast. Here again Geddes' ideas have waited more than a generation for anyone to perceive their importance and translate them into contemporary terms. The work of exploring city and region, adding fresh data and bringing existing knowledge up to date, should become a continuous educational enterprise, in which both children and adults might take part. The Land Utilization Survey of Britain showed how such a useful task might be carried through on a national scale with the aid of amateur investigators and school children; but in local areas an even richer kind of survey is needed — one uniting the past, the present, and the possible. In the very spirit of Geddes' thought, the educational authorities in Philadelphia have recently used the public schools to get their students to survey and replan their neighborhoods. Thus the seed that Geddes originally planted is now beginning to send forth rootlets; and in time every town planning authority should have as a constant aid in the process of development both a continuous survey — rather than one hastily put together for some immediate use — and a body of citizens who themselves, as school children, have already explored their city and dreamed about its potential development: people capable of making effective demands and informed criticisms. In all these efforts we still have a long distance to go before we come abreast with Geddes' teaching and example, if only because we lack the passion and fury that made him live, like one of the ancients in *Back to Methuselah*, in the center of a vortex of highly activated thought.

By both training and general habit of mind Geddes was an ecologist, long before that branch of biology had attained the status of a special discipline: he had come directly into contact with the three men — Ernst Haeckel, Ray Lankester, and Peter Kropotkin — who had laid the foundation for the study of the cooperative activities of all organisms. And it is not as a bold innovator in urban planning, but as an ecologist, the patient investigator of historic filiations and dynamic biological and social interrelationships, that Geddes' most important work in cities was done. He distrusted sweeping innovations and clean slates; as a biologist he knew that small quantities, as in traces of minerals in the diet, might be as important for urban life as large ones, and could be far more easily over-looked by stupid wholesale planning, done at a distance by people who over-valued T-squares and tidiness. Character-istically, one of his first innovations toward improving the congested slums of Edinburgh was not to map out an ideal system of open spaces, but to get hold of every small patch of unusable or unused vacant land, and, with voluntary effort, turn that into a tiny patch of garden or park. The process of " conservative surgery," as Geddes called it in one of his Indian reports, was essentially what he stood for: a process that respected the native style of life and sought to recapture and further its best intentions. He felt that if the right method were established, one which enlisted the interest and service of the plain man and woman, even of the schoolchild, a little leaven would in time leaven the whole loaf.

What Geddes' outlook and method contribute to the plan-ning of today are precisely those elements that the administra-tor and the bureaucrat, in the interest of economy or effi-ciency, are tempted to leave out: time, patience, loving care of detail, a watchful interrelation of past and future, an in-sistence upon the human scale and the human purpose, above all merely mechanical requirements, and finally a willingness to leave an essential part of the process to those who are most intimately concerned with it — the ultimate consumers or citi-zens. "The resorption of government," to use a phrase Geddes and Branford coined, was an integral part of the de-velopment of citizenship, and so of the improvement of cities. Like William James, Geddes was against all bigness, and against all the obvious manifestations of success. "On pain of economic waste, of practical failure no less than artistic futility, or even worse, each true design," Geddes noted, " each valid scheme should and must embody the full utiliza-tion of local and regional conditions and be the expression of local and regional personality. ' Local character ' is thus no mere accidental old world quaintness, as its mimics think and say. It is attained only in course of adequate grasp and treatment of the whole environment, and in active sympathy with the essential and characteristic life of the place concerned." This insistence upon sympathy and human-heartedness as the mark of a right attitude and relationship is one of the distinguishing marks of Geddes' planning philosophy.

In describing Geddes' great virtues as civic educator and planner one has also defined his limitations. Though no one in his generation probably knew more about urban development, as both historian and sociologist, than Geddes did, his name is associated with no great constructive departure in city design itself. The garden city, the neighborhood unit, the unification of fields, factories, and workshops — those master concepts in modern planning — were the products of other minds. Geddes appreciated these innovations and understood their importance; but his own contribution was of another kind. To say this is not to belittle Geddes or to lose sight of the value of his work as town planner; it is rather to call attention to the field in which Geddes' method and outlook were permanently valuable: the realm of education. Few of us can approach Geddes' thought here without becoming conscious of weaknesses in our equipment, of defects in our preparation. From Patrick Geddes, both citizen and planner can learn how to look at cities, how to interpret their origins, their life, their cumulative history, their potentialities, how to understand not merely the daily life of place, work, and folk, but those developments from acropolis to cathedral, from university to concert hall, from cloister to laboratory, that transform the very nature and goals of human life. Above all, Geddes was the exponent of life in unity, life in its fullest development and expression: he was the enemy of those frustrations and miscarriages that we too easily regard as " normal " to civilization. At every level in the organic world, he saw that over-specialization produces arrests, regressions, failures of inventiveness; and he tirelessly sought to encourage the processes of insurgence, of self-transcendence, of creativity. For him the union of the artist and the scientist, the practical man and the idealist, the rural mind and the urban mind, was imperative: this was the condition of remolding our cities and regions to the best uses of life. That lesson makes *Cities in Evolution* even today one of the classic contributions to civic improvement — indeed to the general renewal of life.

J. E. Spingarn

Spingarn belongs among the dark stars in American letters.

Long before his death, J. E. Spingarn had achieved something of the immortality that comes with legend. No one else in his literary generation had produced so decisive an effect with such a fine economy of means. Even his abstention from literary effort, during the last dozen years of his life, created, at least among those who knew him, a stir of uneasiness. Like a late guest for whom a place has been set at dinner, he occupied the attention of the whole table almost as much by his absence as those present could do by their visible efforts. His death, on July 26, 1939, only removed the sense of expectancy that his life perpetually aroused.

Through the dark half year that preceded his death, those who knew J. E. Spingarn as a friend would sometimes measure their private feelings about the man, as one who bore greatness, against the visible achievements of his life, which posterity would finally assay. Were the few books he had written to be weighed confidently against the massive industry of a More, a Babbitt, or even of Spingarn's old master, Woodberry? Had this rich spirit, proud, impulsive, courageous in the face of danger and no less courageous in the face of pain, ever adequately published himself?

I shared those doubts and even on occasion uttered them; for a man's friends, precisely because they demand the hidden utmost of him, are often more stern in their appraisals than is the world. But on mature reflection, I feel that these judgments ignore the very protean essence of his life; one had better be guided here by Spingarn's own critical dictum: " The tragic does not exist for Criticism, but only Aeschylus and

Calderon, Shakespeare and Racine." So one may say that the scholar, the teacher, the soldier, the business man do not exist: only the man exists. The question is not, did he fulfill this or that extraneous demand, but did he fulfill himself?

On that point the answer is plain. Spingarn's life itself was more important than its several professional phases, for he renewed, in terms of modern opportunities, the Renaissance ideal of the gentleman: the man equally at home in a garden, a library, an office, or on a battlefield. It is not an accident that one of his confessed ambitions had been to write a monumental study on the Birth and Death of the Gentleman.

But while Spingarn valued the untrammeled routine of the gentleman, he never accepted the amateur's position of good-natured inferiority. Whatever the task before him, he set before himself the professional's rigorous standard of preparation. His knowledge was no less exact and exhaustive than his bibliographies, whether the subject were the culture of the Renaissance or the culture of clematis. He attacked every task with grave passion; and he applied to it a mind as adept in dealing with ideas as a surgeon's fingers are in making ligatures. Combatting the vice of specialization, he nevertheless managed to retain its virtues.

In pondering my friend's life on the night of his death I was struck for the first time by a parallel in American literature I had never suspected before. It will not do to push this parallel too far; but one cannot altogether neglect it — an inner connection between this austere man, who cried he had " gnawed the heart of night and care to keep myself from gnawing mine own heart," and Herman Melville. Like Melville, Spingarn ran away from home as a lad in his teens, in search of something yet unwon and unknown; and though his abrupt departure ended more swiftly than Melville's whaling cruise, it was followed by a similar meteoric career. Even their poems bear a curious resemblance to each other: born of similar temperaments, not imitation. And above all, they were alike in their towering pride, a pride that often created a barrier between them and their colleagues and in turn perhaps limited the work they were most fit to do.

Joel Elias Spingarn was born in 1875. By 1899 he had already published a volume of great erudition and critical discernment: his classic *History of Literary Criticism in the Renaissance*. Presently he was associated with George Woodberry as professor in the new department of Comparative Literature at Columbia: *the* brilliant young man of the university. There are many stories about his work as a professor. One of the best of them tells of his lecturing with furious intensity for half an hour and then saying: " That is all I have to express on the subject; the class is free for the rest of the hour." Spingarn used to say that this story was apocryphal; but like many such stories, it picks out the essential quality of its subject: his aversion to tedious pedantry, his hatred of the dry punctilio of habit.

His academic career came to a sudden climax through his dismissal in 1911, following a quixotic attempt on his part to pit his powers against the sodden forces of official routine. Apart from the fact that this act took a great scholar out of his natural sphere, I would not overstress the purely personal results of this conflict: the breach must have come sooner or later. But the social context was significant, as in every other major act in Spingarn's life.

Spingarn fought for professorial dignity against bureaucratic convenience; he fought for truth and freedom against lies, subterfuges, and double dealings; he fought for an autonomous faculty, against a system that gave all effectual power to the board of trustees and the president. The issues he raised in this controversy have remained alive in the very form he raised them. It is not too much to say that his sturdy campaign eventually paved the way for the notable revision of the whole system that is now being worked out in the City Colleges of New York.

In the prime of his life (1915), Spingarn gave up his literary and academic career in order to bear his part as a soldier in the World War. Presently, in 1917, he published his *Creative Criticism*. This book became the center of a long critical conflict that arose as much out of misunderstanding as out of judicious disagreement. Its main thesis has by now become something of a truism: a work of art must be criticized primarily *as* a work of art, in its totality, not in terms of the author's success in inculcating virtue or effecting practical reform. Spingarn did not deny that the artist was a moral and social man, fed by every stream of real experience. He merely said that the work of art existed in its own right, with the self-sufficiency and self-justification that characterizes all living forms.

To a parochial professor at Urbana, Illinois, this doctrine was simply un-American, despite the fact that, as Spingarn later pointed out, it could be found in Emerson and Lowell. To a crusading humanist at Harvard, Spingarn's doctrine was a romantic denial of the artist's moral responsibility. But the fact is that the most damning criticism of the whole cult of art as an independent entity was written by Spingarn himself; for his mind, in its impeccable rationality, never spared his own prejudices. The criticism was contained in a poem he first called " The New Palace of Art " and then wryly changed, in his collected *Poems*, to " Art (A Nightmare)." Here Spingarn pictured the real dilemma of art from the beginning of human culture — that this supreme manifestation of life has flourished only by brutal human sacrifice: " Leisure she craves — and straightway men must sweat." " I find no pleasure in her lovely face," he concluded, " I find no quiet in her dwelling place. . . . We shall not enter Eden till she die."

It was Spingarn's gift, it was indeed the mark of his deep vitality, that his contributions, though never quantitatively great, were always timed for the moment when they were capable of having their maximum impact. Such a man might seem aloof, even impassive, but in fact he was always quicker to react than his contemporaries; so, for example, early in the twenties, before fascism had yet defined itself as systematic barbarism, he freely predicted the coming of a blacker period, with a reversion to caste and even slavery — a future that made mock, not only of his own hopes as an American, but of his lifelong devotion to the liberation of the Negro.

At a time when all his scholarly colleagues were laming themselves by servile imitation of quantitative " science " on the German model, Spingarn renewed the pan-European tradition of scholarship. Precisely at the moment when pragmatism was completing its apparent triumph, he introduced Croce to America. So, too, he brought over the contemporary thought of Italy itself, reviving De Sanctis, bringing out Gentile, Borgese, even Pareto. It was Spingarn, finally, who as early as 1922, addressed a manifesto to the younger generation, preaching a return to tradition and to history.

Spingarn belongs among the dark stars in American letters; his place is alongside Hawthorne, Melville, Poe — men who brooded on the world's darkness and knew all its gradations of horror, not because they despised the light, but because they kept their eyes open even when daylight had departed. These men are often closer to the approaching dawn than those who make their easy, midday observations, unquickened by pain, anguish, terror, and dismay. Theirs, in the last line of Spingarn's early poem, " The New Hesperides," is an " inner travail breeding nobler pain, an outer struggle for the golden day." Spingarn by his life made those young anticipatory words become visible. His final testament to us is the book that he lived, but never lived to write.

Henry Wright

Wright was . . . a poet who used statistics, who leaned for inspiration over a drawing board, a poet whose plans for houses and communities rose " to meet the expectation of the land."

In the midst of a busy life, Henry Wright died at the age of fifty-eight. All those who seek to build Jerusalem in this green and pleasant land will mourn his going and bitterly regret the loss. For Wright was perhaps the most fertile mind in that small group of architects, geographers, and sociologists who have been preparing the way for a renascence in our urban culture; and his boldness of thought, his selfless devotion to the public interest, and his scorn of pecuniary standards and evaluations, gave him a special authority among his contemporaries and his students.

This community planner and architect bore an odd resemblance to Robert Frost — the same long humorous upper lip, the same erect brush of gray hair, the same ashen complexion, the same innocent, upraised eyebrow and gray-blue eyes behind which a demon lurked. Wright was indeed a poet in his proper person: but a poet who used statistics, who leaned for inspiration over a drawing board, a poet whose plans for houses and communities rose " to meet the expectation of the land." If to plant a tree, to build a house, and to beget a baby is, as Emerson taught, a sign of maturity, then Henry Wright was a mature man; and his work foretold the erection of communities in which men and women capable of enjoying maturity could live. The nineteen-twenties will be remembered in American architecture as a decade in which the tricksters and shysters were building windy skyscrapers, suggesting green tiles as a substitute for grass and invoking, by the environment they created, a wholesale sterility, if not universal suicide. It will also be remembered for the powerful impetus that Henry Wright gave to the movement back to common sense, to the earth, to social realities, to the human scale.

Who was Henry Wright? The man lacked either the facility or the desire to dramatize himself; that is why, though he did not avoid public work and public appearances, his name remained largely unknown to the reading public. My first memory of Wright goes back to 1923 — a week-end meeting at the Hudson Guild Farm in Netcong, New Jersey, attended by a small group of architects and planners and their friends. Mr. Alexander Bing was there, cautiously feeling his way toward new experiments in housing — Wright had been brought on from St. Louis to meet him — and Patrick Geddes was there, alert, explosive, insistent, sitting cross-legged under the trees, like a venerable Hindu sage. As we sat down to supper the first night, I noticed that Wright had been pushed into the periphery of our circle, away from the bigwigs and the talkers: he was cheerfully sitting down at a table with a few adolescents and one of the hired hands.

This modesty and unassumingness were characteristic of the man: he was always being talked down by people with louder voices, pushed to one side by people with more active elbows; yet somehow, with an inevitability that bore witness to both his passion for ideas and his persistence, he would presently be in the center of the group. In a committee of architects, a conference of city planners, an association of ousing experts, it would be Henry Wright who (his eyes uietly dancing with excitement) would bring forth the ideas that got beneath the preconceptions or uncriticized assumptions of his associates. He was ever on guard against a coercive unanimity: emblem of thought that had gone dead. If, among his closest associates, he found that last year's fresh discovery was becoming this year's deadly platitude, he would even turn savagely on his own views and tear them to shreds.

He had the instinct of the old pioneers when he found his intellectual neighbors were beginning to crowd round too close: he would pull up stakes and look for a less settled country. Yet, with all this adventurousness, no man ever hewed more steadfastly to his own line: the planning of really human communities was food and drink and recreation and dream for Henry Wright. No bait of money or authority ever diverted him from the main preoccupation of his life.

Before 1923 Wright's most important work in community planning had been with the United States Shipping Board during the war; after this, his opportunities came in quick succession. With Clarence Stein, he became co-designer of the first fresh housing experiment after the war, that of the City Housing Corporation at Sunnyside, and later he presided over the design of Radburn.

Wright would have been the first to disclaim sole credit for the important innovations of either Sunnyside or Radburn; indeed, in an article published in *The Western Architect,* " The Autobiography of Another Idea," he traced in considerable detail the various experiments that came to a head in the plan of Radburn. But there is no question about Wright's pre-eminence as a strategist in site-layout and community planning: in any given situation, he would have six ideas to another's one; for like a great strategist — and his favorite game was chess — he carefully prepared plans A, B, and C, and then promptly and cheerfully ditched them to improvise plan F when the critical moment arrived.

The three important features of the Radburn plan, as worked out by Wright and Stein and their associates, were first the superblock, which consisted of a series of dead-end streets, terminating in a public park and surrounded by avenues for wheeled traffic; second, the continuous park-belt, weaving through the scheme of superblocks and forming a continuous system; and third, the organization of domestic neighborhoods about the local school and playing field, en-

suring the safety of children, as well as adult pedestrians, by
a complete separation of footpaths from traffic avenues. The
plan of Radburn — paralleled but not anticipated by similar
schemes on a smaller scale in Europe — was the most important innovation in city planning since Sir Raymond Unwin's
demonstration of the economic fallacy of overcrowding.
Henry Wright's claim on posterity's attention might well rest
alone on his contribution to that plan.

Only second to Radburn was the work that Henry Wright
did for the New York State Housing and Regional Planning
Commission under Mr. Stein's chairmanship — work that cul-
minated in the report of 1926. In a field where there were no
precedents or guideposts in any country, Wright developed
a fresh method of approach, projected a series of economic
and social objectives, and staked out new territory in the field
of planning: he showed that a rational development of New
York would neither congest all its population into the two
great port-termini of Buffalo and New York, as had been
steadily taking place since the eighties, nor attempt to decen-
tralize them aimlessly through the entire area; he showed
rather that there was a natural belt of settlement along the
Mohawk and the Hudson Valleys, where new garden cities
might be built, or existing smaller towns expanded with new
housing and new communal facilities, and that there was even
a neglected region, along Lake Ontario, ill served by railroads
and relatively undeveloped, that had finer qualities of soil and
climate than many more intensively occupied areas. When
Wright's report finally appeared, it was plain that it was a
classic; but so cleanly did this survey set itself against plans
for metropolitan aggrandizement that the dominant school of
" regional " planners — as full of stale illusions as the skyscraper architects — ignored it for well-nigh a decade.

Almost alone among his generation of architects and planners in the East, Henry Wright was sympathetic to the new
vernacular architecture of the machine, and he found much

to admire in its exponents in Europe — the community plans of Ernst May in Frankfort, the apartment houses of Mies van der Rohe in Berlin, and the modern suburb of Neubühl near Zürich. Such a man was bound to become a teacher of the younger generation: he was one of the few planners who understood their lingo, their desires, their hopes. During the thirties he maintained a small summer school for a chosen few at his farm in New Jersey; and this school, together with the Housing Study Guild, which he helped to found in 1932, did more to train the younger generation of architects for public service in housing than any other institution.

Despite his unique gifts and his abundant experience, none of the government departments at Washington was prepared to make full use of Wright's services; and he naturally looked with scorn upon the muddle of contradictory organizations that had been rigged up to promote — and equally to obstruct — public housing. So, while he did not disdain the opportunity to serve as part-time consultant, first under the PWA, later in the Resettlement Division, his heart was elsewhere. By 1934 he had decided to devote himself in the main to teaching; and Columbia University wisely availed itself of the opportunity by creating a professorship for him. Had he lived, a whole generation would have borne the stamp of his humane mind, now eager and adventurous, now cautious and critical, always profoundly analytic, always aware of unsuspected alternatives: above all sturdily conscious of the human objectives that are crystallized about a tree, a house, and a baby.

In Henry Wright's book on *Re-Housing Urban America*, his vast observation and experience as a planner were, in a measure, summed up. But though much of the book is of a technical nature, there is one chapter that defines the essence of the man: the chapter on the quality of space. For Wright, however eagerly he might seek to reduce costs and cut corners, approached the problem as one who had lived on a modest scale most of his life, and who knew, from his own domestic experience, how unwise it is to save on space if the result is an infant's discomfort, a young lover's embarrassment, or a married pair's domestic jangling. That guiding sense of human realities made him the ideal tutor of a generation that must plan, not for the well-to-do and not for a fictitious economy of abundance, but for the masses of common men and women who wish to recover the essential sanities of a living environment, and who will not forever be bribed and put off by purely mechanical substitutes. In Henry Wright's personality one recovered a sense that the best Americans give — one finds it in Emerson, Thoreau, Sullivan — a sense of the perpetual novelty and freshness of life, the miracle of a blade of grass, the elation of a baby discovering its toes. The light that came over Henry Wright's face at the first morning-shiver of a new idea always had a hint of dawn in it, a promise of repeated dawns. That quality does not die: there are generations still unborn in communities still unplanned who will be more helpful neighbors, happier lovers, more responsive parents, because Henry Wright was so passionately interested in the quality of space, and put life itself before all the minor instruments of living.

4
Art and Civilization

The Imperial Facade

Architecture, like government, is about as good as a community deserves.

The decade between 1890 and 1900 saw the rise of a new period in American architecture. This period had, it is true, been dimly foreshadowed by the grandiose L'Enfant, but if the superficial forms resembled those of the early republic, and if the precedents of classic architecture again became a guide, the dawning age was neither a revival nor a continuation.

In the meanwhile, fresh influences had entered. The generation of students who had studied in the Ecole des Beaux Arts after the Civil War was ready, at last, to follow the lone trail which Richard H. Hunt had blazed. Richardson's most intimate disciples reacted against the stamp of his personality and sought a more neutral mode of expression, consecrated by established canons of good taste. On top of this, the introduction of steel-cage construction removed the necessity for solid masonry, and placed a premium upon the mask. The stage was set for a new act of the drama.

All these influences shaped the style of our architecture when it arose; but the condition that gave it a substantial base was the rise of a new order in America's economic life. Up to this time, the chief industrial problem had been to improve the processes of mechanical production and to stake out new areas for exploitation. One may compare these economic advances to the separate sorties of an army operating on a wide front: any lone adventurer might take his courage in his hands and exploit an invention, or sink an oil well, if

NOTE: Reprinted from *Sticks and Stones*, published by Dover Publications, Incorporated ($1.60).

he could find it. By 1890 the frontier had closed; the major resources of the country were under the control of the monopolist; it became more important to consolidate gains than freshly to achieve them. Separate lines of railroads were welded into systems; separate steel plants and oil plants were wrought into trusts; and where monopoly did not rest upon a foundation of natural advantage, the " gentleman's agreement " began its service as a useful substitute. The popular movements which sought to challenge the forces of this new regime — the labor movement, socialism, populism — had neither analyzed the situation with sufficient care nor attracted the adherence of the majority. The defeat of Henry George as a local political candidate was symbolic: by 1888 a humane thinker like Edward Bellamy had already accepted the defeat, had embraced the idea of the trust, and had conceived a comprehensive utopia on the basis of letting the process of monopoly go the limit, so that finally, by a mere yank of the levers, the vast economic organizations of the country would become the " property " of the people.

The drift to the open lands came to a full pause. The land empire had been conquered, and its overlords were waxing in power and riches; the name " millionaire " became the patent of America's new nobility. With the shift from industry to finance went a shift from the producing towns to the spending towns: architecture came to dwell in the stock exchanges, the banks, the shops, and the clubs of the metropolis; if it sought the countryside at all, it established itself in the villas that were newly laid out on hill and shore in the neighborhood of the great cities. The keys to this period are opulence and magnitude: " money to burn."

These years witnessed what the Roman historian, Ferrero, has called a " *véritable recommencement d'histoire*." In the new centers of privilege there arose a scale of living and a mode of architecture which, with all its attendant miseries, depletions, and exploitations, recalled the Rome of the first and second centuries after Christ. It is needless to say that vast acres of buildings, factories, shops, homes, were erected which had no relation at all to the imperial regime; not everyone participated in either the benefits or the depressions that attended the growth of monopoly, but the accent of this period, the dominant note, was an imperial one. While the commonplace building of the time cannot be ignored, it remains, so to say, out of the picture.

II

Hardly had the process of concentration and consolidation begun before the proper form manifested itself. The occasion for its appearance was the World's Columbian Exposition, opened in 1893. In creating this fair, the enterprise and capacity for organization which the architects of Chicago had applied to the construction of the skyscraper transformed the unkempt wilderness of Jackson Park into the Great White City in the space of two short years. Here the architects of the country, particularly of New York and Chicago, appeared for the first time as a united profession, or, to speak more accurately, as a college. Led by the New Yorkers, who had come more decisively under European influence, they brought to this exposition the combination of skill and taste in all the departments of the work that had, two centuries earlier, created the magnificent formalities of Versailles. There was unity of plan in the grouping of the main buildings about the lagoon; there was unity of tone and color in the gleaming white façades; there was unity of effect in the use of classic orders and classic forms of decoration. Lacking any genuine unity of ideas and purposes — for Root had initially conceived of a variegated oriental setting — the architects of the exposition had achieved the effects of unity by subordinating their work to an established precedent. They chanted a Roman litany above the Babel of individual styles. It was a capital triumph of the academic imagination. If these main buildings were architecture, America had never seen so much of it at one time before. Even that belated Greco-Puritan, Mr. Charles Eliot Norton, was warm in praise.

It would be foolish to quarrel with the style that was chosen for these exposition buildings, or to deny its propriety. Messrs. McKim, White, Hunt, and Burnham divined that they were fated to serve Renaissance despots and emperors with more than Roman power, and unerringly they chose the proper form for their activities. Whereas Rome had cast its spell over the architects of the early Renaissance because they wished once more to enter into its life, the life of its sages and poets and artists, it attracted the architects of the White City because of its external features, because of its stereotyped canons and rules, because of the relatively small number of choices it offered for a lapse in taste, because of its skill in conspicuous waste, and because of that very non-committal quality in its massive forms which permitted the basilica to become a church, or the temple to become a modern bank.

Of all the Renaissance architects, their impulses and interests were nearest, perhaps, to Robert Adam, whose church at West Wycombe could be turned into a ballroom by the simple act of removing the pews, and permitting the gay walls and decorations to speak for themselves. Behind the white stiff façade of the World's Fair buildings was the steel and glass structure of the engineer: the building spoke one language and the " architecture " another. If the coming of the skyscraper had turned masonry into veneer, here was a mode of architecture which was little but veneer.

In their place, at the fair, these classic buildings were all that could be demanded: Mr. Geoffrey Scott's defense of the baroque, in *The Architecture of Humanism*, applies particularly to its essential manifestations in the garden and the theater — and why not in the fair? Form and function, ornament and design, have no inherent relation, one with the other, when the mood of the architect is merely playful: there is no use in discussing the anatomy of architecture when its only aim is fancy dress. As a mask, as a caprice, the classic orders are as justifiable as the icing on a birthday cake: they divert the eye without damaging the structure that they conceal. Unfortunately, the architecture of the Renaissance has a tendency to imitate the haughty queen who advised the commons to eat cake. Logically, it demands that a Wall Street clerk shall live like a Lombardy prince, that a factory should be subordinated to esthetic contemplation; and since these things are impossible, it permits "mere building" to become illiterate and vulgar below the standards of the most debased vernacular. Correct in proportion, elegant in detail, courteous in relation to each other, the buildings of the World's Fair were, nevertheless, only the simulacra of a living architecture: they were the concentrated expression of an age which sought to produce "values" rather than goods. In comparison with this new style, the romanticism of the Victorian Age, with its avid respect for the medieval building traditions, was honesty and dignity itself.

The Roman precedent, modified by the work of Louis XIV and Napoleon III, by Le Nôtre and Haussmann, formed the basis not merely for the World's Fair, but for the host of city plans that were produced in the two decades that followed. It seemed for a while as if the architect might take the place of the engineer as city planner, and that the mangled regularity of the engineer's gridiron plan, laid down without respect to topographic advantage or to use, might be definitely supplanted in the remodeled central districts and in the new extensions and suburbs of the American city. The evil of the World's Fair triumph was that it suggested to the civic enthusiast that every city might become a fair: it introduced the notion of the City Beautiful as a sort of municipal cosmetic, and reduced the work of the architect to that of putting a pleasing front upon the scrappy building, upon the monotonous streets and the mean houses, that characterized vast areas in the newer and larger cities.

If the engineer who had devoted himself to sewers and street-plans alone had been superficial, the architectural city planner who centered attention upon parkways alone, grand avenues alone, and squares like the Place de l'Etoile alone, was equally superficial. The civic center and the parkway represented the better and more constructive side of this effort: in Cleveland, in Pittsburgh, in Springfield, Massachusetts, harmonious groups of white buildings raised their heads above the tangle of commercial traffic, and in the restoration of L'Enfant's plan for Washington, the realities of the imperial regime at length caught up with the dreamer born out of his due time. A good many of these plans, however, were pathetically immature. One of the reports for Manhattan, for example, devoted pages and pages to showing the improvement that would follow the demolition of the wall around Central Park — and the importance of clipped trees in the design of grand avenues!

Plainly, the architect did not face with sufficient realism the colossal task with which he was confronted in the renovation of the city. He accepted his improvements too much at the value placed upon them by the leaders of Big Business — as a creator of land-values, as an element in increasing the commercial attractiveness of the city. Did not Mr. Daniel Burnham himself point to the improvements in Periclean Athens, not as the embodiment of Athenian citizenship and religion at its highest point, but as a measure for increasing the attractiveness of the city to visitors from abroad? Cut off from his true function to serve and beautify the community, made an accessory of business itself, like the merest salesman or advertising agent, it is no wonder that the architect speedily lost his leadership, and that the initiative went once again into the hands of the engineer.

The main merit of all these efforts to perpetuate the

World's Fair is that they sought to achieve some of the dignity and decisiveness of the formal plan. Their weakness was that they neglected new elements, like the billboard, the sky-sign, the subway, the tall building, which undermined the effects of the plan even when it was achieved. In their efforts to escape from the welter of misguided commercial enterprise, the advocates of the city beautiful placed too great reliance upon spots of outward order and decency; they took refuge in the paper symmetry of axial avenues and round-points, as one finds them in Haussmann's Paris, and neglected the deeper and more genuine beauties of, let us say, the High Street in Oxford or Chipping Camden, or of many another European town that had achieved completion in its essentials before the nineteenth century.

In short, the advocates of the city beautiful sought a remedy on paper which could be purchased only by a thorough reorganization of the community's life. If all this applies to the better side of the World's Fair, it touches even more emphatically the worse.

The twenty years between 1890 and 1910 saw the complete rehabilitation of the Roman mode, as the very cloak and costume of imperial enterprise. The main effort of architecture was to give an effect of dignity and permanence to the façades of the principal thoroughfares: the public buildings must dominate the compositions, numerous boulevards and avenues must concentrate the traffic at certain points and guide the stranger to the markets and amusements; where possible, as in the Chicago plan, by Messrs. Burnham and Bennett, avenues must be cut through the gridiron pattern of blocks in order to achieve these effects. If this imperial street system is somewhat arbitrary, and if the necessary work of grading, filling, demolishing, and purchasing existing property rights is extremely costly, the end, nevertheless, justifies the means — the architecture impresses and awes a populace that shares vicariously in its glories. Should the effect prove a little too

austere and formidable, the monuments will be offset with circuses and hippodromes.

In all this, the World's Fair was a precise and classic example, for it reproduced in miniature the imperial order.
When the panic of 1893 kept people away from the exhibitions of art, industry, and culture, sideshows were promptly
introduced by the astute organizers. Beyond the serene classic façades, which recalled the elevation of a Marcus Aurelius,
sprawled the barkers, the freaks, and the tricksters, whose
gaudy booths might have reminded the spectator of the other
side of the imperial shield — the gaminism of Petronius Ar-
biter. The transformation of these white façades into the Gay
White Ways came during the next decade; the sideshows
achieved a separate existence as " Coney Island." On top of
this came the development of the mildly gladiatorial spectacles
of football and baseball; at first invented for playful exercise,
they became a standard means of exhibition by more or less
professional performers. The erection of numerous amphi-
theaters and arenas, such as the Yale Bowl, the Harvard Stadium, the Lewisohn Stadium, and their counterparts in the
West, rounded out the imperial spectacle.

By a happy congruence of forces, the large-scale manufacture of Portland cement, and the reintroduction of the Roman
method of concrete construction, came during the same period. Can anyone contemplate this scene and still fancy that
imperialism was nothing more than a move for foreign markets and territories of exploitation? On the contrary, it was a
tendency that expressed itself in every department of Western civilization, and if it appears most naked, perhaps, in
America, that is only because, as in the earlier periods, there
was so little here to stand in its way. Mr. Louis Sullivan
might well complain, in *The Autobiography of an Idea*, that
imperialism stifled the more creative modes of architecture
which might have derived from our fine achievements in science, from our tentative experiments in democracy. It seems

inevitable, however, that the dominant fact in our civilization should stamp the most important monuments and buildings with its image. In justice to the great professors of the classic style, Messrs. McKim and Burnham and Carrere and Hastings, one must admit that the age shaped them and chose them and used them for its ends. Their mode of building was almost unescapably determined by the milieu in which they worked.

The change in the social scene which favored an imperial setting was not without its effects upon the industries that supplied the materials for architecture, and upon the processes of building itself. Financial concentration in the stone quarries, for example, was abetted by the creation of a national system of rail transportation, and partly, perhaps, by the elaboration of the mechanical equipment for cutting and trimming stone beyond a point where a small plant could work economically. The result was that during this period numerous small local quarries, which had been called into existence by Richardson's fine eye for color contrasts, were allowed to lapse. Vermont marble and Indiana limestone served better the traditions that had been created in the White City.

The carrying of coals to Newcastle is always a pathetic practice; it remained for the imperial age to make it a subject for boasting. Just as many Connecticut towns, whose nearby fields are full of excellent granite boulders, boast a bank or a library of remote marble, so New York City, which has a solid foundation of schist, gneiss, and limestone, can point to only a handful of buildings, notably the College of the City of New York and Mr. Goodhue's Church of the Intercession, in which these excellent local materials were used. The curious result of being able by means of railway transportation to draw upon the ends of the earth for materials has been, not variety, but monotony. Under the imperial order the architect was forced to design structures that were identical in style, treatment, and material, though they were placed thousands of miles apart and differed in every important function. This ignorance of regional resources is not incompatible with grand effects, or even on occasion with decently good architecture. But it does not profit by that fine adaptation to site, that justness of proportion in the size of window and slope of roof, which is an earnest of the architect's mastery of the local situation. Substitute Manila for the military colony of Timgad, or Los Angeles for Alexandria, and it is plain that we have here another aspect of Ferrero's generalization. Even architects whose place of work was nearer to the site of their buildings were, nevertheless, compelled to copy the style of the more successful practitioners in New York and Chicago.

In government, in industry, in architecture, the imperial age was one. The underlying policy of imperialism is to exploit the life and resources of separate regions for the benefit of the holders of privilege in the capital city. Under this rule, all roads lead literally to Rome. While, as the German historian W. H. Riehl points out, the provincial highroads served to bring the city out into the countryside, the railroads served to bring the major cities together and to drain the products of rural regions into the metropolis. It was no accident that the great triumphs of American architecture during the imperial period were the railroad stations, particularly the Pennsylvania and the Grand Central in New York, and the Union Station in Washington. Nor is it by mere chance that the Washington and the Pennsylvania stations are the monuments to two architects, McKim and Burnham, who worshiped most wholeheartedly at the imperial shrine. With capital insight, these men established the American Academy at Rome: they recognized their home.

Esthetically considered, it is true, perhaps, that the finest element in the Pennsylvania station is the train hall, where the architect has dealt sincerely with his steel elements and has not permitted himself to cast a fond, retrospective eye upon the Roman baths. When all allowances are made, however, there remains less for criticism in the railway stations and the stadiums — those genuinely Roman bequests — than in any of the other imperial monuments. Indeed, so well does Roman architecture lend itself to the railroad station that one of the prime virtues of such a building, namely ease of circulation, was even communicated to the New York Public Library, where it is nothing but a nuisance, since it both increases the amount of noise and diminishes the amount of space for reading rooms that are already overcrowded.

Here, indeed, is the capital defect of an established and formalized mode: it tends to make the architect think of a new problem in terms of an old solution for a different problem. Mr. Charles McKim, for example, found himself hampered in competition over the New York Public Library because the demands of the librarian for a convenient and expeditious administration of his business interfered with the full-blown conception which Mr. McKim had in mind. All this happened after years of demonstration in the Boston Library of Messrs. McKim and White's failure to meet that problem squarely; and it apparently was not affected by Mr. McKim's experience with the great Columbia Library, which has ample space for everything except books. In short, the classic style served well enough only when the building to be erected had some direct relation to the needs and interests of the Roman world — the concourse of idlers in the baths or the tiers of spectators in the circuses and hippodromes. When it came face to face with our own day, it had but little to say, and it said that badly, as anyone who will patiently examine the superimposed orders on the American Telegraph Building in New York will discover for himself.

III

With the transition from republican to imperial Rome, numerous monuments were erected to the divine Cæsar. Within a much shorter time than marked the growth of the imperial tradition in America, a similar edification of patriotic memories took place.

In the restoration of the original plan of Washington, which began in 1901, the axis of the plan was so altered as to make it pass through the Washington Monument; and at the same time the place of the Lincoln Memorial, designed by the late Mr. Henry Bacon, a pupil of Mr. McKim's, was assigned. This was the first of a whole series of temples devoted to the national deities. In the Lincoln Memorial, in the McKinley Memorial at Niles, Ohio, in the Hall of Fame at New York University, and in their prototype, Grant's Tomb, one feels not the living beauty of our American past, but the mortuary air of archæology. The America that Lincoln was bred in, the homespun and humane and humorous America that he wished to preserve, has nothing in common with the sedulously classic monument that was erected to his memory. Who lives in that shrine, I wonder — Lincoln, or the men who conceived it: the leader who beheld the mournful victory of the Civil War, or the generation that took pleasure in the mean triumph of the Spanish-American exploit, and placed the imperial standard in the Philippines and the Caribbean?

On the plane of private citizenship, a similar movement took place: while before 1890 one can count the tombs in our cemeteries that boast loudly of the owner's earthly possessions and power, from that time onward the miniature temple-mausoleum becomes more and more frequent. In fact, an entire history of architecture could be deduced from our cemeteries; all that has so far been described could be marked in the progress from the simple slab, carved in almost Attic purity with a weeping willow or a cubistic cherub, that characterized the eighteenth century, to the bad lettering and the more awkward headstones of the early nineteenth century; and from this to the introduction of polished granite and iron ornament in the post-Civil War cemetery, down to the mechanically perfect mausoleum, where the corpses are packed like the occupants of a subway train, that some of our more effusively progressive communities boast of today. As we live, so we die: no wonder Shelley described Hell as a place much like London.

The Roman development of New York, Chicago, Washington, and the lesser metropolises, had an important effect upon the homes of the people. Historically, the imperial monument and the slum-tenement go hand in hand. The same process that creates an unearned increment for the landlords who possess favored sites, contributes a generous quota — which might be called the unearned excrement — of depression, overcrowding, and bad living, in the dormitory districts of the city. This had happened in imperial Rome; it had happened again in Paris under Napoleon III, where Haussmann's sweeping reconstructions created new slums in the districts behind the grand avenues, quite as bad, if far less obvious, as those that had been cleared away; and it happened once again in our American cities. Whereas in Rome a certain limit, however, was placed upon the expansion of the city because of the low development of vehicular traffic, the rise of mechanical transportation placed no bounds at all on the American city. If Rome was forced to create huge engineering projects like aqueducts and sewers in order to cleanse the inhabitants and remove the offal of its congested districts, the American city followed the example of the modern Romes like London and Paris by devising man-sewers, in which the mass of plebeians could be daily drained back and forth between their dormitories and their factories.

So far from relieving congestion, these colossal pieces of engineering only made more of it possible: by pouring more feeder lines into the central district of New York, Boston, Chicago, or where you will, rapid transit increased the housing congestion at one end and the business-congestion at the other. As for the primary sewer system devised for the imperial metropolis, it could scarcely even claim, with rapid transit, that it was a valuable commercial investment. The water outlets of New York are so thoroughly polluted that not merely have the shad and the oyster beds vanished from the Hudson River, where both once flourished, but it is a serious question whether the tides can continue to transport their vast load of sewage without a preliminary reduction of its content. Like the extension of the water conduits into the Adirondacks, all these necessary little improvements add to the per capita cost of living in an imperial metropolis, without providing a single benefit that a smaller city with no need for such improvements does not enjoy. In the matter of public parks, for example, the Committee on Congestion in New York, in 1911, calculated that the park space needed for the East Side alone, on the scale provided by the city of Hartford, would be greater than the entire area of Manhattan Island. In short, even for its bare utilitarian requirements, the mass-city, as the Germans call it, costs more and gives less than communities which have not had imperial greatness inflicted upon them.

As to the more positive improvements under the imperial regime, history leaves no doubt as to their dubious character, and current observation only reinforces history's lesson. In discussing the growth of the tenement in Rome after the Great Fire, Friedlander says:

The motives for piling up storeys were as strong as ever: the site for Cæsar's Forum had cost over £875,000 compensation to tenants and ground landlords. Rome had loftier houses than modern capital. A disproportionately large part of the area available for building was monopolized by the few, in consequence of the waste of space in the plethoric architecture of the day, and a very considerable portion was swallowed up by the public places, such as the imperial forums, which took up six hectares, as well as by the traffic regulations and extensions of the streets. The transformation and decoration of Rome by the Cæsars enhanced the scarcity of housing, as did Napoleon III's improvements in Paris. A further adjutory cause of the increase in the price of dwellings was the habit of speculation in house property (which Crassus had practiced in great style) and the monopoly of the proprietors, in consequence of which houses were let and sublet.

It would be tedious to draw out the parallel: given similar social conditions in America we have not been able to escape the same social results, even down to the fact that the palliatives of private philanthropy flourish here again as they had not flourished anywhere on the same scale since the Roman Empire. So much for imperial greatness. When an architect like Mr. Edward Bennett can say, as he did in *The Significance of the Fine Arts:* " House the people densely, if necessary, but conserve great areas for recreation," we need not be in doubt as to who will profit by the density and who will profit, at the other end, by the recreation. It is not merely that the park must be produced to remedy the congestion: it is even more that the congestion must be produced in order to provide for the park. To profit by both the disease and the remedy is one of the masterstrokes of imperialist enterprise. Mr. Daniel Burnham said of the World's Fair, according to Mr. Bennett and Mr. Charles Moore, " that it is what the Romans would have wished to create in permanent form." One may say of our imperial cities that they are what the Romans did create — but whether the form will be permanent or not is a matter we may leave to the sardonic attentions of history.

For my own part, I think we have at last acquired a criterion which will enable us to sum up the architecture of the imperial age, and deal justly with these railroad stations and stadiums, these sewers and circuses, these aqueducts and parkways and grand avenues. Our imperial architecture is an architecture of compensation: it provides grandiloquent stones for people who have been deprived of bread and sunlight and all that keeps man from becoming vile. Behind the monumental façades of our metropolises trudges a landless proletariat, doomed to the servile routine of the factory system; and beyond the great cities lies a countryside whose goods are drained away, whose children are uprooted from the soil on the prospect of easy gain and endless amusements, and whose remaining cultivators are steadily drifting into the ranks of an abject tenantry. This is not a casual observation: it is the translation of the last three census reports into plain English. Can one take the pretensions of this architecture seriously; can one worry about its esthetics or take full delight in such finer forms as Mr. Pope's Temple of the Scottish Rite in Washington, or Mr. Bacon's Lincoln Memorial? Yes, perhaps — if one refuses to look beyond the mask.

Even in some of its proudest buildings, the imperial show wears thin; and one need not peer into the slums beyond in order to realize its defects. The rear of the Metropolitan Museum or the Brooklyn Museum, for example, might be the rear of a row of Bronx tenements or Long Island City factories, so gaunt and barren and hideous is their aspect. If the imperial age was foreshadowed in the World's Fair, it has received its apotheosis in the museum. In contrast to the local museums one still finds occasionally in Europe, which are little more than extensions of the local curio cabinet, the imperial museum is essentially a loot-heap, a comprehensive repository for plunder. The sage Viollet-le-Duc once patly said that he preferred to see his apples hanging on a tree, rather than arranged in rows in the fruit shop: but the animus of the museum is to value the plucked fruit more than the tree that bore it.

Into the museum come the *disjecta membra* of other lands, other cultures, other civilizations. All that had once been a living faith and practice is here reduced to a separate specimen, pattern, or form. For the museum, the world of art has already been created: the future is restricted to a duplication of the perfected past. This animus is identic with that which made the Romans so skillful in copying Greek statues and so dull in carving their own — a desirable habit of humility were it not for the fact that the works of art in the past could not have been created had our ancestors been so punctual in respect to finished designs. The one thing the museum cannot attempt to do is to supply a soil for living art: all that it can present is a pattern for reproduction. To the extent that an insincere or imitative art is better than no art at all, the Imperial Age marked an advance: to the extent, however, that a living art is a fresh gesture of the spirit, the museum confessed all too plainly that the age had no fresh gestures to make; on that score, it was a failure, and the copying of period furniture and the design of period architecture were the livid proofs of that failure.

The museum is a manifestation of our curiosity, our acquisitiveness, our essentially predatory culture; and these qualities were copiously exhibited in the architecture of imperialism. It would be foolish to reproach the great run of architects for exploiting the characteristics of their age, for even those who in belief and design have remained outside the age — such resolute advocates of a medieval polity as Dr. Ralph Adams Cram — have not been able to divert its currents. In so far as we have learned to care more for empire than for a community of freemen, living the good life, more for dominion over palm and pine than for the humane discipline of ourselves, the architect has but enshrined our desires. The opulence, the waste of resources and energies, the perversion of human effort represented in this architecture are but the outcome of our general scheme of working and living. Architecture, like government, is about as good as a community deserves. The shell that we create for ourselves marks our spiritual development as plainly as that of a snail denotes its species. If sometimes architecture becomes frozen music, we have ourselves to thank when it is a pompous blare of meaningless sounds.

The Metropolitan Milieu

Wherever Stieglitz turns his head in this city, he looks for a touch of life, seizes it, emphasizes it.

Ever since I began walking about the streets of New York, noting its people, its buildings, its industries, its activities, I have planned to write an extensive interpretation of my native city's development. The time to have done this was in 1939, when I returned for a winter's residence, after three years spent mainly in my Dutchess County home; but the mounting menace of fascism drove all such thoughts from my mind. If I never live to write that book, the following essay must serve as a substitute.

"The Metropolitan Milieu" is a subjective interpretation of the city: subjective in the sense that it is focussed in a succession of human personalities: Whitman, Ryder, and above all Alfred Stieglitz; it is an attempt to show how a particular environment not merely molds the human personality but often reactivates it, developing compensatory interests that offset its evils and make possible a fuller human growth.

Much of the material in this essay derives directly from my own experiences and impressions. Through my grandfather, Charles Graessel, with whom I used to stroll about the city up to the age of ten, I had a direct connection with a remoter past, with sweet old Bastian, the German bookbinder on University Place, who loved Leatherstocking, *or with the custom bootmaker on Canal Street who still made my grandfather's boots. I saw the sordid seventies through the eyes of my mother, who grew up in a gloomy house that still stands in the shadow of St. Marks-in-the-Bouwerie. I saw the immigrant's city through the eyes of our faithful maid, Nellie Ahearn,*

146

who gave me entry to the struggling but generously hospitable Irish Catholics of the middle West Side; as a boy in the public schools, above all during my high school period at Stuyvesant, I became intimately acquainted with a later wave of immigrants, the Polish and Russian Jewish migration; in short, long before I began deliberately to think about the city, I had absorbed much of it through my pores.

Only a born New Yorker, perhaps, could do justice to the work of such a genuine New Yorker as Stieglitz: we had a common bond even in our remembered fondness for the horse races at Belmont Park, Sheepshead, and Brighton. Indeed, it is out of our love for what the city has given us that we have attempted to stand fast against its slippery ways, to break with its more inhuman routines and its money-bound activities, and to rally together the forces of spirit for an attack upon its sleek materialism.

Stieglitz's integrity and his concentration upon essentials, his implacable refusal to be diverted by the trivial or the loudly advertised or the pseudo-good, give his personality a unique place in the development of the city. When all its showy splendors have been reduced to their proper significance, when its inflated values have fallen, when the city itself finally saves itself by re-grouping in units that have some relation to the human scale, there will still be this to be said for the expansive New York of Stieglitz's generation: it produced an Alfred Stieglitz. [Author's note, 1945]

THE COLOR OF THE CITY

Before the Civil War, New York shared its intellectual distinction with Boston, its industrial place with Philadelphia, and its commercial supremacy with Baltimore and New Orleans. Though it had become the mouth of the continent, thanks to the Erie Canal, it was not yet the maw. After the Civil War, despite the energetic rise of Chicago, New York City became an imperial metropolis, sucking into its own whirlpool the wealth and the wreckage of the rest of the country and of the lands beyond the sea.

When Dickens first visited America, voracious pigs rooted in the streets of Manhattan. Less than a generation later, through the holy transmutation of war, most of them were turned into financiers and industrial enterprisers, and they confined their operations to Wall Street, where the troughs were deep and the wallow good. Poets became stockbrokers; Pan took a flier in railroad securities; satirical humorists hobnobbed with millionaires and turned the lance of their satire against purely legendary kings, the Cooks, the Vanderbilts, the Rogerses, the Rockefellers. New York had become the center of a furious decay, which was called growth and enterprise and greatness. The decay caused foul gases to form; the gases caused the physical body of the city to be distended; the distention was called Progress.

So the city grew. Brownstone mansions, often grotesquely scratched with Eastlake ornament, wheeled into position along Fifth Avenue; and brownstone houses, in solid speculative rows, lined the side streets as the city stumbled rapidly northward. On either side of them, in the cheaper quarters, were the new tenements, with common toilets in the halls, and dusty vestibules where, in the 'seventies, a row of pitchers would be exposed through the night, to be filled with milk in the morning. The crosstown traffic became less important, as the rivers ceased to provide the main entrances to the city; but the tangle of wheels on the avenues thickened: shafts interlocked, hubs scraped, horses reared, presently a bridge was built over Broadway for the pedestrian. The vivacious dangers of congestion had all appeared: exasperated drivers exchanged oaths as deadly as bullets, and gangsters, lining up for fights on the dingier side streets, exchanged bullets as lightly as oaths. Respectable folk hunched their shoulders, lowered their heads, and hypnotized themselves into somnolence by counting sheep: at all events the population was increasing.

Beer saloons, four to as many corners in most parts of the city, brought together in their more squalid forms the ancient forces of hunger and love and politics: " free lunch," " ladies' entrance," and the political boss and his underlings. The main duty of the latter was to protect vice and crime and to levy a constant tax upon virtue in whatever offensive form it might take — as justice, as public spirit, as intelligence. Whisky and beer ruled the wits and the emotional life of the city: whisky for aggressiveness and beer for good-natured befuddlement. Barber shops specialized, until the present century, in painting out black eyes that did not yield to the cold iron of the lamppost. The swells, of course, drank their wine convivially at Martin's or Delmonico's; but that was as far from the beer saloon as Newport or Narragansett were from Coney Island. In the 'nineties Messrs. McKim, Mead, and White began to make over the city for the more polished classes: they designed the Century Club, Gorham's, Tiffany's, Delmonico's, and many mansions in the city for the new Borgias and Sforzas. But these cultured architects of course remained aloof from the principal buildings of the populace, the tenement and the saloon. The dingy brown front of the saloon, with the swinging doors and the sawdust floors and the slate carrying the day's menu and the soap-decorated mirrors, remained unchanged by fashion for two generations or more, obeying the biological law that the lowest organisms tend to remain stable.

In the 'seventies, elevated railroads were built; and for miles and miles, on each side of these ill-designed iron ways, which contrasted so unfavorably with those Berlin built only slightly later, tenement houses were planted. Thousands of people lived under the shadow of the elevated, with the smoke of the old-fashioned locomotives puffing into their windows, with the clank and rattle causing them to shout in daily conversation to overcome the roar outside. The obliviousness to low sounds, the indifference to cacophony which makes the ideal radio listener of present-day American, was part of the original acquisition of Manhattan in the Brown Decades. This torment of noise troubled sleep, lowered waking efficiency, depleted vitality; but it was endured as if it were an irremediable fact of nature. In the lull of the elevated's thunder, the occasional tinkle of the cowbells of the ragman on a side street, or the solemn " I-I-I-I- cas' clo's " of the secondhand clothing buyer, would have an almost pastoral touch; while *Carmen*, on an Italian's clanking hand organ, could splash the sky with color.

Within the span of a generation, the open spaces and the nature vistas began to disappear. The older beer gardens, like Niblo's Garden, gardens that had frequently preserved the trees and open space of a whole block, were wiped out: only in the further reaches of the city did they remain, like Unter den Linden on upper Broadway, and like the roadhouses which dotted the more or less open country that remained on the West Side above 125th Street until the end of the century. The rocky base of Manhattan, always unkind to life, steadily lost its filament of soil. The trees in the streets became more infrequent as the city grew; and their leaves grew sear before autumn came. Even the great Boulevard above Sixty-fifth Street, which the ignoble Tweed had planted along Broadway for his own pecuniary benefit, sacrificed its magnificent trees to the first subway; while only the ailanthus tree, quick growing and lean living, kept the back yards occasionally green, to gladden the lonely young men and women from the country, who faced their first year in the city from hall bedrooms on the top-floor rear of unamiable boarding houses. And as the city grew, it grew away from its old markets: one of the last of these, to prove more reminiscent of the old than anticipatory of the new, was the Jefferson Market, with its medieval German tower, at Eighth Street. Vanishing from the consciousness of most Manhattanites were the open markets that had once brought the touch of the sea and the country to its streets, connecting farmstead and city home by means of little boats that plied the Hudson and Long Island Sound.

The waterfront kept a hold on the city, modifying its character, longer than the countryside did. The oyster stands remained on South and West streets; and " mast-hemmed Mannahatta " was still an accurate description up to the end of the 'nineties: Alfred Stieglitz has indeed recorded for us the bowsprit of an old sailing vessel, thrust like a proud harpoon into the side of our Leviathan. But most of the things that had made life pleasant and sane in the city, the old houses, red brick, with their white doorways and delicate Georgian fanlights, the friendly tree-lined streets, the salty lick and lap of the sea at the end of every crosstown street, as Melville described it in the opening pages of *Moby Dick* — all these things were disappearing from the eye, from the nose and touch, and so from the mind.

The water and the soil, as the prime environment of life, were becoming " immaterial " — that is to say, they were of no use to the canny minds that were promoting the metropolis, unless they could be described in a legal document, appraised quantitatively, and converted ultimately into cash. A farm became for the speculator a place that might be converted into building lots; in that process, indeed, lay the meaning of this feverish growth, this anxious speculation, this reckless transformation of the quick into the dead. People staked out claims on the farther parts of the city in the way that prospectors stake out claims in a gold rush. There was always the chance that some negligible patch of earth might become, in the course of the city's growth, a gold mine. That was magic. In the atmosphere of magic, the desire to get something for nothing, a whole population hoped and breathed and lived. That in reality the environment was becoming unfit for human habitation in the process did not concern the midas-fingered gentlemen who ruled the city, nor did it affect the dull-fingered million who lacked that golden touch: their dreams were framed within the same heaven. Lacking the reality, they fed on the gilded lubricities of Mr. Bennett's, Mr. Pulitzer's, and Mr. Hearst's newspapers.

THE CULT OF PAPER

The ledger and the prospectus, the advertisement and the yellow journal, the world of paper, paper profits, paper achievements, paper hopes, and paper lusts, the world of sudden fortunes on paper and equally grimy paper tragedies, in short, the world of Jay Cook and Boss Tweed and James Gordon Bennett, had unfolded itself everywhere, obliterating under its flimsy tissues all the realities of life that were not exploitable, as either profits or news, on paper. Events happened to fill the paper that described them and to provide the daily titillation that relieved a commercialized routine. When they came reluctantly, they were manufactured, like the Spanish-American War, an event to which Newspaper Row contributed rather more than statesmanship did.

Behold this paper city, buried in its newspapers in the morning, intent through the day on its journals and ledgers and briefs and " Dear-sir-in-reply-to-yours-of-even-date," picking at its newly invented typewriters and mimeographs and adding machines, manifolding and filing, watching the ticker tape flow from the glib automatons in Broad Street, piling its soiled paper into deep baskets, burying its dead paper in dusty alphabetical cemeteries, binding fat little dockets with red tape, counting the crisp rolls and bank notes, cutting the coupons of the gilt-edged bonds, redeemable twenty years hence, forty years hence, in paper that might be even more dubious than the original loan issued. At night, when the paper day is over, the city buries itself in paper once more: the Wall Street closing prices, the Five-Star Sporting Extra, with the ninth-inning scores, the Special Extra, All-about-the-big-fight, all about the anarchist assassination in St. Petersburg — or Pittsburgh.

The cult of paper brings with it indifference to sight and sound: print and arithmetic are the Bible and the incense of this religious ritual. Realities of the world not included in this religion become dim and unreal to both the priests and the worshipers: these pious New Yorkers live in a world of Nature and human tradition, as indifferent to the round of the seasons and to the delights of the awakened senses and the deeper stores of social memory as an early Christian ascetic, occupied with his devotions amid the splendid temples of a Greek Acropolis. They collect pictures as they collect securities; their patronage of learning is merely a premature engraving of their own tombstones. It is not the images or the thoughts, but the report of their munificence in the newspaper, that justifies their gifts. The whole social fabric is built on a foundation of printed paper; it is cemented together by paper; it is crowned with paper. No wonder the anarchists, with more generous modes of life in mind, have invented the ominous phrase: " Incinerate the documents! " That would wreck this world worse than an earthquake.

Beneath this arid ritual, life itself, attenuated but real, starved but still hungry, goes on. Lovers still become radiant and breathless; honest workers shave wood, rivet steel beams, dig in the earth, or set type with sure hands and quiet satisfaction; scholars incubate ideas, and now and again a poet or an artist broods by himself in some half-shaded city square. In rebellion against this arid and ugly new environment, some country-bred person, a William Cullen Bryant or a Frederick Law Olmsted, would attempt to preserve faltering rural delights: a picnic grove here, a park there. Just before the Civil War the building of Central Park began; and despite the raids of political gangsters, despite the brazen indecent robbery of the Tweed gang — so malodorously like the political gangs of our own day — a stretch of green was carved out, not merely carved out, but actually improved, from barren goat pasture and shantydom into a comely park.

Meanwhile, the city as a whole became progressively more foul. In the late 'seventies the new model tenement design, that for the so-called dumbbell apartment, standardized the habitations of the workers on the lowest possible level, encouraging for twenty years the erection of tenements in which only two rooms in six or seven got direct sunlight or a modicum of air. Even the best residences were grim, dreary, genteelly fusty. If something better was at last achieved for the rich in the eighteen-nineties, on Riverside Drive and West End Avenue, it remained in existence scarcely twenty years and was replaced by mass congestion.

During the period we are looking at, the period of Alfred Stieglitz's birth and education and achievement, we are confronted with a city bent on its own annihilation. For New York used its intense energy and its taut, overquickened life to produce meaner habitations, a more constricted environment, a duller daily routine, in short, smaller joys, than it had produced during the modest provincial period. By denying itself the essentials of a fine human existence, the city was able to concentrate more intently upon its paper figments. It threw open its doors to the Irish of the 'forties, to the Germans of the 'fifties and 'sixties, later to the Italians, and to the Russians and Jews of eastern Europe: the outside world, contemptuous but hopeful, sneering but credulous, sent many of its finest children to New York. Some of them pushed on, to the cornlands, the wheatlands, the woodlands, the vinelands, to the iron mines, the coal mines, the copper mines; while those that remained were forced to huddle in utmost squalor. But the congested East Side, for all its poverty and dirt, was not the poorest part of the city: it still had its open markets with their color, its narrow streets with their sociability and their vivid common life and neighborly help, its synagogues with at least the dried remnants of a common vision.

This New York produced the elevator apartment house at the end of the 'sixties, and the tall building, called the sky-scraper after the topmost sail of its old clipper ships, a little later; and it used these new utilities as a means of defrauding its people of space and light and sun, turning the streets into deep chasms, and obliterating the back yards and gardens that had preserved a humaner environment even when people drank their water, not from the remote Croton River, but from the Tea-water Pump.

The spirit of pecuniary pride was reckless and indiscriminate; it annihilated whatever stood in the path of profit. It ruined the ruling classes as well as their victims. As time went on it became even more positive in its denial of life; so that in more elegant parts of the East Side today there are splendid "modern" mansions that are practically built back to back, even worse in some respects than the vilest slums on Cherry Street. This negative energy, this suicidal vitality, was the very essence of the new city that raised itself after the Civil War, and came to fullest bloom in the decade after the World War. Beholding it in its final manifestations, a German friend of mine wrote: *Dies ist die Hölle, und der Teufel war der Baumeister.* Men and women, if they survived in this environment, did so at the price of some sort of psychal dismemberment or paralysis. They sought to compensate themselves for their withered members by dwelling on the material satisfactions of this metropolitan life: how fresh fruits and vegetables came from California and Africa, thanks to refrigeration, how bathtubs and sanitary plumbing offset the undiminished dirt and the growing tendency toward constipation, how finally the sun lamps that were bought by the well-to-do overcame the lack of real sunlight in these misplanned domestic quarters. Mechanical apparatus, the refinements of scientific knowledge and of inventive ingenuity, would stay the process of deterioration for a time: when they failed, the jails, the asylums, the hospitals, the clinics, would be multiplied. Were not these thriving institutions too signs of progress, tokens of metropolitan intelligence and philanthropy?

But in the end, the *expectation* of health and wholeness, like the expectation of honesty and justice, tended within the great metropolis to disappear. In the course of its imperialistic expansion the metropolis, as Patrick Geddes put it, becomes a megalopolis, concentrating upon bigness and abstract magnitude and the numerical fictions of finance; megalopolis becomes parasitopolis, dominated by those secondary pecuniary processes that live on the living; and parasitopolis gives way to patholopolis, the city that ceases effectively to function and so becomes the prey of all manner of diseases — physical, social, moral. Within such a town, graft and corruption are normal processes; the greater part of the population shares the animus of the criminal, applauds him when he " gets away with it," and condones his crime when he is caught redhanded. The city that has good words for its Commodore Vanderbilts and Tweeds and Crokers, to say nothing of contemporary gamblers and shysters who have practiced on an even larger scale, which multiplied these antisocial types a thousand times, is a city in which a deteriorated social life, without elementary probity or public spirit, has become normalized into the accepted routine.

So every profession has its racket, every man his price. The tonsil-snatcher and the ambulance-chaser and the insurance-fixer and the testimonial-writer have their counterparts in the higher reaches of the professions. The more universal forms of dishonor become honorable, and graft and shakedowns, like the private toll exacted for automobile and marriage licenses, become so common that they even escape notice. Those who actively oppose these customary injustices and these systematic perversions of law and decency are looked upon as disappointed men who have set their own price too high. Force, fraud, lying, chicane, become commonplaces; the law is enforced by illegal methods, the constitution protected by unconstitutional practices; vast businesses are conducted in " peace " by judicious connivance with armed thugs — now passive blackmailers, now active strikebreakers — whose work proceeds under the amiable eyes of the very agents supposed to combat it. No one believes that the alternative to living with honor is to die with honor: it is easier, it is more comfortable, to live sordidly, accepting dishonor.

In such a city, an honest man looms high. He is a lighthouse on a low and treacherous coast. To attain even a human level becomes, in this megalopolitan environment, an arduous, almost a superhuman, task.

EARTH, WATER, SKY, MEN

Any fair picture of New York must confess the underlying sordidness of a large part of its preoccupations and activities. It is not that manufacture and shipping and the exchange of goods are necessarily antivital or antisocial processes: quite the contrary. But when these activities become central to life, when they are themselves perverted to serve chiefly as instruments in an abstract accountancy of profit and power, the human hierarchy of values is displaced; and, as in some perversion of the physiological functions, the head becomes cretinous, and the subordinate members become gigantic *and useless*. What I have elsewhere called a purposeless materialism became the essential principle of the city's life.

One must not flinch, then, from recognizing the dark elements of the picture. But one would have no true image — in fact, no image at all — if one forgot to add the light that defines and relieves the blackest shape; and even at its worst, these elements were always present. There is, to begin with, the physical magnificence of the scene: the sweep and curve of the bay, the grand spaciousness of the river, the rhythm of the tides that encircle it, the strike of its mica-gleaming schists as they crop out in the park or the temporary excavation, and finally, the proud upthrust of the Palisades themselves. In the very shape of the island is something tight, lean, athletic: a contrast to the glacial till of Long Island, with its fat Dutch landscape, its duckponds, its feathery asparagus beds. The skyscrapers, despite their disorder, have not diminished those positive lines in their stalagmitic upthrust: they are almost as geometric as gypsum crystals. And before the skyscrapers were built, from Brooklyn Heights, from the Palisades, from the Belvedere in Central Park, from Morningside Heights, one could see and feel the hard flanks of Manhattan.

Above all, there is the sky; pervading all these activities is the weather. The sharp crystalline days of early autumn, with intense blue sky and a few curls of cloud drifting through space like the little jets of steam that were once such characteristic outlets of the older skyscrapers; the splendors of sunset on the waters, over the Palisades, crossing the Brooklyn Ferry, looking toward the Jersey shore from the Brooklyn Bridge; the swift, whiplike changes from heat to cold, from fog to clarity, from the sharp jeweled contours of John Bellini to the soft tones of Whistler and Fuller. Occasionally, too, the sulphurous hell of the dog days, to whip up appetite for the dank clouds in the west and the brave crackle of lightning and the drenching showers. At the other extreme the benignity and quiet of a city quenched by snow: the jingle of sleighbells in the eighteen-nineties, the cold flash of electricity on the elevated tracks twenty years later.

The niggling interests of the day might lead to a neglect of these fundamental beauties; but they could not obliterate them. Nature remained, ready to nourish the first person who opened his eyes and breathed in the air — the clear, slightly salt-laden air, grey wings swooping and circling through it. This clear air and this intense sunlight are no small encouragements to the photographer. And the landscape as a whole has definition, a disciplined line. The rocks run as due north and south as the points of the compass, and the very sides of the island, once scraggly, have been shaped by the hands of man into sharp lines, like the margin of a Dutch canal. No matter how great the confusion on the surface, beneath it all, in the rocks themselves, is order: no matter how shifty man's top layer, the foundations are solid. If the streets are dingy, there is the dazzle of the sky itself; if the alleys and streets are foul, heavy with ancient dirt, with the effluvia of the sewers or the factories, there is the sanative taste of salt in the first wind that blows from the Atlantic. The cold sea fog in spring, sweeping inland in the midafternoon, calls one to the ocean as imperatively as the proud, deep-throated roar of the steamer, claiming the channel as she passes out to sea. So the ocean and the sky and the rivers hold the city in their grip, even while the people, like busy ants in the cracks and crevices, are unconscious of these more primal presences, save when they read a report in the morning paper, and reach for an umbrella, an overcoat, a fan.

Along with its great landscape, New York has had its men. Even in the worst periods of the city's deterioration, there has always been a saving remnant, that handful of honest souls whose presence might have saved the Biblical cities of the plain.

There was, for one, Walt Whitman himself, " of Mannahatta a son," whose visits to the city, with even occasional public appearances, continued after the Civil War, and whose brief pictures of the city are precious records of its life. Whitman, who had rambled about every part of the city, who knew it coming inward from his native Huntington, from Coney Island when that spot was just a fishing hamlet, from the rocky wilds of the upper part of the island, where he would go walking with Bryant — Whitman knew the city at its best. While he realized the evil significance of so much of its vitality, and the impoverishment of its wealth — see his description of the fashionable parade in Central Park in 'seventy-nine — he was nourished by it and fed steadily on it, opera, theater, bookstalls, libraries, lecture halls; above all, the million-headed throng on the streets.

Drinking at Pfaff's, loafing on the Fifth Avenue stages with the coach drivers, crossing the Brooklyn Ferry, Whitman had caught something in the common life that was dear and permanent. He who really touches the soil of Manhattan and the pavement of New York touches, whether he knows it or not, Walt Whitman. Beneath the snobbery of the commercial elite, there was in New York a genuinely cosmopolitan spirit. In those who like Whitman and Melville were well rooted in the provincial soil, this spirit was capable of reaching out for elements that were still foreign to the new country — the philosophy of Hegel and Schopenhauer, the criticism of Carlyle and Ruskin, the vision of Michelet and Hugo — and transporting them to our unfinished landscape. Melville, who had been a common sailor, and Whitman, a common printer and carpenter, were not caught by the bourgeoisie and debased into accepting their prudent paper routine. Both of them were capable of a passionate aristocracy that reserved for the spirit its primacy in the affairs of men. Whitman's democracy was the prelude to a broader-rooted aristocracy, and none knew that fact better than he.

The Roeblings were in New York, too, during the 'sixties, and Washington remained on, though an invalid, until the Brooklyn Bridge was finally completed in 1883. Not alone did they compose the poem of granite and steel that is the Brooklyn Bridge, one of the first of those grand native works of art that Whitman had demanded of the sayers and delvers, but they brought that arduous habit of intellectual exertion, that capability for heroic sacrifice on behalf of immaterial things, that strict obligation to self-discipline, which came directly from the great Germany of Kant and Goethe and Hegel, a Germany the elder Roebling — who was a pupil of

Hegel's — so well knew. It was right for a New Yorker who was interested in science or engineering to seek Berlin during this period; so that even though Stieglitz was unaware of the fact that he was following in the footsteps of the great engineer who built the bridge, it was as natural for him to go to Berlin as it was for Louis Sullivan, a little earlier, to follow the footsteps of Richardson to the Ecole des Beaux Arts in Paris.

Though none of the new buildings in New York could compare in beauty with the High Bridge, in its original stone form, or with the Brooklyn Bridge, there was a stir in architecture in the 'eighties and 'nineties, due chiefly to the work of Richardson, whose influence remained even though he changed his residence from Staten Island to Boston. Beginning with the De Vinne Building on Lafayette Street, an excellent structure created for a scrupulous and craftsmanlike master of printing, the finest works of New York architecture were the series of loft and factory and storage buildings that arose in the 'eighties: buildings whose round arches, solid stone courses, and subtle brickwork set a mark that few later buildings have surpassed. These buildings, moreover, were better than the very best Europe could show in this department at the same period, and contemporary European travelers of discernment noted and admitted this.

Finally, there was Albert Pinkham Ryder, the most sensitive, the most noble mind that appeared in New York after the war, a worthy companion in the spirit to that other postwar recluse, the author of *Moby Dick*. If the bold sunlight of Broadway made its sheet-iron buildings look flimsy and unreal, the moonlight of Ryder's inner landscape gave body to reality: Ryder with his intuitions of human destiny, Death Riding around a Racetrack, with his wistful melodies of love, the vision of Perette, Siegfried and the Rhine Maidens, with his presentation of fate in the little boats with a tiny sheet of sail on a broad moonlit sea, to which he so often returned — this mystic had a strength and a purpose that the ephemeral

162

activities of the outer world did not possess. A benign figure, ranging up and down the streets after dark, penetrating life in its stillness and peace more bravely than those who flung themselves into the noisiest corners of the battlefield, Ryder also became part of the soil of Manhattan. No one can be aware of the rich vitality of the city who does not know its Ryder as well as its Whitman. He needed little from the city; he gave back much.

THE LIVING ENVIRONMENT

The problem for the creative mind in the 'nineties, whether he was a young writer like Stephen Crane or a young man with a passion for photography like Alfred Stieglitz, was to face this New York of boundless misdirected energy and to capture a portion of that wasteful flow for his own purposes, using its force without accepting its habitual channels and its habitual destinations. But there was still another problem: and that was to conquer, with equal resolution, the gentility, the tepid overrefinement, the academic inertness and lack of passionate faith, masquerading as sound judgment, which were characteristic of the stale fugitive culture of the bourgeoisie. The genteel standards that prevailed were worse than no standards at all: dead objects, dead techniques, dead forms of worship, cast a morbid shadow on every enterprise of the mind, making mind itself a sham, causing vitality to seem somehow shameful. To put the choice with the crudest possible emphasis, the problem for the creative mind was how to avoid the gangster without turning into the spinster.

Now, during the nineteenth century, great forces were at work in the world. People who prefer the tight securities of the eighteenth century or the adolescent turbulence of the seventeenth century only prove their own timidity and ineptness when they belittle these forces merely because they destroyed old patterns and worked creatively on unfamiliar lines. But if the artist was to become a force in his own right once more, as confident of his mission as the scientist or the engineer, it was important that he should not identify himself with the senseless acts of imperialist conquest, or with the senseless mechanical negation of life. When I use the word senseless I use it in both its usual meanings — first, foolish and stupid; and on the other hand, without benefit of the senses, shut off from the experiences that come through the eye, the hand, the ear, the nose, the touch of the body. For the weakness of the mechanical ideology that had put itself at the service of capitalism — and that colored even the minds that rejected it — was that it had limited the provinces of the senses, and confined its operations to a blind world of matter and motion.

Following partly from this mechanical philosophy, partly from the new routine of industry, the senses were in fact denied and defeated in all the new industrial centers; not least, certainly, in New York, which concentrated the industry and the finance of the Western continent. To become a force in this society, this city, it was necessary to open up once more all the avenues of human experience; to sharpen the eye, quicken the touch, refine the senses of smell and taste, as a preliminary to restoring to wholeness the dwarfed and amputated personalities that had been produced — the Gradgrinds, the M'Choakumchilds, the Bounderbys. In a world where practical success canceled every other aspiration, this meant a redoubled interest in the goods and methods that challenged the canons of pecuniary success — contemplation and idle reverie, high craftsmanship and patient manipulation, a willing acceptance of the emotions and an enlargement of the erotic ritual, a shift from the specialized masculine interests leading to an exploitation of power to the more generalized, more centrally biological interests symbolized in love: an emphasis on the ecstasy of being rather than a concentration on the pragmatic strain of " getting there."

In the Bhagavad Gita, Krishna says that the way to contemplation may be found through action as well as through exercises that are directly meant to intensify and illuminate the spiritual life. And it was by action, by utilizing one of the fine mechanical instruments that had been produced by the scientist and the inventor, that Stieglitz, on returning to New York in the eighteen-nineties, approached the world around him and helped restore those values that had been left out of the narrow *Weltbild* of his contemporaries. While Stieglitz, through his very use of the camera, allied himself with the new forces at work in the world, he did not, like those who have denied their own humanity, become smaller through his use of the machine. For mark this: only those who live first and who keep alive have earned the right to use the machine. Those who use machinery because they are incapable of facing the stream of life and directing it, those who seek order in automatons because they lack the discipline and courage to achieve order in themselves, become the victims of their instruments and end by becoming mere attachments to a mechanical contrivance. Not so with Stieglitz: from the beginning the machine was as subordinate to his human direction, through his understanding of its potentialities and capacities, as is the breathing of a Hindu guru. When used thus, as part of man's organic equipment rather than as a substitute for a deficient organ, the machine becomes as integral as the original eyes or legs. Assimilating the machine in this fashion Stieglitz was armed to reconquer the lost human provinces that had been forfeited by the one-sided triumph of the machine.

In the surviving photographs of Stieglitz's early discovery of New York with the camera, one is conscious at first chiefly of his sure and resolute approach to the outward aspects of the city that had been regarded as " unpaintable," and therefore, in a fashion, as unusable. He watches the changing of the horses on a horse car in a snowstorm; he looks at a row of ugly brownstones or hovers above a maze of railroad tracks in a railroad yard, with the locomotives puffing magnificently at the sky. In his interest in these things, he is on a par with another realist, who used paint as his major medium, rather than photography, Thomas Eakins — but his scope is broader, his interests less traditional. Stieglitz does not, like his Parisian contemporary, Atget, range the city from morning to night, deliberately composing a documentary history of its life, after the fashion of Zola. He not merely observes: he waits; he eliminates, he selects. Certain aspects of the city he touches only by implication. Instead of merely mining the pitchblende, he extracts the minute particle of radium, which accounts for the strange behavior of the entire mass.

There are many parts of New York that Stieglitz ignores or leaves no record of, parts of it that have not entered his life or nourished him; there are other parts of his experience, like the grand spectacle of the horse races, which mean much to him and still are preserved only in a print or two. It is not for lack of love or interest that the epic of New York is not caught by his camera, chapter by chapter, as it unfolds from the 'nineties onward; to seize this was indeed part of his conscious intention. But the point is that it is not the document but the life that made it possible that he searches for and holds to: and as Emerson says, the essential fact is unaltered by many or few examples. If one doubts Stieglitz's awareness of the deeper transformations of feeling and thinking and acting that took place in his metropolis one need only examine his photographs more carefully. The external change in the city itself was profound. Within the darkened alleyways of the financial district, people lost their sense of day and night, just as they lost the occasional glimpse of the sky which makes the worst routine bearable. In the new subways they lost even the glimpse of the sun over the roof tops of Manhattan, which had once been theirs from the ramshackle elevated roads. Nature in its most simple form, the wonder of the morning and the night, was missing from the metropolitan routine; and *therefore* — I say " therefore " because such reac-

tions are rarely accidents — these elements establish themselves in Stieglitz's photographs with a new force.

The chief instrument of photography is light; and the fact
that Stieglitz always worked by natural light, never by artifi-
cial light, with its studied arrangements and its temptations to
trickery, is an important one. But all the hours of the days
become important to him: so he takes the first night pictures
that have esthetic significance. The weather, likewise, is an
important element for his vision: hence, too, he takes the first
photographs in snow and in rain. He does not have to escape
to the country to find nature, any more than he has to escape
to antiquity to find beauty, in the way that the purse-proud
art collectors of the period, the Mrs. Jack Gardners and the
Pierpont Morgans, were doing. All these necessary elements
in life were still present in the city, though they had been excluded from the routine of getting and spending. Just as
Ryder continued to be in touch with nature when he had his
ailanthus tree and his patch of sky, so Stieglitz found the
necessary germs of a living environment even in a metropolis
that had lost the most rudimentary sense of the soil, and was
turning itself, step by step, block by block, into a stony waste.

During the nineteen hundreds, too, the city was losing its
sense of the rivers, despite the extension of Riverside Park.
For sewage pollution had driven the North River shad away
and made all other kinds of fish that might be caught noxious;
so that the old gaffers with their set-lines and bells had disappeared from the Hudson, along with the groups of happy
naked swimmers, and another link with nature was broken,
even as, because of pollution from the oil-burning steamers,
the waters of the Lower Bay lost the bluefish and weakfish
that had once been so plentiful there. But Stieglitz, not less
than Whitman, preserved the sense of the waters surround-
ing Manhattan. He photographed the ferry boats coming
into their slips, the boatload of immigrants, the skyline of

Manhattan from the Jersey shore, with the water establishing a base in the foreground. Water and sky come into his pictures, again and again: the river, the ocean, the bathing beach, the rain, the snow, and finally, dominating the whole landscape in every sense, the clouds. Shut out by the tall buildings, shut out by the dark courts of the new apartment houses, the very stars at night put at a distance by the myriad lights of the city, flaring, as Tennyson said, like a dreary dawn — the sky remains under all conditions the essential reminder of nature and the cosmos. In the course of Stieglitz's own development, the sky becomes a more and more essential part of his pictures; and finally, it becomes the symbol whereby Stieglitz unites his sense of the universal order with the sense of the personality, as developed in the relations of men and women.

In the stoniest pavement of the city there are cracks. And out of the bleakest soil, between these cracks, a few blades of grass will sooner or later show, whose seeds are borne by the birds; here, even, the germ of a tree will take root and spring up, if no foot disturbs it. It is in the cracks between the new buildings that Stieglitz finds the sky; it is in the surviving cracks in the pavement that Stieglitz finds his trees; and in his most characteristic pictures of the city, so far from emphasizing the massiveness and the obduracy of its stones, he emphasizes the presence of life. One of the most moving and impressive pictures he ever made was that of a little tree in Madison Square Park, young and vernal in the rain, with a street sweeper in the foreground and the dim shape of a building in the background: the promise of life, its perpetual reawakening and renewal, are in that print.

Wherever Stieglitz turns his head in this city, he looks for the touch of life, seizes it, emphasizes it; and by this means he sets himself in opposition to those who would glorify the negation of life and sanction its subordination to metropolitan business, material concentration. Meanwhile, all the forces of urban aggrandizement are on the make: advertising, insurance, and high finance, the divine trinity that rules the world of industry and perverts its honest labors for its own ends, gather together in the city and out of its egotism and self-inflation rose higher and higher skyscrapers, first in the southern end of the island, then, forming a sort of double vertebral column, from Thirty-fourth Street upward, in the new central district. The new office buildings and lofts are flanked by apartment houses as stupidly planned, as extravagantly designed, as crazily and as dishonestly financed as the business buildings themselves. The megalopolitan architects who designed these puerile structures gloated over the prospect of a whole city composed of skyscrapers, with aerial drives for the rich, and in the murky canyons below the working and living quarters for the poor — artificially lighted! artificially ventilated! — a city in which sunlight would be supplied by sunlamps, grass by green tiles, and babies, presumably, by mechanical incubation. (No extravagance of Aldous Huxley's satire was beyond the serious commonplace luncheon conversation of the self-infatuated schoolboys who were financing and planning and building the " city of the future," on paper.)

A generation after his first pictures of New York, Stieglitz surveys the city once more, now from the seventeenth story of an office building at Fifty-third Street, surrounded by the architectural bluff and fraud of the boom period. He ironically portrays these structures with no further hint of nature than the indication of the hour of the day, through the degree of light and shadow that falls on their trivial façades. He shows the skyscraper — the mock city of the future — in the last state of mechanical perfection and human insignificance, devoid at last of even the possibility of earning money: financial liabilities, as well as the social liabilities their reckless misuse had already made them. There, in effect, is the ultimate result of putting nature at a distance and subordinating all the values of living to the paper routine of pseudo-work and profit-pyramiding. These skyscrapers of Stieglitz's last photographs might be the cold exhalations of a depopulated world.

And at the end, with a sardonic gleam in his eyes, he photographs the turning point: the tearing down of a seven-story building at Sixtieth Street and Madison Avenue in order to make way for a new two-story building. The nightmare was over. The human scale had begun to return. Finally, the sterile dream of imperialist conquest externalized itself in that last gesture of the impotent: Rockefeller Center. But this was already an aftermath, which, like an auto rolling backward downhill, continued on its course because the driver preferred the sensation of motion, even if it were motion backwards, to the recognition of his inability to reverse the direction and go forward.

SYMBOLS OF VITALITY

While the tree and the sky are dominating symbols in Stieglitz's work, brought to sharper focus by their steady exclusion from the urban landscape, there are two others that were important, both in his personal life and in his vision: the race horse and the woman. The thoroughbred horse, quivering in every muscle, nostril open, eyes glaring, hooves delicately stamping, ready for the race or the rut: symbol of sheer animal vitality, bred and nurtured with a single eye to that final outburst of speed which carries horse and rider down the home stretch to victory. From the black heavy-flanked Waterboy or the low-slung, short-legged chestnut Sysonby, to the great Man o' War and his present-day successors, these horses represented the pinnacle of animal achievement: proofs of man's skill and intelligence in alliance with the world of life, symbolic of those new strains of wheat, those new hybrids or sports in flowers and fruits, whose conquest was ultimately more important to man than were half the mechanical contrivances on which the metropolitan mind doted.

And if the horse was animal vitality, woman was — if one may combine the words — animal spirituality, that form of spirit which, unlike the lonely ascetic endeavors of man, fulfills itself in the very organs of the body, in the warmth of the arms, in the tenderness that emanates from the breast, in the receptivity of the lap, in the utilization of every physical fiber for the higher ends of life, making the body not the enemy of the mind but the friendly guide and initiator; favoring the warm intellect, touched by the earth, the intellect of Goethe, as contrasted with the cold intellect, the intellect divorced from the earth, the intellect of womanless men like Leonardo. Man tends to overvalue his eyes and his muscles: the organs of definition and of physical conquest. Woman teaches him to use his lips, his sense of touch, and to diffuse some of the fierce tactile sensitiveness that is at first concentrated so exclusively in his generative organ. Here is a vitality even deeper-fibered than that of the thoroughbred horse; for it reaches, through the very structure of woman's body, toward a completer biological fulfillment, never being fully organized or alive except when the relationships lead, through the lover or the baby, to the ultimate breast and womb.

The masculine world, with its strife of markets, with its stultifying ambitions to corner wheat or to cheapen steel, to invent this or that substitute for organic life, to conquer by an equation or a formula this or that territory of the intellect, this masculine world, particularly in our own cultural epoch, has tended toward an asceticism that has left little energy or time for the fundamental biological occupations. The seed was sound and fruitful: the great outburst of vitality marked by the rising birth rate of the nineteenth century proved it; but the soil was too dry and sour and lacking in humus to give the plant itself full growth. So that it was the classes at the periphery of our mechanical civilization, more often the not-serious people, the unbusinesslike, the wastrels and gamblers and sports, the " low " and the " vicious," among the males, who still preserved an alert eye appreciative of the flanks and fetlocks and neck of a horse, or the flanks and belly and buttocks of a woman.

Compare the stock exchange and the race track. Economically, both are mainly gambling devices; and humanly speaking they are both low forms of activity. But one is indoors; it is conducted in a clamorous jumble of noises by means of a series of telegraphic symbols; the realities with which the gamble deals, the automobile factories and packing plants and mail-order houses and banana plantations, are present only as verbal abstractions. The other activity is held outdoors under the sky; the track, heavy or fast, is affected by accidents of the weather; the gamble has to do with visible horseflesh and visible human skill and courage; and in the procession to the post, the suspense of the start, the stretching out of the field, and the final climax of the home stretch, there is a superb esthetic spectacle. The drama itself does not terminate abruptly with the end of the race: the tension is prolonged by the return of the jockey to the judge's stand, where he awaits for an instant, with upraised arm and whip, the nod that gives him the victory in a fairly won race.

Degas came closer than anyone else among the painters to representing this drama; but there is something, in the four-dimensional continuity of it, that evades even the most skilled of painters; indeed, the impulse to grasp this continuity was responsible for the critical steps in the invention of the motion-picture camera. At the bottom of this interest is the horse himself; and until the automobile usurped this interest, the horse and the gambling connected with the races were ways in which the American, caught in his artful commercial merry-go-round, kept a little of his residual sense of the primitive and the organic. Right down to the end of the first decade of the present century, the Speedway at 155th Street was maintained as a common race track for trotters; and the designer of Central Park, a generation earlier, was forced, in the interests of more general recreation, to plan his horse drives so as to curb racing.

If Stieglitz did not photographically utilize this deep interest of his in the horse races — there is, however, the fine print of " Going to the Post " — it was only perhaps because its intensity was incompatible with that patient suspended animation which makes photography possible. Stieglitz was too near the race horse, as one is too near the lover in an embrace, to be able to photograph him. And yet the horse symbolized to him, as it did to the author of *St. Mawr* and to the author of *Roan Stallion* in a later generation, something essential in the life of man: that deep animal vitality he had too lightly turned his back on and renounced in his new mechanical preoccupations. So Stieglitz conceived, though he never carried out, a series of photographs of the heads of stallions and mares, of bulls and cows, in the act of mating, hoping to catch in the brute an essential quality that would symbolize the probably unattainable photography of a passionate human mating.

SEX AND LOVE

Just as the old rural interest in animals could enter the city only deviously by way of the race track, so sex itself, despite its endless manifestations, had no central part in the routine of the civilization that had reached a mechanical apex in New York. Where sex was most obvious, in the burlesque houses and musical comedies and in the murky red-light district, it was also most furtive and shamefaced: a grudging admission, not a passionate conviction; an itch, not an intensity; a raw piece of flesh flung to a caged animal, who responded in his reflexes, like a Pavlovian dog, without benefit of mind. Foreign observers noted that women tended to dominate the pioneer society of America, and to hold its males in nominal subservience to ideals of courtesy and chivalry toward womanhood. But although the traditional scarcity of women in a new country gave woman a privileged position and permitted her a freedom of travel and a freedom of choice in mating unknown among similar classes in Europe, the result was to widen the political scope of woman at the expense of her sex life. Instead of ruling with and through her sex, the American woman, despite her studious attention to her own beauty, her figure, and her dress, learned to preserve her freedom and power by keeping sex at a distance. It was on the assumption that " nothing could happen " that the sexes came together so easily, and that women in America, up to the second decade of the present century, were given their " freedom."

And in any fundamental sense nothing did happen, even after the American girl extended her flirtations to the length of concluding them in bed. The whole business of sex remained peripheral: sexual expression symbolized freedom or sophistication; indeed, it often sank so low as to justify itself as hygiene. People married and became the parents of children and were driven to seek divorce before they had even scraped the surface of intimacy. This negation of sex was helped, perhaps, rather than hindered by the devices of birth control. Contraceptive devices put between passion and its fulfillment a series of mechanical or chemical obstacles which, though small in themselves, could never be completely routinized into oblivion: the least objectionable device from the standpoint of intercourse was also the most dangerous in the possibilities of serious lesion. If this is still largely true today, a hundred years after the initial movement toward birth control in America, it was even more true a generation ago, when the crudeness and uncertainty of the various devices used added to the clumsiness and anxiety that attended their employment. With sex, the dish often became lukewarm before it could be served; and with the loss of warmth and flavor went a loss of appetite; for why, if the final result were favored by lukewarmness, should people ever bother to reach in the first place a hotter temperature?

Lusty men and passionate women of course remained in this society; but the whole tone of sex remained practically as low as it had been in Victorian days. Although talk about sex, and even possibly physical indulgence, became more common, the actual manifestations often remained placidly anemic: a girl might have a dozen lovers without having known an orgasm, or have a dozen orgasms without having achieved any fundamental intimacy with her lover. On the surface, decorum or the defiance of decorum; beneath it, irritation, frustration, resentment — resentment on the part of the male for the unarousableness of the female, about whom the faint aroma of anxious antisepsis clung like an invisible petticoat; resentment on the part of the female against the male both for his bothersome insistence and his lack of really persuasive aggression. In the course of business, the work in the office and the factory, the activities of the home, the club, the social gathering, men and women saw each other too little on their more primitive levels to overcome all these obstacles and find each other. They sought by the chemical means of drink to reach these levels more quickly — only to lose the sting and sharpness of sex, when what they needed was patience and leisure and sympathy and above all free energy and vitality, for all of which a tumescent animal befuddlement was in no sense a substitute. For what was left for sex but the dreary crowded moments before sleep, when all energy had been spent upon every aspect of living except sex?

One emphasizes the state of sex in American society because here again Stieglitz was to preoccupy himself with symbolic representations of the elements that were lacking in the scene around him. As a young student in Europe, he had found his own sense of manliness and sexual confidence re-enforced and cultivated by the great traditions of the arts, above all by Rubens, whose portrait of Hélène de Fourment, an exuberant naked girl wrapped in fur, he had seen on his first visit to Vienna, at a critical moment when it had re-echoed and eloquently justified the impulses he found within himself. The health, the animal vitality, the unashamed lushness of sex in Rubens's paintings, are all as conspicuous as the absence of these qualities in the unhealthy sentimentality that has hung around sex in the Western world, since Christianity attempted to transfer to heterosexual relations the sick moonlight glamour of unfulfilled yearning that derived ultimately, perhaps, from the romantic homosexual love of the Greeks. Rubens was a long step back to reality from the misty mid-regions inhabited by Poe's pallid maidens, girls who were reproduced in paint in the adolescent sweetness of George Fuller's paintings in the 'seventies, and still further attenuated in the popular Dewing ladies who ruled the 'nineties. The ideal maiden of adolescent America was a sort of inverted pariah: untouchable by reason of her elevation. In defiance of Nature, her womanliness and her untouchability were supposed to be one. But what was sex, how could it exist, how could it nourish the personality, if it were not in fact the most essential demonstration of touchability — if the intercourse of lovers, at all its levels, from the intuitions at a distance to the final stages of union, were not accompanied at every moment by that direct sense of touch, that tact, which removes the need for words and signs and breaks down the formidable distance between object and subject, between thine and mine?

In all the manifold meanings of the adjective, sex was primarily the realm of tactile values. Stieglitz was to discover these values and intensify them in his photography even before Berenson had used them, too narrowly, as a key to the great painting of the Italian Renaissance. The blindness of love, debased as a mere figure of speech, is indeed one of the most characteristic of its attributes. It is blind in the fact that it reaches deeper levels of consciousness, below the open-eyed rationality of practical achievement. It is blind in the way that it often shuts out the outer world in order to concentrate upon the inner stimulus, blind as in terror, blind as in prayer;

and finally, it has the beautiful compensation of blindness, for
it learns to see with its fingertips, and to offset the closed eyes,
reacts more quickly than the other available senses in every region of the body.

It was Stieglitz's endeavor, at first mainly instinctive, finally,
through a better self-knowledge, with a fuller awareness of
his actions, to translate the unseen world of tactile values as
they develop between lovers not merely in the sexual act but
in the entire relationship of two personalities — to translate
this world of blind touch into sight, so that those who felt
could more clearly see what they felt, and so those who could
merely see might reach, through the eye, the level of feeling.
Observe the work of Stieglitz's contemporaries in photography,
moved perhaps by the same desires but deeply inhibited. See,
in the many reproductions in *Camera Work* — which doubtless helped pave the way to the sun-bathing and easier nudity
of a later day — see how they portray the nude body. However honest their efforts, they nevertheless surround the body
with a halo of arcadian romanticism; note how resolutely they
equip their naked models with glass bubbles; how they com-
pel these naked girls painfully, for the first time in their lives,
to pour water out of narrow-necked jugs; how they lash them
to tree stumps or make them shiver at the edge of icy pools.
Sex must be disguised as art — that is, as artiness — before
one may peep at it without blushing. Undisguised, the girl
averts her face from the camera, so that the self-conscious
and self-righteous face shall not acknowledge the powers of
the body. The efforts of these earlier photographers are not
to be despised; but the tantalizing fear of sex, a fear of its
heady realities, is written over their pictures, with their dutiful
aversions, their prescribed degrees of dimness, their overarch
poses.

It was his manly sense of the realities of sex, developing out
of his own renewed ecstasy in love, that resulted in some of
Stieglitz's best photographs. In a part by part revelation of a
woman's body, in the isolated presentation of a hand, a breast,

a neck, a thigh, a leg, Stieglitz achieved the exact visual equivalent of the report of the hand or the face as it travels over
the body of the beloved. Incidentally, this is one of the few
aspects of photography that had not been anticipated in one
fashion or another by the painter, since the dismembered
anatomical studies of the Renaissance, which casually resemble
these photographs, are purely instruments of factual knowledge: they make no appeal to sentiments and feelings. In
more abstract, yet not in less intimate form, Stieglitz sought
to symbolize the complete range of expression between man
and woman in his cloud pictures, relying upon delicacies and
depths of tone, and upon subtle formal relationships, to rep-
resent his own experiences. Earth and sky, root and topmost branch, animal intimacy and spiritual expression — these
things, which were so remote from the routine of the metropolitan world, or which there existed in such loud disharmony,
were restored to their natural integrity in Stieglitz's life and
work. What was central became central again; what was
deep was respected for its profundity, instead of being ignored; what was superficial was thrust behind the essential.

Stieglitz was never a better son of the city he loved and
identified himself with than when he turned his back on her
desiccated triumphs and recalled, in word, in photography, in
the tenacious act of existence, the precious elements that the
city had excluded. With Whitman, with Ryder, with the
handful of other men that each generation has produced in
New York, Stieglitz has served his city, not by acquiescing in
its grandiose decay, nor yet by furthering its creeping paralysis: he has served it by nurturing in himself, and in those who
have witnessed his work, the living germs that may reanimate
it, quickening the growth of the higher forms of life it has
excluded. For, as Whitman said, the place where the great
city stands is not the place of markets and stretched wharves
and multiplying population and ships bringing goods from the
ends of the earth: it is the city of the faithfulest lovers and
friends.

Pierre-Auguste Renoir

In a civilization impoverished by abstractions — progress, the machine, the state, financial power, imperialist exploitation — Renoir renewed the natural appetites; he turned men's eyes toward bread and wine and sunlight and sex, the sources and symbols of life.

The Renoir exhibition at the Metropolitan Museum was fitly prefaced this spring [1937] by the Manet show at Wildenstein and the quite ravishing Degas show at Durand-Ruel. It is the last big show of the season, and fortunately for lovers of Renoir — perhaps I should say fortunately for all lovers — it will remain on through the summer.

Pierre-Auguste Renoir was born in 1841 at Limoges. This makes him a close contemporary of Rodin and Claude Monet, and a little younger than Manet and Degas, who were born in the early eighteen-thirties. His birthplace, where the famous enamels were made in the Middle Ages, is the great pottery center, and in 1854 he went to work as a china-painter in a porcelain factory. By honest origin, then, Renoir was one of those creatures who are so often talked about nowadays — a proletarian painter; and I think he disposes of the patronizing middle-class superstition that a proletarian painter would naturally spend all his life depicting the grandeurs and miseries of proletarians.

Not merely did Renoir originally have to seek a living as a factory worker; he lost his job because the fashionable machine processes that were being introduced in the fifties did away temporarily with the need for china-painters — an early victim of technological unemployment. At seventeen, he entered the studio of Gleyre, where he met Monet and Sisley. So Renoir rose into the new aristocracy of the unemployed —

the painters and sculptors who were in revolt against the tastes and standards of the bourgeoisie; people who created art, as the aristocracy flirted and danced and went to the hunt, because it was, despite the meagerness of the artists' subsistence, a profoundly satisfactory mode of life.

Renoir's first salon picture was shown in 1863, but he destroyed a good part of his early work, and the present show opens with a portrait of Mme. Darras, done in 1871 — a grave piece, carefully modelled, in beautiful repose, the work of a man who was already well within sight of maturity. Meanwhile the Franco-Prussian War had taken place, followed by the tense, exalted period of the Commune and the savage horror of its suppression. Frenchmen were humiliated by the disasters that had overtaken them, but not exhausted, and a gathering and tightening of energies took place among the élite. One marks that sombre intensity in much of Renoir's early work. It achieved its fullest expression toward the end of the seventies; note " La Fillette Attentive," " Two Little Circus Girls," " L'Ingénue," and " La Petite Margot Bérard."

Even in his early maturity Renoir was perhaps more open to the influences around him than any of his peers. He made sorties now in one direction, now in another. " Le Pont Neuf à Paris," one of the new sunlight paintings of the Impressionists, was done as early as 1872. Many of these pictures, even as late as " The Duck Pond," are executed with the fine pointillist stroke of Monet. On the other hand, in " Child with a Hoop," of about 1875, the lace of the collar is put on with a heavy touch that his friend Cézanne applied to his early pictures; only a certain tenderness of contour in the child's face marks it as especially Renoir's.

Through this early period, Renoir's palette was as undecided as his technique. Those who think of Renoir chiefly in terms of those streams of scarlet and carmine that issue out of Rubens and Fragonard and suffuse so many of the paintings of Renoir's old age must bow to the cooler charms of the

olive greens and dull oranges and gray blues of Renoir's
"Melon and a Vase of Roses," painted in the middle seventies.
Some of Renoir's greatest paintings, indeed, are built out of
these cool colors and sombre tones. One of the most marvelous of these is the full-length portrait of Mlle. Durand-Ruel,
now in the Barnes Foundation Collection and not in the present show, but two of the portraits shown are close runners-up
to that picture. There was a moment, marked by "La Pen-
sée," which Renoir's delicacy of touch created forms that
were almost emanations, rather than solid bodies, figures that
remind one of the feminine wraiths that our own George
Fuller evoked during the same period. Yet Renoir's diaph-
anous girls are composed with an underlying firmness that
saves them from dissolution, and even in his most ethereal moments he never lost touch with solid earth. For during this
period, Renoir did the study of Anna that is now in Moscow, I
believe — one of the first of his lush, round-bellied, almost-
pregnant girls.

I cannot leave the Renoirs of the seventies without dwelling
for a moment on the portrait of Mlle. Legrand, "La Fillette
Attentive," and that of "La Petite Margot Bérard." Neither
of these portraits owes any direct debt to the new experiments
in light and color that Renoir was making, even though the
pinafore of "La Fillette" is slashed in with some of Manet's
easy freedom. Their incomparable beauty is due to Renoir's
tenderness in dealing with his subject; they are the visible
outcome of his exquisite sensitiveness and fineness of feeling.
The artist's brush, Renoir once remarked to M. Vollard,
should caress the canvas, and it is in this fashion that he treated
the wide-eyed and wistful children who sat for him. The
pallid delicacy of Margot's skin, the even more transparent
touch of shadow, the soft aura of her hair, are done with a
craftsmanship a Roger van der Weyden might have striven to
surpass. In his later years Renoir showed, no doubt, a deeper
individualization of style, and even when he was crippled by

arthritis he could paint such a richly textured portrait as that
of Mme. Tilla Durieux. But he never surpassed, in sheer ade-
quacy of means to an end, the best work he did in the seventies. A Harvard sociologist has recently suggested that what
we hitherto conceived as development, evolution, progress
should be regarded as mere fluctuations. That is a true figure,
at least, for Renoir's life curve.

There was, indeed, a period of extreme fluctuations, more
rapid and violent than in the years just before, that lasted from
about 1879 to 1888 — changes that perhaps seem especially decisive because the artist himself had become conscious of them.
This period was marked by a series of foreign journeys beginning with a trip to Algiers in 1879, by his marriage in 1880,
and by his fatherhood in 1885. It was perhaps that *crise à
quarante ans* that so often overtakes men of ability in middle
life; the period when they desert their wives, run away to the
South Seas, change their occupations, take to drink, or commit
suicide, a period when they write over the doors of their private chambers an urgent " Now or Never! " or a regretful
" Too Late! " During this decade Renoir was in a state of
uneasy turmoil; some of his best and some of his worst paintings belong to this second adolescence. Not merely did
Renoir find himself fed up with Impressionism and openly re-
nounce it; he had moments of intense disgust when he felt that
he knew nothing about painting and had accomplished nothing. Such revulsions are usually as unsound as they are subjective, but they save the creator from a smug contentment
with minor successes and they often lead to a more disciplined
hold over his weaknesses and a more enlightened exploitation
of his strength.

So with Renoir. It was during this very period of self-
criticism that he reached a new level in, among other pictures,
" Le Dejeuner des Canotiers." In this painting, the somewhat
diffuse composition is brought into focus by sheer mastery of
the color relations, and the faces and the bodies become part

of a double field of interest in which the still life of wine, fruit, and tablecloth plays a major part. The feeble spot in this composition — for there are occasionally feeble spots in Renoir's paintings — is the body of the white-shirted man standing on the left. Here Renoir failed to create the slightest illusion of distance from the girl in front, and the white surface itself remains paper-thin. But the painting, nonetheless, is a superb work, a celebration of the joys of youth, a sort of repainting of the grand picnic that Victor Hugo described in the early pages of *Les Misérables* without the possibility of Hugo's sordid aftermath.

What separated Renoir from his fellow-Impressionists was chiefly his sense that the artist was more important than his palette; he recognized that Velásquez's noblemen were dignified because the painter had endowed them with his own dignity. Though Renoir loved to paint nature, he disdained to paint her *au naturel*. Under the influence of Cennino Cennini, he even sought, by a crisp draughtsmanship, to emancipate himself from the mere transcription of nature, not realizing, perhaps, that he had always done so unconsciously.

But after 1888 the new Renoir definitely emerges; he is really the old one, strengthened, clarified, reunited. Both his palette and his form from this time on tend toward the typical. By a curious irony, he is hardly less the Impressionist than before, but now he is an Impressionist who seeks a conscious dignity of form, a painter whose Impressionism is a tool and a method, not an end. Lack of interest kept him for experimenting with those spatial compositions in which both Degas and Cézanne were to excel; distance lent no enchantment to Renoir's view. The foreground for him was so nearly all-important that, as often as not, the background is silent or is reduced to a lazy hum of color.

The "new" painter was already in existence in 1879. Mark the formal use of red, blue, lilac, and lavender in the "Lady Sewing." Nevertheless, in Renoir's later work there was a marked settling down into type; he even tended to give all his figures certain generic features: slanting, half-closed eyes, wide mouths, broad cheekbones, and ample bosoms, while his palette, now rich and sensuous, rarely returned to the cool end of the spectrum. Of the paintings of the later years, there is perhaps a less adequate showing in the present exhibition, but that of " Gabrielle with Jean and a Little Girl " is very fine, while " After the Bath " is a representative sample of those nude figures to which he so often reverted. " Claude at the Easel," done around 1906, is one of the most happy of his later studies of children, and if the face here is less completely realized than that of Margot — if perhaps something precious has indeed been lost — the painting as a whole is more completely individualized. Every inch of it is " signed."

So much for Renoir's paintings *as* painting. But what of his symbols? Is Renoir an example of the proletarian artist gone wrong? Is this an old story of youthful integrity turned into bourgeois compromise and middle-aged escapism? Or is Renoir a proper subject for a medical biography which would show how his arthritis produced a special love for tender flesh and flexible joints and healthy bodies whose very limbs seem tumescent with ecstasy? None of these things is true. Renoir, like his great predecessor Rubens, is one of those artists whose harmonious relations with life were too deep to be disrupted by war, disease, pain, and social frustration; artists whose only form of rebellion or criticism is a renewed gusto in creation. Such people encounter tragic defeat like the pair of birds that Ernst Toller describes in his autobiography. When their nest is broken, they build it again, and when it is broken a second and a third time, they return, with insistent vitality, to the task of rebuilding it. The period in which Renoir painted was blighted at both ends by a catastrophic war and was sharp with economic and political crises, but one searches Renoir's canvases in vain for an expression of these facts. Or, rather, one does not search in vain. He has an answer. He opposes to misery, cruelty, and barbarism the rejuvenating images of life.

Roger Fry, who conquered with difficulty a temperamental aversion to Renoir's art, referred in his *Vision and Design* to the commonplaceness of Renoir's vision. In one's first approach to Renoir, he explained, one was reminded of pictures that would be the " delight of servants' halls." Renoir would not have been embarrassed by that snobbish allusion. He enjoyed the servants around him and said that a woman's hands were not worth painting unless they had been molded by housework. It was natural that his symbols should be commonplace enough and vital enough to break through the factitious standards of caste. In a realistic sense far different from the warped mysticism of the Nazis, Renoir was the artist of blood and soil, the veritable commonplaces of life. He painted glowing landscapes and animated flowers. He painted men and women in acts of simple enjoyment, dancing in the country or the city, picnicking, boating, bathing, eating, conversing, flirting. He was the painter of all those relaxed, sunlit moments whose immediate reward is grace, laughter, ecstasy, and animal health. He makes one feel it is good to be a lover and taste the appeasing sanity of a lover's body; good to be a parent, watching a child's miraculous passages of growth. Renoir brought to these elemental biological states all the force of his imagination. In a civilization impoverished by abstractions — progress, the machine, the state, financial power, imperialist exploitation — Renoir renewed the natural appetites; he turned men's eyes toward bread and wine and sunlight and sex, the sources and symbols of life. So he extracts from lovers their rapture and gives it back in double measure. And today, no matter how the world wobbles at its poles, Renoir remains close to the hub of human reality, perhaps closer than any other artist in his century.

Surrealism and Civilization

Like the modern psychoanalysts, the surrealists have approached the normal by way of the pathological.

At the moment [1936], the town is practically crawling with surrealist exhibitions. There is Joan Miró at the Matisse Gallery, and Salvador Dali at the Julien Levy Gallery, and Man Ray at the Valentine Gallery; and, for good measure, Bedlam and Bloomingdale and Cloud-Cuckoo-Land and Cockaigne have broken loose at the Museum of Modern Art. If you don't know yet what surrealism is, you will never have a better chance of finding out for yourself — or increasing your present confusion. Is it a passing fashion or a new sphere of painting? Is it a variety of art or a metaphysical theory of the universe or a subversive political weapon or a series of practical jokes? Is it a meaningless revolt or a revolt against meaning? Or merely paranoia become playful? All these are weighty questions. One or two of them, incidentally, have something to do with art.

Usually, one of the easiest ways to place a movement is to ask where it began and who started it. Some say surrealism began with a group of young European exiles who sat in a café in Zurich in 1916, concocting a revolution in art called Dada (the art to end all art) — at the very moment that V. I. Lenin, a lover of the classics, was planning a revolution in politics. The two revolutions split at that point, but both were deeply in revolt against the heavy platitudes, the unctuous moralities, and the drab acceptances of the world of " reality," and they came together again in 1925, when everything fashionable had suddenly to prove its right to exist by showing that it was connected with Marxism. Most of the books and

manifestoes that have been written on surrealism confine themselves to these Continental origins. They therefore neglect
the wild surrealist element that has been present in American
art and in American humor from the very beginning.

One of the great merits of the Modern Museum show is
that it presents the immediate origins and achievements of surrealism against a broad background of fantastic and irrational
art that goes back to the Middle Ages. Scarcely anything that
has conceivably paralleled the present movement or contributed anything to it has been neglected by Mr. Alfred Barr:
now a painting by Hieronymus Bosch, now a photomontage
from the New York *Evening Graphic*. The final result of
such inclusiveness and exhaustiveness is that one begins to find
surrealist images sticking out of every hole and cranny, and
one loses sight of two or three of the great landmarks in painting that lead up to surrealism. These landmarks, though included in the show, are swamped in the weltering, dreamlike
confusion of it. If I single them out, it may make the going
a little easier.

The main divisions of surrealist art are distinct, but have a
common foundation in the mind: the pathologically irrational,
the comic, and the unconscious. Each of these sides is in opposition to the conceptions and practical needs of everyday
life; each of them stresses the private and the subjective and
the whimsical, and belittles the public and the objective and
the dutiful. The first, and at the moment the most engrossing,
side of surrealist art begins with Goya. He etched a whole
series of prints, called " Caprices," which for more than a
century seemed only a perverse mystery to most lovers of art,
prints with strange demonic figures leering savagely or ob-
scenely at the spectator, or with natural figures in crazy attitudes, committing obscure follies. These prints seem to rise,
like a miasma, from the murder and torture Goya depicted in
the plates on the horrors of war. Today, Goya's images recur
too frequently in the photographic sections of the newspapers

to be dismissed as " unreal," and it is perhaps no accident that a country that has known brutal irrationality in so many forms should have contributed so many leaders to the surrealist movement today — Picasso, Dali, Miró. If this were all there is to surrealism, one might justify Mr. David Gascoyne's beginning his *Brief Survey* with Gilles de Retz and the Marquis de Sade.

The comic side of surrealism is familiar to the English-speaking world from " Mother Goose " onward. " Hey-diddle-diddle, the cat and the fiddle," the Jabberwocky, the Yonghy-Bonghy-Bò, and the folk tales of Munchausen and Paul Bunyan have had their counterparts in an equally crazy folk art, like the china cat decorated with flowers in the present show. This part of surrealist art flourishes on the incongruous and the unexpected. It is at its best, in painting, in Dali's picture of the wilted watches, in those curious collections of objects that Ray assembles in his canvases, or in those marvelous montages of old woodcuts that Max Ernst has put together with such loving patience. One does not have to read Bergson's disquisition on the significance of laughter to enjoy this part of surrealism. Surely, the very worst compliment one can pay it, even when it is savage or sinister, is to greet it with a respectfully solemn face. If Goya contributed the sadistic nightmare, Edward Lear discovered the magical release of nonsense. (But surrealism has its practical side, too. It was a surrealist experimenter who had the courage to put sugar into a concrete mix to make it stronger.)

The last ingredient in surrealism is the unconscious. Ever since the Renaissance, painters have conscientiously been painting only what they could see with their eyes. " I don't paint angels," said Courbet, " because I have never seen one." But images of all sorts are perpetually welling up out of the unconscious: modern man, concentrated upon conquering Nature and piling up riches, penalizes daydreaming and forces these " irrelevant " images back or keeps them from germinat-

ing; he has invented a score of contraceptives for the imagination, and then is surprised to find his life has become a sterile
one. At night, however, the repressed images spring up again.
These products of the unconscious are not necessarily sinister
or macabre. In a more benign form, they took shape in the
paintings and prints of Odilon Redon, as they had done in
those of William Blake before him, and though Redon has had
very little influence over the French, German, or Catalonian
surrealists, the benigner unconscious activity he exhibited can
be seen in the works of modern Americans like O'Keeffe and
Dove.

If one judges surrealism by the aesthetic and human values
that lie outside it, a good part of it is rubbish; its value lies not
in what it so far has found but in the fact that it has opened
up the gallery of a mine which may, with more adequate tools,
be exploited for more precious ore than that which has so far
been brought to the surface. One of the most powerful and
inventive of the European surrealists, Max Ernst, is only a
moderately good painter; and if the earlier surrealist paintings
of Chirico, spacious and noble in composition, still remain
very fine, if Roy is always an admirable craftsman, and if
Masson and Miró both have a graceful and deft touch, the
quality of the paintings remains an incidental if not a negligible part of the whole movement. To judge the art fairly,
one must realize that it is a symptom — a symptom of the disorder and brutality and chaos of the " real " world; an attempt
through disintegration — as in a Freudian analysis — to dig
down to a point solid enough to serve as a fresh foundation.
With all its praise of the irrational, there is method in the surrealist madness.

Until a generation ago, only soothsayers and ignorant folk
believed in dreams. It took the genius of Freud to combine the
ordinary consciousness of the neurotic with the ordinary
dreams of the normal man, and to see that there was an underlying identity; *dreams meant something*, and in a sense, the

more irrational they were, the more they meant. We can no longer go around pretending that the world is the same world it was before Freud gave us this clue. What we can see and measure and count is only a part of the picture. The complete picture is not so clear and not so orderly as the mind, for practical purposes, would like to have it.

This is one of the great commonplaces of our generation; and the proof is that it has made its way into literature so thoroughly that no one bothers there to call it surrealist. In Virginia Woolf's *Mrs. Dalloway* the returned soldier, Septimus, is suffering from a psychoneurosis, and this is the way she describes his feelings: " He lay very high, on the back of the world. The earth thrilled beneath him. Red flowers grew through his flesh; their stiff leaves rustled by his head. Music began clanging against the rocks up here. . . . It cannoned from rock to rock, divided, met in shocks of sound which rose in smooth columns (that music should be visible was a discovery) and became an anthem, an anthem twined round now by a shepherd piping." Need I point out that one has only to transfer these images onto canvas to have a complete surrealist painting?

Anything that can be imagined is real, and nothing is so real as an obsession. In those words one might sum up the present attitude of the surrealists. Like every new school, they have wilfully lost sight of the partial reality which they wish to supplement or replace; they deny the orderly, the rational, the coherent, the visible. But what they are doing, in fact, is to increase the scope of reality. They are exploring foul underground caverns where one hears only the whir and whistle of invisible bats; they are holding the manacled hands of prisoners in moldy dungeons; they are making their way, by touch rather than by sight, through slimy passageways that may bring them up to the surface of " normal " life with a better comprehension of what lies beneath. Like the modern psychoanalysts, the surrealists have approached the normal by way of the pathological. That follows inevitably from the fact that the willing, wishing, urging, passionate part of man's life has been slighted, stifled, and even banished altogether in favor of practical routines. Distrusting the imagination, we let it sneak back into life only in the guise of fancy dress or an even fancier disease — just as many of us never get a real opportunity for pleasurable idleness until we find ourselves on our backs in a hospital, recovering from the birth of a baby or an operation for appendicitis.

But it would be absurd to dismiss surrealism as crazy. Maybe it is our civilization that is crazy. Has it not used all the powers of the rational intellect, all the hard discipline of the practical will, to universalize the empire of meaningless war and to turn whole states into Fascist madhouses? There is more here than meets the eyes. Demons, for the modern man, are no less real than electrons; we see the shadow of both flitting across the screen of visible reality. Surrealism makes us conscious of this fact; it arranges the necessary apparatus. Before we can become sane again, we must remove the greatest of hallucinations — the belief that we are sane now. Here surrealism, with its encouraging infantile gestures, its deliberately humiliating antics, helps break down our insulating and self-defeating pride. Even in perverse or sinister or silly forms, the surrealists are restoring the autonomy of the imagination.

The America in Europe

What was perhaps salutary in the American revolt against history was what had been salutary in the Renaissance itself: the discovery that the historic past is a repository of possibilities, and that one is not committed to any determinist form of continuity.

For most Europeans, perhaps, the effort to define America, particularly the United States, confines itself to those features which, seemingly, are not European. In that light, the United States becomes something fabulous and monstrous: a place where the entire population lives in skyscrapers, dines in drugstores, works on assembly lines, pays blackmail to gangsters, and exists in a combination of luxury and squalor, of sophistication and infantilism. That image of America has, one grants, partly been molded by Hollywood: it is in fact the grotesque elaboration in dream of elements that actually exist in daily life, under more human circumstances. But this picture explains nothing about America's past or its potentialities; and though it inflates the European ego, it does less than nothing to improve the relations between these two domains of our common Western culture.

To achieve understanding, a quite different approach seems to me needed. This requires, on the part of the European, an act of self-examination, based on the historic fact that the New World was, from the beginning, a European conception. The important thing to grasp is that the forms and values of American life first took shape in the European mind before they achieved, by a certain detachment and isolation, the qualities that the European designates — not without disapprobation — as American. What has happened in America has also, at the same time, happened in Europe. The only thing that keeps this fact from being more obvious is that in

Europe the New World is still partly concealed under the débris of history: old buildings and cities, old rituals, usages, customs, institutions, that were left behind in the migration to America. The American, so to say, is a European stripped of the historic garments of his culture, clothed in the new, machine-made clothes that his ancestors first dreamed of as the proper costume for post-Christian man. Why did Poliziano, in his Epistle to the King of Portugal, in the same decade that Columbus discovered America, exult in the very newness of "the New World"? Was it not because Europe was already seeking a new face and a new form, as well as a new theater for its activities?

America was settled by people who deliberately cut themselves off from the existing facts of church, state, city, family, in order to make a fresh start, on their own terms, in the new continent. When they made this decision, they were still Europeans: Europeans who were already partly committed to exploiting a new ideology and a new method of life. This ideology was founded on capitalism and rational calculation, on the physical sciences and the conquest of nature, on the exploitation of power and the denial, or at least the subordination, of the sensuous and the erotic aspects of life. Such a new equipment of ideas, which willingly sacrificed the esthetic to the practical, the historical to the novel and experimental, was an ideal one for subduing a vast continent within a limited space of time. But it was in no wise different from the ideology that, from the seventeenth century on, transformed England and in turn every other country in Europe, and produced a dull, unillumined, busy, barbarous life, wherever its ways and methods dominated. Mechanization, absorption in technical progress, the over-valuation of action and the denial of contemplation, preoccupation with power and with money as the symbol of power — none of these facts, surely, is foreign to Europe. It is not in the pages of Theodore Dreiser or Sinclair Lewis, but in those of Honoré de Balzac, that the fullest documentation of these facts is to be found. Certainly these methods and ideals were not imported from America: they were, rather, Europe's original gift to the New World. Transported to a land where no other forms of culture were solidly established, this mechanistic culture grew to giant size, just as the Canada thistle grew without opposition on the pampas of South America. There is nothing that the severest critics of American culture have said about it during the last thirty years — a period of intense self-examination, inaugurated by Van Wyck Brooks, Randolph Bourne, and Waldo Frank — that John Ruskin and Matthew Arnold had not been forced to say about England almost a century earlier.

Such an interpretation does not justify the wholesale subordination of life to mechanism. Whether this process exists in the fashion that characterizes it in Europe, retarded by old religious and humanist traditions, or in the accelerated mode that it displays in America, it remains in fact monstrous. Indeed, it is perhaps only now, with the approach to complete mechanization, through the replacement of the human organism — indeed, the human personality — by the automaton, that one can see clearly the ultimate destination of the whole movement. Already the machine threatens to annihilate its creator, either by sudden wholesale destruction, in a genocidal " war," or by the slow removal of all the traits and aptitudes that make him fully human. (The last process has been described in a book that deserves to be better known: Roderick Seidenberg's *Post-Historic Man.**) Plainly, a life in which feeling and emotion, tenderness and love, imagination and hope, dream and prophetic anticipation no longer modify human actions, may easily move from a dehumanized rationality to irrational nihilism. Machines have no other reason for existence than those purposes which man bestows on them; and a scientific technology under the putative control of men whose very method of thought has eviscerated emotions, feel-

* Chapel Hill, N. C.: University of North Carolina Press, 1950.

ings, values, may not be sufficiently sane even to save itself. Indeed, if anything is left of science and the machine after the present crisis is past, it will be only through the vigorous counter-action of human qualities that have not been cultivated by mechanical man.

In so far as these tendencies can be most clearly seen and appraised in America, the European has reason to scan this development anxiously. But it is unwise, I think, to overlook the fact that the critical steps that produced this result were taken in Europe, from Roger Bacon and Leonardo down to the galaxy of European scientists whose collective efforts finally unlocked cosmic energies without any prophetic and prudent concern for the social consequences. Furthermore the vast destructive powers that have now been unleashed would not be as dangerous as they actually are, were it not for the general development of moral and political nihilism. This nihilism is very largely the product of Old World disintegration, long in process from Machiavelli and Hobbes to Nietzsche, from Bakunin to Hitler and Mussolini. The mission of America, with respect to all these sinister transformations, has been to translate the idea into the act. But to put the main onus upon America is to misunderstand the nature of the problem. The barbarism and nihilism that now threaten the development of all culture, and that ultimately, with our present weapons, might bring to an end all life on this planet, have sprung up in the midst of our common civilization: Europe and America are equally involved.

Now, in addition to the "machine," Europe has contributed yet another element to American life and thought which is still, again erroneously, regarded as an original American contribution. This component of our life is in some sense a counterweight to the mechanical, the automatic, the compulsive: it is associated with a worship of the vitalities of nature, particularly as expressed in primitive people, primitive customs and usages, primitive occupations like hunting and

fishing, and a rough, simple, hearty life, lived in utmost freedom from human restrictions, in direct communion with the
wilderness. To be willing to live under such conditions was,
indeed, a primary condition for survival in the New World
during the period of pioneering: as such, it needed no extra
justification. But as a system of values, as a utopia, the return
to nature was an early European contribution: one can trace
it, in fantasy and symbol, from the paintings of Piero di
Cosimo to the African primitive period of Picasso. The life
of the frontier in the New World called, not for a docile
mechanical discipline, but for animal energy and audacity:
the romantic impulse thus offered an alternative to those hardy
spirits who refused to be imprisoned in the new mechanical
routine of the counting house and the factory. Europe itself
had known these qualities, while still under Christian discipline, in the settlement of the borderlands of the North and
East in the eleventh and twelfth centuries, and in the fierce
adventurous spirit that made the Crusades possible. But in the
eighteenth century the worship of nature and the belief in a
primeval innocence that antedated the corruption of civilized
society united minds as different as those of Rousseau and
Vico and Diderot. America became a sort of testing ground
for this ideology: necessity conspired with desire. In the
New World, the ideals of the romantic movement were translated into daily realities: here the European met tribes that
lived in a state of nature and, to survive in the same environment, took on many of their habits of life. To this new land,
too, he brought thousands of primitive people from Africa,
who through song and fable and dance had a direct effect
upon the development of American folk culture. In America, precisely because the older European images had become
faint and had lost no small part of their authority, there was a
readier reception of the ways and beliefs of the more primitive peoples. Mark Twain, in his classic *Huckleberry Finn*,
repeats the superstitions of the Negro slaves, whose own pri-

meval terrors infected at least the infancy of their masters; and the beats of the African tom-tom, the orgiastic motions of the jungle dance, resound in the rhythms of modern jazz. In the Latin American countries this mingling of primitive and sophisticated elements went on from an even earlier day.

With this special susceptibility to the natural and the primitive in every form, the American has not merely returned to a source of vitality: he has symbolically, by his receptivity if not by his humility, performed an act that may prove important in the development of a common culture: he has recognized and transmitted values derived from peoples who were once despised because they had existed outside the circle of European tradition. As with the development of the machine, the opening of Western culture to more primitive impulses was not without grave dangers; for if it was accompanied by a great surge of vitality, by a vast increase in the food supply and the population, it likewise multiplied the powers and claims of the id. To make the primitive elements dominate the more cultivated elements is a sort of reversed imperialism; all the worse because it denies, not only the normal hierarchy of values, but the well-tried path of human development. But to accept the primitive as an active component in life, even in its highest manifestations, was a gain, not merely for human wisdom, but for the more universal culture that mankind has still to create. The man who prepares himself to participate in the common culture that will in time emerge, will not merely be prepared to accept a Chinese painting of the Sung dynasty along with the frescoes of Pompeii and the Etruscan terra cotta sculptures: he will be equally prepared to understand a carved ebony idol from the Congo. In that act of humility, the European perhaps needed no aid from America; yet the fact is that, because of accidents of geography and history, this movement went on more fully and rapidly here, and was assimilated most rapidly into the folk culture. One of the greatest works of literature North America has yet produced, Herman Melville's *Moby Dick* (1851), owes some of its abundant power to the fact that it brings together in a single picture the two dominant elements at work to modify the old Classic-Christian culture of Europe: the cult of mechanical man, with its demonic pursuit of power, personified by Captain Ahab's irrational assault on the White Whale that has lamed him; and the cult of the primitive, symbolized both by the nature of the chase and the crew that perform it, a crew drawn from all the nations and races of the world, with the important office of the harpooner given to the primitives — to Tashtego, the American Indian; Queequeg, the South Sea cannibal; and Daggoo, the giant African Negro. Both the human promise of " the New World " and its irrational and destructive potentialities were here prophetically revealed.

One further element in European culture that came to fullest ripeness in America remains to be considered: the attempt to wipe out the past and make a fresh start, an impulse that antedated by many centuries the ideology of the Romantic movement. This effort took many forms: but each was an attempt to break with tradition and to disrupt cultural continuity, either by attempting to restore an archaic moment of the past, or to jump precipitately, without effort to carry the past along or erect any transitional bridges, into a better future. The Renaissance is one name for this anti-historic movement; Protestantism is another; Utopia is a third; and Revolution a fourth. The story of America itself is in no small part the story of an attempt to overthrow history and to re-establish every institution *de novo* on a rational basis. Distance in space from Europe naturally increased the American's sense of distance in time. America's age of innocence, the creative age of Ralph Waldo Emerson and Walt Whitman, was based in part upon the sense that an entirely fresh start was possible, thanks to the virgin continent and the new political constitution and the substantial equality of all men

and ranks in this new world. But within less than a generation, after the Civil War, Whitman himself admitted that the
New World culture he had prophesied must rest solidly upon
the old cultures of Europe and the East, and be continuous
with them; while at the same time a whole generation of
Americans, headed by Henry James and Henry Adams, led
the movement back to Europe, in an attempt to recognize and
do justice to their ancestral selves, to recover their abandoned
inheritance. Neither migration nor revolution — this was the
final moral — was sufficient to undermine the facts of history:
for without the past the present would be meaningless and the
future inconceivable.

The most radical attempts to achieve freedom from the
past — political and economic revolution — have not in fact
justified the hopes that the thinkers of the enlightenment en-
tertained for such emancipation. The more effective the liberation from the past, the more complete the enslavement to
a narrow and compulsive present. America itself, in the
course of two centuries of development, has empirically established the absurdity of the dream of radical discontinuity, as
Russia, in the course of a single generation, has likewise done.
Renewal, not revolution, is the source of creativity. What
was perhaps salutary in the American revolt against history
was what had been salutary in the Renaissance itself: the discovery that the historic past is a repository of possibilities, and
that one is not committed to any determinist form of continuity. In terms of future ends one may reject some element
in the immediate past and seek a new link of continuity elsewhere. It was thus that Emerson and Thoreau turned to the
thought of the East, particularly to the poetry and scriptures
of the Hindus. To that degree, America's attempted detachment from history facilitated the inclusion of non-European
cultures, in a wider historic synthesis. This intercourse took
place at many different levels in the culture of Europe, too,
it goes without saying, from Schelling and Schopenhauer on-

ward; and it has happily been attended by a reciprocal attitude toward European forms among Asiatic scholars and
thinkers: was it not from Thoreau that Gandhi learned the
doctrine of civil disobedience? The paradoxical result, then,
of America's attempt to throw off the shackles of history has
been to widen the province of history: if the New World
personality is less bound up with Europe, he is closer to the
rest of the world. One may say, then, that America is that
part of Europe that is not committed wholly to its past, and
that is not confined to the cultural shell in which that past
originally took form. With this goes a difference of emphasis: the European is still conscious of what " has been ": the
American, coming to an almost untouched land, was more
concerned with what " may be." The very essence of the
thought of Emerson — and in this he was truly representative
of his contemporaries — is the ephemeral and provisional nature of all human institutions. For him the past is not sacred,
because all that it contained of value and significance can be
recreated in the here and now. If the most solid of institutions
vanishes, as in a dream, it is equally possible, for Emerson,
that a dream may shortly become solid, palpable, visibly active. The Europeans who settled America were not merely
relatively flexible and adaptable to new circumstances: they
had confidence in possibilities not validated by previous human experience. This is just the opposite of the doctrine that
haunts Greek and even Jewish thought, the repetitious nature
of all human activities: vanity of vanities! From the European standpoint, with its sense of human limitations, of com-
mitments not lightly to be thrown off, this American futurism
is naive. But perhaps it explains a kind of Quixotism in
American behavior, which the European is tempted to interpret — as he often interpreted the purpose of the Marshall
Plan — by orthodox materialist criteria. Like the original
New World impulse itself, this is perhaps a necessary counter-
poise to Europe's tendency to surrender passively to its own

past, with its sad if not cynical remembrance of failures, dis-appointments, frustrations, tragic defeats. In a letter to his daughter Martha, in 1787, Thomas Jefferson wrote: " We are always equal to what we undertake with resolution. It is part of the American character to consider nothing as des-perate." Is not this reservoir of confidence and vitality pre-cisely what we must now draw on to overcome the catastro-phes that now threaten mankind? Those American politicians who see no alternative to the state of exacerbated insecurity and fear they themselves have created, have here, as in so many other places, betrayed their country's deepest traditions.

In appraising America, then, it is important for the Euro-pean to realize that he is looking, more often than not, at a detached fragment of himself. This fragment, because of its very detachment, has grown to gigantic size; but it is nevertheless directly related to him: indeed, it is largely a product of his own impulses, dreams, conceptions. Yet such changes as the New World transplantation and mingling of cultures has brought about, the mixing of nations and races, the receptivity to the primitive, the mass equalizations and uniformities of " the machine," the openness to universal ele-ments, drawn from non-European cultures as well as from Europe — all these changes parallel or prophesy similar trans-formations within Europe itself. The detachment of Ameri-can culture, the overgrowth of mechanical and primitive ele-ments, need not lessen the European's sense of shock, nor should it diminish his anxiety. But it should at the same time increase his awareness of his own deep involvement, for the problems that America poses were first occasioned by changes that took place in European thought, and must ultimately be faced and solved within the Old World as well as the New. For the New World culture of Europe and Asia, and the New World culture of the Americas can survive only on the same terms that individual states and nations and cities can now survive — by the further creation of a One-World culture, which will enclose and reconcile, and yet transcend, all the existing energies, vitalities, humanities, and divinities. Here as elsewhere survival is bound up with continued growth and renewal.

Monumentalism, Symbolism and Style

. . . While the ideal of architecture is surely to give a maximum satisfaction to all functions, there is a tendency in our age to regard the mechanical functions as naturally dominant ones, even to view with suspicion any deliberate attempt to produce visual animation or excitement at any sacrifice of either comfort or mechanical perfection.

THE EXPRESSIVE FUNCTION

In recent years, Dr. Sigfried Giedion has given a new turn to architectural criticism by suggesting that there is a need for the monumental in modern architecture. " Monumentality " is a dangerous concept to use, for it has by now many unfortunate connotations of empty grandeur, of pretentious display, of over-forced impressiveness; so that there is almost as much danger in reviving the term as in forgetting the important function of architecture to which Dr. Giedion has thereby called our attention. The qualities that Dr. Giedion would like to reinstate are, if I understand him rightly, manifold: they might be treated under the heads of symbolism, of visible hierarchic order, of esthetic expressiveness, of civic dignity. Unfortunately, these terms are almost as full of insidious meanings as monumentalism and are as capable of being misunderstood. Perhaps the best way to restate Giedion's thesis would be to say that it is not enough for a modern building to be something and do something: it must also say something. What is this, however, but a return to " commodity, firmness and delight " with the emphasis once more on delight? Is it not in effect a restatement of Ruskin's belief that architecture begins where building leaves off; though not with Ruskin's reduction of architecture proper to the effects produced through the use of painting and sculpture?

This new interest in the expressive element seems to me healthy; it means, or it should mean, that modern architects have mastered their grammar and vocabulary and are ready for speech. Awaiting that day, Dr. Walter Curt Behrendt called his book not *Modern Architecture*, but *Modern Building*.

EVOLUTION WITHIN MODERN ARCHITECTURE

Once we admit that a building should not merely facilitate function but disclose human intention, we open up the grand problem of style: the expression of an informing idea and purpose. Contrary to Mr. Thomas Creighton's position in *Progressive Architecture*, the modern architect, in abandoning his long tedious flirtations with historic styles associated with different cultures than his own, has not earned the right to disregard style entirely: rather he has made it possible to make more fundamental choices in form, choices between ponderosity and lightness, between magnificence and humility, between complexity and simplicity: choices which are ultimately not pragmatic and technical, but esthetic, ethical, personal. It was not until modern forms were accepted as the common underlying foundation that such choices could be rationally made.

Before one can talk intelligently about the problem of style today one must first define what one means by " modern " in architecture. As usual in dealing with historic processes there are two schools, those that emphasize the element of continuity, and those that emphasize discontinuity. In his first book on modern architecture Mr. Henry-Russell Hitchcock gave these schools the names of " New Traditionalists " and " New Pioneers " — a happy differentiation; all the happier, it seems to me, because the New Traditionalists in their further development (witness Fritz Schumacher and the Perrets and the elder Moser) moved closer to the New Pioneers, and because the Pioneers on approaching maturity promptly reached

back for certain elements they had dropped in their first one-
sided absorption in expressing technical processes: Mies van
der Rohe's traditional use of fine materials in the Barcelona
Pavilion was an early departure in this direction. In *Modern
Architecture*, his first essay, Hitchcock even allowed for the
fact that the New Pioneers would not be forever identifiable
through the starkness and nakedness of their forms: he pointed
to the possibility of the same kind of maturation that other
primitive styles had gone through, with the development of
the ornamental and the symbolic. Such change might take
place rapidly or slowly; it might be extraneous and effortful,
or organic and intrinsic; but surely no definition of the modern can be framed that would not include as part of the very
concept of modernity the possibility of further change. The
unforgivable error, from the standpoint of either philosophy
or historic scholarship, would be to identify the modern with
one phase or one moment of the modern movement, as if " art
stopped short at the cultivated court of the Empress Jose-
phine," in W. S. Gilbert's properly mocking words.

MODERN ARCHITECTURE AND THE " INTERNATIONAL STYLE "

There are two ways, then, in which one may consider modern architecture. The sound way, it seems to me, is to associate it with the increasing use of new materials, of new
technical processes, of new forms of construction, along with
an esthetic infused with the conceptions of time, space, energy, life and personality that have been developing since the
sixteenth century. Viewed in this way, modern architecture
has been long in process; and it has left over the landscape of
the Western world a succession of significant buildings and
monuments, sometimes faintly adumbrated, sometimes almost
completely realized, in terms of their immediate intentions,
like Paxton's Crystal Palace or Root's Monadnock Building,
to mention only the work of earlier generations. Modern
architecture is accordingly an inclusive name for an effort

which has a single trunk but many different branches — branches that sometimes flourished and then withered, like *L'Art nouveau*. In this movement it is the technical basis that has been most firmly established: but the final process of expressing human purpose, of interpreting in new terms our fresh conceptions of life and personality, has been late in its development, more tentative, more self-contradictory in its achievements, ranging there from Frank Lloyd Wright to Mies van der Rohe, from Baillie Scott and Mackintosh to Aalto and Mendelsohn.

But there is another way of defining modern architecture: that of restricting the term to that segment of the modern movement which was affected by the cubist theories of painting and by the mechanocentric attitude that Le Corbusier sought to translate into esthetic terms in the early twenties. This narrow canon of modernity gives an arbitrary starting-point for the movement and produces a new kind of academicism in which a very limited system of architectural forms takes the place of the classic five orders. This restrictive definition of modern architecture was popularized by the Museum of Modern Art show of 1932 in New York, and it is still maintained by Alfred Barr: see his address at the Museum's symposium in February, 1948, on "What Is Happening to Modern Architecture." The criteria of the International Style, as Hitchcock and Johnson set them forth in the Museum catalogue, were three: emphasis on volume rather than on mass, regularity rather than axial symmetry, and proscription of arbitrary decoration. These canons of style were vague enough to seem innocent, but in application they carried with them certain other very positive esthetic preferences, which a glance at the buildings selected under the canon immediately disclosed. Positively, the International Style favored two-dimensional façades, cantilevered walls, flat roofs, smooth surfaces, compositions as elementary as a Mondrian painting; negatively, it not merely proscribed " arbitrary decoration " but favored black and white, opposed color, disliked contrasts in texture, recoiled from three-dimensional composition as revealed in overhangs, setbacks, and interpenetrations of mass and volume.

As an emblem of revolt the International Style was exciting, but as architectural achievements the purest of its buildings had the misfortune, too often, to be esthetically dull precisely in proportion to their programmatic correctness. Fortunately for the modern movement vigorous personalities like Breuer, Aalto, Sert never kept to the letter of the law. Nevertheless the law itself did something less than justice to the vitality of the movement as a whole, for the fashionable criteria had the effect of pushing to one side many excellent architects like Wright, Mendelsohn, Dudok, Wijdeveld, whilst various inferior designers whose work fitted into the limitations of the 1932 formula were thrust into positions of eminence their work did not entitle them to. " Wright," said the Museum of Modern Art catalogue in 1932, " belongs to the International Style no more than Behrens or Perret or Van de Velde." I should hesitate to resurrect those words at this late date were it not for the fact that they disclose the limitations, not of modern architecture, but of the concept of the International Style.

Plainly, one can make this criticism without in the least rejecting the creative contributions that Le Corbusier, Gropius, Mies van der Rohe, Neutra and their immediate followers and colleagues actually made. From the standpoint of an organic architecture, adequately tapping all the positive forces in our society, the modern was enriched by the conscious attempt to formulate, more rigorously and more artfully than the nineteenth-century engineers, the technical bases of modern expression: the scientific, the mechanocentric, the objective, the non-humanistic. Any valid formulation of the modern must include the so-called International Style in its exploratory, experimental efforts to establish the limits of mechanism, functionally and esthetically — not least esthetically. But modern life cannot stop at that point. Having invented, for example, the neat, compact, shipshape " laboratory kitchen," we are now in the process of reconverting the kitchen, where means are available, once more into a humanly conceived living room, because we have discovered that other functions must be served in a kitchen besides those of organic chemistry. Similarly we may no longer identify a modern composition by the fact that the outer wall is post-free or its first floor rises free of the ground like those neolithic Swiss lake dwellings Le Corbusier's unconscious ancestral memories have, perhaps, revived: similarly to avoid the use of columns or pitched roofs merely to prove one is modern is too simple a means of self-identification. It is just its freedom from the dry International Style formula that has perhaps called down such abuse on " Bay Region cottage architecture." In loyalty to their original premises the advocates of the International Style have deliberately rejected every manifestation of the modern but their own. Here time has brought about a sweet revenge, for by now their formula is old-fashioned, indeed dated.

THE INFLUENCE OF PAINTING

What influence should painting have on the development of modern architecture? Perhaps some of the most acrimonious differences that have developed in recent years can be traced back to the way in which this question is answered. Obviously the cubists, the suprematists and the purists had a direct influence upon the brilliant young Dutchmen and Frenchmen who were developing modern architecture during the twenties; indeed the International Style, as it came to be defined, owed more to the painter than it did to the engineer. To some extent one may say that the control of the machine liberated the architects of this school from the canons of architecture and enabled them to superimpose on their compositions the canons of painting. In this respect the cubists and

suprematists with their geometrical figures had the same effect
upon construction as the advocates of the Wavy Line had
a generation before upon ornament — though many of the
Art nouveau buildings were often far more audacious as technical achievements. My own answer to this vexed question
is that the direct effect of painting upon buildings is a bad one,
to the extent that it tempts the architect to treat his building
as if it were a composition uninfluenced — as architecture on
the contrary must be — by the passage of the spectator towards
it, around it, and through it. Living in the same environment
of ideas, the modern architect will necessarily draw from the
same sources as the modern painter, even as he draws from
the same sources as the scientist and the philosopher, who
attempt to interpret the emergent forces of his age. So one
should expect to find an underlying kinship between architecture and painting and sculpture; each will tend to express the
same ideas and feelings, in forms that will be deeply rather
than superficially related. But the imitation of painting by
architecture is a backward step. The relation between sculpture and building, on the other hand, is a closer one; and there
are modern sculptors like Naum Gabo, a man of original
genius, whose work is much closer to architecture than that of
many architects. Yet here, too, the development of the two
arts should be parallel; and the interaction should be mainly
a spiritual one, for the architect should not and cannot limit
himself to the problems that the sculptor faces, since buildings
must be used in a quite different sense from the way in which
sculpture is used. This standard of judgment works both
ways: not merely should a building not seek to imitate a
painting, but one should never judge the success of a building,
even esthetically, merely by looking at a photograph of it.
Though the eye embraces both painting and architecture, the
two arts are, from my standpoint, almost as far apart as dance
and music. Does this negative judgment also apply to the
modern architect's use of Arp's irregular curved surfaces for

all kinds of flat surfaces, instead of more orderly geometric figures? I am afraid it does, except as a momentary gesture of freedom. Such forms come properly under the ban on "arbitrary ornament," for here the International Style fashion has plainly defied its own canons.

THE IMPORTANCE OF STYLE

On this interpretation the epithet "International Style" was ill-chosen. For, in the Western world at least, every genuine style has been international in its development: romanesque, gothic, renaissance, baroque, even the pseudo-styles of neo-classic and neo-gothic have been the expression of our whole civilization. This universalism is precisely what distinguishes style — the forms by which men express their purposes, values and ends — from the little local and temporal eddies of fashion. But limiting the modern to the current fashions of Paris and Berlin failed to do justice to the deepseated internationalism of the contemporary movement, belittling the contributions of the British at the beginning of the present century and forgetting the work that had been done in California at the same time — work not unaffected by contact with the Japanese and the Chinese, to say nothing of the Polynesians and the Hindus. (If one examines the bungalow Robert Louis Stevenson built for himself in Samoa, for example, one will discover how much merely living in the tropics did to alter the traditional relation of window and wall, and the very words "bungalow," "verandah," "lanai," suggest a new relationship between the house and its green surroundings.) If modern architecture is truly indigenous to our culture, one should expect to find it springing up independently in various areas, gathering into the main stream various regional experiments; and that is what has actually been happening, now with Chicago dominating, now with Brussels or Paris, now with San Francisco or Rio de Janeiro. In such a movement the regional will bear the universal stamp and the uni-

versal, fully embraced, will incorporate and further the regional. Where the canon of the " International Style " has
been strictly followed there is a certain esthetic uniformity
in all its examples. But for an inclusive kind of modernism
what one should seek is not uniformity but unity, the working out of fresh adaptations and forms, with all the wealth
of expression that life and personality provide.

This interplay of the universal and the regional is what the
pseudo-International Style denies: often with absurd results
as in the transplantation of façades of glass, that visual tag of
modernism, to cities like Moscow where the climate invites
extra protective devices for the winter, and to regions like
North Africa where the great architectural problem is protection against the sun rather than fullest exposure. In the
current conception of the International Style one discovers
not internationalism but the covert imperialism of the great
world megalopolises, claiming to dominate the culture of their
time and rejecting all forms of art except those which have
been created by the few to whom it has given the stamp of
approval. Once these severe criticisms have been made, however, I would join with the exponents of the International
Style in an emphasis of the conscious international intention
which should pervade all architecture today, warning against
any idiom so local, so exclusive, so indigenous that it denies
rather than affirms the common elements upon which our
whole civilization rests. Hence the Russian return to the pon-
derous forms of classicism, the typical architecture of autoc-
racy and bureaucracy, is not merely esthetically reactionary:
it is a denial of that common world which men of good will
in all countries seek to build; and its official adoption in the
thirties warned all sensitive observers in advance of the turn
towards isolationism and imperialism that Russian policy was
taking.

THE PROBLEM OF SYMBOLISM

Architecture grows to self-consciousness and mature expression out of the elemental processes of building, mainly by concern over symbolism. However constant the mechanical functions of a building may remain — so that the form of a court of justice could be taken over by the Christian church because both buildings were designed to hold a crowd — the needs of language differ from generation to generation as each fresh experience of life gives us something new to communicate or as new evaluations change the relationship of one social institution to another. There are many points of difference between verbal expression and plastic expression, but the need to assimilate and record new experience is common to both. All this is plain in the transformation of historic forms: no internal technical development in building will explain the abandonment of the audacious verticality and sculptural exuberance of medieval building for the more elementary technical forms of renaissance building, with their horizontal lines, their repeating patterns, their standardized ornament; nor will any purely esthetic reaction explain the positive hatred with which by the end of the eighteenth century, especially in France, all gothic building was viewed by " progressive " minds. What is superficially a change of form turns out to be something far deeper: a change of meaning. Ornament and decoration sometimes record changes of feeling, sentiments, and attitudes faster than construction. But construction itself is the main language of expression and is at the service of many different human purposes other than those satisfied by building proper. The height of a spire meant religious aspiration in the thirteenth century; in the form of a skyscraper, it means publicity and self-advertisement in the twentieth century. Yet in more than one medieval church, from Lübeck to Florence, the height and scale of the church also represented the conscious self-assertion of the bourgeoisie

over the clergy: so there is a significant connecting link between the two.

Now we live in an age that has not merely abandoned a
great many historic symbols but has likewise made an effort
to deflate the symbol itself by denying the values which it
represents. Or rather our age has deflated every form of
symbolism except that which it employs so constantly and
so unconsciously that it fails to recognize it as symbolism and
treats it as reality itself. Because we have dethroned symbolism, we are now left momentarily with but a single symbol
of almost universal validity — that of the machine. We
should understand certain aspects of modern architecture during the last generation a little better if we realized that many
modern architects were trying to pour into this restricted
mode of symbolism all the feelings and sentiments that had
hitherto flowed freely into love and religion and politics.
Much of what was masked as functionalism was in fact fetish-
ism: an attempt, if I may use Henry Adams' well-worn figure,
to make the Dynamo serve for the Virgin. Those who had
devaluated the personality compensated for this error by over-
valuing the machine, which alone, in an otherwise meaningless world of sensations and forces, represented the purposes
of life.

THE MACHINE AS ARCHITECTURAL SYMBOL

Because a large part of our world has been created through
physical science with the aid of mechanical invention, no
honest construction in our own time can avoid expressing this
immense debt. From Rennie and Paxton and Roebling onward, the most significant structures have usually been those
which most fully explored the new media of expression. Unfortunately the theoretic exposition of the machine as the
exclusive source of modern form was not expressed with any
boldness until Le Corbusier published his famous tract, *Towards a New Architecture;* and the architects who adopted

Le Corbusier's line glorified the machine age with conscious exaggeration not in 1820, when its limitations had still to be revealed, but in 1920, when the weaknesses of the mechanical ideology had been in fact fully disclosed. Most of these architects concealed what they were actually doing even from themselves by fancying that they had sloughed off symbolism altogether: they were thinking in terms of efficiency, economy, *Sachlichkeit*, objectivity, physical science. Consciously or unconsciously they gave to their buildings the stamp of the factory, as their predecessors had given to their buildings that of the church, or those in the baroque period that of the palace. As fact and symbol the machine took the measure of man.

What we are beginning to witness today is a reaction against this one-sided symbolism and this distorted picture of modern civilization. We can no longer treat the machine as an exclusive architectural symbol at a moment when the whole ideology of the machine is in process of dissolution, for culture is passing now from an ideology of the machine to an ideology of the organism and the person — from Newton and Descartes to Geddes and Whitehead. We know that the mechanical world is not the real world but only an aspect of the real world, deliberately abstracted by man for the purpose of expanding his physical power and multiplying the energies he commands. We know, too, that in this over-concentration upon power many important elements were left out of account — especially those needed for the development of life and personality. *As an integral part of modern culture, the machine will remain as long as modern culture remains:* let me italicize that statement. But as a dominant element, wholly subduing life to the demands of mechanization, reducing the personality and the group to a mechanical unit, performing its limited function in a greater mechanism, concentrating on quantity and denying quality and purpose, the machine is an enemy of human development rather than an agent. The problem of quantity, the problem of automatism, and the problem of limitless power, which our very success in perfecting machines has raised, cannot be solved in terms of the machine. We must erect a new hierarchy of function in which the mechanical will give place to the biological, the biological to the social, the social to the personal. For this new order the machine can no longer serve as symbol: indeed, the emphasis on the impersonal, the anti-organic, the non-humanistic, the " objective " must now be counteracted by a temporary over-preoccupation, perhaps, with the organic, the subjective, the personal. On these terms Frank Lloyd Wright in 1900 was far in advance of Le Corbusier in 1920; indeed in a sense *L'Art nouveau* was, despite its ill-conceived ornament, often closer to the human and the organic than the architects of cubism were. To say this is not to desert functionalism in architecture, but to relate it once more to every human function.

DO WE WANT ARCHITECTURE AT ALL?

At intervals for the last century or more people have been predicting the death of painting and sculpture; and without doubt engineering and photography and the motion pictures, the new popular arts, have come to perform many of the functions that these more singular and personal arts, when they were at the service of the reigning ideology, once performed. But rationalists a hundred years ago were also confident that religion would within a measurable time dissolve: yet the most dogmatic, authoritarian, and antirational forms of it have actually gathered strength rather than lost it during this period, so that one must assume that Benjamin Kidd, who predicted the revival of religion in the nineties, was a better sociologist than those who opposed him. But how is it with architecture? If the focus of architectural interest shifted wholly from expression to mechanical content, there would come a time when engineering, through the sheer complication and expense of its constantly proliferating devices, would supplant architecture and nullify all efforts at visual expression. With air conditioning and a host of other mechanical instruments, building might return once more to the environment from which it started — the cave; in which the exterior, if visible at all, would become a blank shell which revealed nothing of what went on within it and made no effort to organize exterior and interior into a unified whole. At that point we should be driven to ask a critical question: Do we or do we not want architecture? If we do, it may be necessary to retrace some of our steps and seek a new point of departure. For if we want architecture, we must ask for a margin of freedom — a margin above the necessary, the calculable, the economic. It is in that margin for free choice and free decision that architecture moves and breathes and produces a visible effect, designed to impress the human spirit.

The canon of economy remains basic in modern form, then, not as an end in itself but in order to provide just that extra margin of wealth, energy and vitality through which the human imagination may more freely express itself. With reason the architect will continue to make his structure light, spare, elegant, severe; in a large part of his work he will avoid any superfluity, any structural or spatial over-emphasis, any ornamental elaboration, any departure from standardization and modular forms; and an escape from such forms must be looked upon with distrust, if not with downright disfavor. Yet all this restriction is for the sake of freedom: the freedom, say, to provide an open corridor with a view on a garden, rather than a shorter corridor with rooms on both sides, as economy might dictate; the freedom to enlarge an entrance for the sake of " effect " or to employ rich materials and to refine the craftsmanship of visible details; the freedom to provide an approach and a setting that will heighten the visual interest of the spectator, to give him a special sense of the building's purposes and activities by the very means employed in its organization. When human purposes rather than mechanical requirements prevail, style becomes the very mirror of personality. But one must not, like Benedetto Croce and Geoffrey Scott, seek to separate the esthetic moment from the practical, the ethical and the meaningful attributes of the same activity. A practical miscalculation like the use of material that weathers badly in a few years' time, or an ethical and political error like the human overloading of the land in an otherwise admirable apartment house design, may from the present standpoint undermine the esthetic result. A humanistic canon of architecture will provide accordingly for all the dimensions of the human personality, arranged in the order of their value and significance and united into an organic, interrelated whole. Translated into practical domestic terms, this means that an architect may deliberately forego adding an extra bathroom in order to increase the dimensions of the living room or to panel it in a more attractive species of plywood.

THE VARIETIES OF FUNCTIONALISM

The phrase " form follows function " has a long and honorable history. The underlying perception belongs to the biologist Lamarck: a recognition of the fact that all structures in organic nature are purposive and that all purposive activities become, as it were, formalized, ingrained in structure. The American sculptor, Horatio Greenough, an intellectual man who had doubtless absorbed Lamarckianism, as Emerson had, long before Darwin became fashionable, translated this perception into architecture with a clarity that still remains admirable. A generation or so later Louis Sullivan reiterated the same truth in his *Kindergarten Chats*, perhaps rediscovering it for himself, perhaps unconsciously repeating Greenough; and he elaborated the various corollaries that follow its acceptance: namely, that new purposes and new functions demand new forms; that old forms are not adequate for the expression or fulfilment of new functions; that functionless form denotes atrophy, purposelessness, inertia —

and so forth. Since modern man has invented a host of new functions through his command over nature, and since democratic society embodies purposes not accepted by a theocratic or feudal order, this new criterion of form drew a new series of guiding lines for the architect. No one who rejects this fundamental discovery can be a modern architect, and forms that are deliberately defiant of function, even if applied in a superficially modern building, are weak forms no matter how powerful the first esthetic impression. But if Lamarck's doctrine is thoroughly sound as a foundation, it does not apply in its purely physiological form to the whole of architecture any more than it applies to the whole of organic nature. The beautiful, Emerson remarked, rests on the foundations of the necessary; Emerson did not make the error of saying that the necessary and the beautiful were one. Darwin himself observed that the sexual functions seemed often to promote excrescences or change of plumage in birds of a purely decorative nature — useful only because, on a human parallel, they seemed to attract the interest of the opposite sex. In short, there are subjective interests derived from spectator and user that must be taken account of in any sound architectural canon. A building may be functionally adequate from the standpoint of engineering and yet be a failure from that of physiology or psychology. Take the ideal of a constant, equable, unvarying environment which most engineers and even many architects regard as desirable for building interiors. This ideal may well prove to be in opposition to the biological need for small variations and readjustments as one of the very conditions of life. So with every other aspect of architecture: there is not a single function to be satisfied but a whole interrelated series. In his public buildings Richardson deliberately slighted the equipment and finish of his interiors in order to have all the means he needed to produce on the exteriors an impressive monumental effect, believing that the impression the building made on the passing citizen was a more important function than the immediate gratification it might give to the actual users of the structure.

Now, while the ideal of architecture is surely to give a maximum satisfaction to all functions, there is a tendency in our age to regard the mechanical functions as naturally dominant ones, even to view with suspicion any deliberate attempt to produce visual animation or excitement at any sacrifice of either comfort or mechanical perfection. But as modern architecture matures it must become multi-functional, giving increasing weight to biological, psychological, social, and personal criteria. There is nothing new in this suggestion. Did not the formulators of the " International Style " deliberately reject functionalism? Le Corbusier's cartesian sense of order rests for example on an esthetic foundation: he would even select the tenants for his skyscraper village in Marseilles on the basis of their esthetic response to his architecture rather than their human need. This esthetic is, alas, a very limited one; but in so far as it shifts the focus of design to the human purpose or idea it makes possible the kind of freedom that good architects have always exercised. In this respect the path of modern architectural development is that of all organic development: from the mechanical and the conditioned, the realm of physical necessity, to the vital and the free, the realm of personal choice.

EXTROVERSION AND INTROVERSION

On one dogma almost all believers in modern architecture are agreed: namely on the open plan, particularly in dwelling houses, as the very essence of modern expression: free-flowing space, rooms divided by hardly even a visual partition, have become the patent of modern building. Look at a book of modern plans and you will find that only in the bathroom is anything like complete privacy and isolation permitted; even the bedrooms in many new houses present walls of glass that give out on an equally open garden. As a movement towards freedom, as an effort to achieve flexibility, this over-emphasis on openness, coming as it did first of all from the Middle West, that land of extroverts, must have our sympathetic assent. But there is nothing final in this achievement, for the open plan is the symbol of an entirely public and outward-turning life. There must come a time when modern architecture will recognize equally the deep human need for the cell: the room with the locked door, secure against all intrusion, giving out not on open space but on a garden or walled yard equally inviolate to unwanted visitors. With respect to the needs of the human personality, a good part of modern architecture is lopsided; it provides no means for withdrawal, for solitary meditation or prayer, for the sense of solidity, of security, even of continuity — represented, say by a wall two feet thick. One would think that nothing ever was, could be, or should be performed in private.

Now I am all for open planning and removable partitions; of the latter for both wall and interior we have yet to make the fullest use; indeed there has been a singular lack of mechanical ingenuity here, despite the example of the Japanese. But in the very effort to achieve this openness and flexibility the architect must not forget that there are moments of life that call for darkness and retirement, for recesses and nooks and hide-aways; those moments in life should not be represented grimly only in the form of air-raid shelters. Hence, while accepting gladly the current innovations of the extrovert, I would, looking towards the future, provide the corrective contradiction: more light, yes, but some darkness. More openness, yet some enclosures. More volume, but some mass. More flexibility, yet some rigidity. As the modern movement matures, an organic architecture will do justice to the introvert no less than to the extrovert, to the subjective no less than to the objective, to the dark, primitive, unconscious forces as well as to the cold illuminations of science and reason; in short, it will take into account the functions and purposes of the whole man and not try to whittle him down to the size and shape that will fit some less-than-man-size formula.

WHAT IS MONUMENTALISM?

The other name for monumentalism is impressiveness: the effect produced upon spectator or user by the scale and setting of a building, by its height and reach and splendor, by the dramatic emphasis of its functions and purposes through the means available to the architect — mass, volume, texture, color, painting and sculpture, gardens, water-courses and the disposition of the buildings that form the background. It is by its social intention and not by its abstract form that the monument reveals itself, hence the Eiffel Tower is a monument and the chimney of a power plant, even when it is made over into an overbearing classic form, is not. The esthetic monumentality of Wright's Larkin Building in Buffalo was betrayed by its own limited uses and by the drab neighborhood in which it was set; but one might look far to find a more effective monument — peace to the International Stylists! — than Dudok's Town Hall at Hilversum, to whose impressiveness the architect brought every possible visual aid. In essence the monument is a declaration of love and admiration attached to the higher purposes men hold in common. An age that has deflated its values and lost sight of its purposes will not, accordingly, produce convincing monuments. Dignity, wealth, power, freedom, go with the conception of monumentality; and its opposites are meanness, poverty, impotence, standardization. Pride and luxury, it is true, often produce bad monuments; but poverty and humility if left to themselves would never produce any monuments at all. Most ages to make the monument possible have (in Ruskin's terms) lighted the lamp of sacrifice, giving to the temple or the buildings of state not their surplus but their very life-blood, that which should have gone into the bare decencies of life for the common man. This fact is responsible for democracy's distrustfulness, its grudging attitude towards the monument. But though often painful in the giving, these sacrifices were not without their reward even to the giver, whether that gift was voluntary as often in the building of the cathedrals, or exacted by physical force as in the taxes that made possible the pomp and grandeur of great courts. Denying the claims of the flesh and the prosperity of the household, buildings of permanent value, enriching the eye, sustaining the spirit, not for a few passing days but for generations and centuries, actually came forth.

CAN WE JUSTIFY MONUMENTS TODAY?

To remind oneself of these conditions is almost to explain why we have lost to such a large degree the capacity to produce monuments in our time. If surplus wealth were sufficient to produce monuments, we might produce them today as easily as we produce much more costly things like cyclotrons and atomic piles. Never before, surely, has so much physical power and physical wealth been available. But for all this we spend money for monuments with a bad conscience when we spend at all. This bad conscience is the product of middle-class convictions and middle-class standards, of course; the poor, precisely because their lot is so constrained, have never lost the sense of life which produces the monument: consider how they will spend on a wedding, and even more on a funeral, the money that might have been " better " spent — but who shall define and justify this better? — for their children's food or clothes or education. To raise all living standards to a decent level, at least to the " minimum of existence," is the aim of modern man, not to elevate and sanctify one side of life at the expense of every other aspect. Plainly, there is reason for this choice: too easily did the upper classes in other periods tend to justify the poverty of the poor and the deprivations of the needy to make possible the grand, the superfluous, and the beautiful. But as we approach a high general level of comfort today, the danger is rather just the opposite; that we forget the function of sacrifice, which means ultimately the arrangement of the goods of life, not in the order that produces merely physical survival but in the order that conduces to continued spiritual development. If we were better prepared to accept sacrifice there might be less immediate danger to mankind from the cyclotrons and atomic piles to whose existence we dedicate every available penny. We spend lavishly on mechanical means; we scrimp on the ultimate human needs. That is why modern monuments are far to seek.

Last year's discussion of monumentalism in the *Architectural Review* suffered a little from a general lack of concrete reference to any monuments later than fifty or seventy-five years ago, and my present thoughts are in the same danger: so let me point to a relatively recent example of monumentality that well illustrates my point, though it does not refer to the kind of structure that is ordinarily termed a monument. I refer to the great semicircular retaining wall that set off Frankfort-Römerstadt from the allotment gardens that spread in serried order below. Since I saw Römerstadt in 1932 and never revisited it, I may have an exaggerated impression of its original brilliance and of the sense of spacious order contributed to the design itself by this monumental feature. Nevertheless I must record my conviction that it remains one of the high points in the architectural expression of our time, not by the excellence of its individual buildings but by the ordered relation of the whole: it shows what modern man might do with his freedom once he controlled the forces at work in his society sufficiently to touch every part of it, field and road, house and garden, highway and public building. The only modern architectural work that has given this same impression to me in similar fullness and for similar reasons is the dam, the powerhouse, the road system, and the park around the Norris Dam in Tennessee — though I must exclude the town pattern and the houses beyond. Why are these examples of true monumentality and in what does their impressive effect specially lie?

The first thing to note is the very fact of impressiveness: the retaining wall boldly separates the community itself on the upper level from the orderly arrangement of small garden plots and tool sheds below. With a slight loss of land the retaining wall might have been omitted entirely; by merely grading the land down and planting it with appropriate vines and bushes, the soil itself would have been held back. In the layout of such a suburb it would, again, have been simpler to have united the allotment garden with spaces continuous to the dwelling house, as in the open English plan; but the architects of this project used the very opportunity that came with the low-lying land of the Nidda to separate these two elements, thereby creating in the gardens and open land behind the houses a sense of spaciousness and " aristocratic " ease. As with almost all examples of true monumentality one must pay in some way for the esthetic effect produced: in this case by a walk to the allotment gardens and by the provision of special tool sheds on the garden plots — sheds which, erected at the beginning, of uniform material and design, add to the sense of order and give scale to the broad sweep of land in the foreground. But note: these arrangements cannot be justified on the score of economy; quite the contrary. The retaining wall itself was far more costly than any grading of the land would have been. Such a monumental treatment of the landscape and city implies a greater amount of wealth, a greater amount of leisure, indeed perhaps a greater capacity for esthetic enjoyment than the actual inhabitants of Römerstadt possibly ever possessed.

Such planning cannot be justified in terms of immediate needs; hence later housing developments in Frankfort, seeking to meet the requirements of the *Existenz-minimum*, became more sparing of any form of visual freedom and luxury, more rigorous, more *sachlich* — and more barren of any stirring human reference. But in the long run the treatment provided at Frankfort-Römerstadt would sustain the spirit by gladdening the eye, while more economical planning would leave the spirit unmoved or actually depressed; and in that case the original cost and effort, seemingly so much in excess of what the day's needs would justify, might turn out to be exceedingly small, as is the case with the great monuments that have existed from three hundred to three thousand years. On this matter, William Butler Yeats's words to the Dublin philanthropist who wanted to make sure that the common people would enjoy art before he gave any more bequests should be remembered and heeded. Monumental architecture is to be justified not in terms of present necessity and popular demand but in terms of future liberation: to create a " nest for eagles."

5

Notes for a New Age

Program For Survival

We have now to devise, under pressure of the greatest crisis mankind has yet faced, the political and moral protective devices that will keep our knowledge, not merely from ruining civilization, but from causing life, in all its organized forms, to disappear from the planet.

THE CRISIS OF THE CRISIS

At the present rate of progression since 1600, it will not need another century or half century to tip thought upside down. Law, in that case, would disappear as theory or a priori principle and give place to force. Morality would become police. Explosives would reach cosmic violence. Disintegration would overcome integration.

Those words were written by Henry Adams in a letter to Henry Osborn Taylor in 1905; and he elaborated them in his essay on the " Phase Rule in History." However outwardly arbitrary the formula upon which this prediction was based, Adams's forecast was the product of the keenest historic insight that has been recorded in modern times; for not merely did Adams date the turn in the transformation of the physical sciences and technics almost to a year, but he understood the nature of the political and moral changes that would accompany that event.* With the invention of the atomic bomb

---

* Adams predicted a change of phase in 1917; actually, Rutherford's critical discovery of the possibility of smashing the atom by striking the nucleus took place in 1918.

NOTE: This essay is, in effect, a continuation of the final chapter in *The Condition of Man*. The opening section of that chapter might be profitably read in connection with the present argument, since it shows that it did not need the actual invention of the atomic bomb to convince intelligent observers like Burckhardt and Henry Adams that the elements that might lead to a complete disintegration of modern civilization were already at hand.
— L. M.

every item in the prediction was fulfilled except one: the disappearance of law and morality. That took place when the bomb was actually used.

Every human being must now consider the implications of this cosmic event; for we have now to devise, under pressure of the greatest crisis mankind has yet faced, the political and moral protective devices that will keep our knowledge, not merely from ruining civilization, but from causing life, in all its organized forms, to disappear from the planet. No previous crisis in mankind's history can compare with this: even the Ice Ages, because of their slow coming, were less of a menace to the biosphere. The question is no longer whether this or that nation, this or that civilization, can survive. The question is whether mankind has enough imagination to mobilize, on behalf of peace and co-operation, forces men have hitherto conscripted only for war and destruction. Unless the crisis produces such a dynamic will, man himself is lost.

There is one element in this problem that makes the outcome especially hazardous: the element of time. Since Henry Adams's formula has already proved to be accurate, we must have sufficient respect for his historic judgment to note that in the series of epochs into which he divided the modern age, the length of each period became progressively shorter. The age of atomic energy opened with A. H. Becquerel's discovery of radioactivity in 1896. With the invention of the first machine for releasing atomic energy on a large scale (the atomic bomb itself) that age has possibly already almost reached its end. If we fail to establish the necessary political controls and to impose the necessary moral disciplines, our world will come to a close in a quick orgy of annihilation, brought on by unsupportable anxiety and fear.

But if we learn the art of control soon enough to prevent the suicidal misuse of scientific knowledge, we will, by that very fact, have outlived the Atomic Age itself, the age of unqualified, indiscriminate power. The unification of knowledge and life will put an end to the current pursuit of power divorced from the ends of life. In the very act of saving the race, man will be compelled to master the perverse impulses that caused him to regiment and repress life itself; and that conquest will make the Atomic Age — in which the machine dominated and threatened the existence of man — obsolete.

Grave as the situation is in itself, the time element infinitely increases its gravity. Mankind, already weakened and debauched by war, cannot give itself time to idle on the oars, while deliberating at length over the changes that must be made in our educational and political institutions, if we are to control the terrible genius that has risen out of the cyclotron and the atomic bomb, as the jinn rose out of Aladdin's lamp. We must think swiftly, plan swiftly, act swiftly. And our thinking must be as unsparing of our foibles and habits as the atomic bomb itself is unsparing of all the structures and organisms within its range of disintegration. *This means that there is no part of our modern world that we must not be ready to scrap, if the need to scrap it is the price of mankind's safety and continued development.*

The age of atomic disintegration cannot tolerate absolutism in any form: even in the form that regards scientific knowledge as an absolute. If science itself were the main obstacle to mankind's continued existence, reasonable men, fully awakened to the danger, would demolish science as readily as they would demolish a Congo fetish. They would know that if intellectual progress had caused mankind to reach the edge of the abyss, it is better to recoil than to take the last step that will send us hurtling downward. If that were the price of survival, we would have to pay it, as cheerfully as the Erewhonians did when they made the invention of machines a criminal offense.

In the first moment of appraising our situation it would be premature, to say the least, to advance the abandonment of modern science and technics as the only way out: that is far from my purpose. But our only hope of ensuring mankind's safety at a smaller price lies in our willingness to think in terms that would be as drastic and unconditional. If we cannot control ourselves sufficiently to create a harmonious world order, then we shall have to destroy our machines, as the only other means of guaranteeing our survival. But note: the most complete transformation of the self must take place among those who have been least concerned with the psychological and moral nature of man. If our leaders remain fossilized and fixed, if they remain unimaginative, limited, brutish, if they continue automatically along the path on which they have been going, they will bring on catastrophe.

This is not an idle threat, nor is it the panicky reaction of mere laymen: it has come first from those whose theoretic and practical knowledge of atomic energy gives them the fullest authority to predict the consequences of its misuse. In the course of an atomic war, as one of the distinguished Nobel Prize winners, Dr. Irving Langmuir, has pointed out, the planet itself may be made permanently uninhabitable — the countryside no less than the cities. As a result, not only man's civilization but the human race, not merely human life but all forms of life, may be exterminated forever. That doom would be a heavy price to pay for the promotion of untrammeled curiosity and unbridled power.*

Never has mankind faced such a total danger before. In the race between education and catastrophe, which Mr. H. G. Wells pointed out long ago, we can already see the finish line. And at the moment, catastrophe is in the lead.

IS HUMAN LIFE SACRED?

Nothing is sacred but human life. I have affirmed this dogma as if it were indisputable; but in doing so I do not deny

* See Dr. Langmuir's address at the American Philosophical Society, Philadelphia, November 16, 1945.

or forget that Dr. Sigmund Freud has found a death wish in the heart of our civilization; so there is a possibility, if not a probability, that part of mankind itself is now in a psychotic state and is possessed of a strong impulse to work destruction upon the world and death upon itself. To measure the destructive potentialities of the atomic bomb it is not enough to estimate the amount of energy a single machine may release: we must also make some appraisal of the forces of love and hate, creation and destruction, that are at work in the user, in modern man himself. To what extent does modern man act on the premise that life is sacred?

Two sets of forces have worked side by side in modern civilization; and they have likewise operated side by side within science and technics themselves: one negates life, the other affirms it. The physical sciences, as first formulated by Galileo and Descartes, displaced the whole man from the investigation of the physical world. By eliminating the human equation, as far as possible, by repressing not merely emotions and desires but even the secondary qualities of matter which touched these emotions and desires, they achieved an astounding measure of skill in observing, measuring, and controlling the processes of nature. In developing along these lines they followed the classic path of capitalism.

The results had great human significance and produced measurable human benefits: an increase in power, goods, vitality. But the results were the by-product of a method that was not, as such, concerned with human benefits beyond those that accrued directly to the scientist in his search for verifiable truth.

The very success of the physical sciences in their applications to technics has given support to their metaphysical assumptions and their daily regimen. Projecting this mechanical world out of one side of his personality, man has in turn been influenced by it; in the act of contriving automatons he himself has become one: he has conceived a personality whose main characteristic is the displacement of the human by the mechanical.

Under the influence of a more humanitarian Christian insight, Leonardo suppressed the invention of the submarine, because, as he wrote in his Notebooks, man was too devilish to be entrusted with such an invention. This kind of inhibition has become almost inconceivable to the orthodox scientist or engineer. In the pursuit of truth or in the pursuit of practical success, there is no road that they will not follow to its end, even should that end prove inimical to man. Professing to eliminate questions of value and purpose from scientific thinking, this kind of man attributes value and purpose chiefly to one kind of human activity: that which he himself practices. It needed nothing less than the atomic bomb itself to shatter the shell of this orthodoxy.

Under the guise of rejecting absolutes, the technician has made science an absolute. One might smile on this charitably as a natural human foible but for this fact: Western man has accepted the scientist at his own value. The piety and superstition that led men once to worship the golden calf now leads them to worship the machine. For most Americans, certainly, almost any religious heresy might be uttered without awakening a word of protest, except the heresy that I am now actually uttering — the assertion that the machine is a fetish, an object of irrational devotion. Yet it is in this very irrationality of our reaction to the machine that one of the main problems of controlling it lies. If the machine is indeed our true god, what worshipper would dare to control it? The very suggestion savors of blasphemy.

From the standpoint of the physical scientist, as scientist, the notion that life is sacred is meaningless. The highest exponents of physical science, from Kepler and Newton to Clerk-Maxwell and Einstein, have never accepted the mechanistic dogma that robbed man himself of primacy and bestowed value only on his creations. But for all that, it is the guiding principle of modern research. In the physicist's world, life is non-existent, and the values of life are, if anything, merely accessory to the triumphs of physical science. This, at least, is the traditional view. Significantly, a succession of physical scientists in our own time have challenged the dubious assumptions upon which this dehumanized world-view was built up; and one may regard this reaction, which I shall refer to later, as a protective development within science itself, against the forces of disintegration it has unleashed.

But there is another side to science and its applications, fortunately for the world. This side of science has its origins in medicine, whose first object is the maintenance of health and the healing of disease; and here a radically different conception has flourished. Biology has established, not only the interdependence of the entire world of life, but the fitness of the planet itself for the nurture of life. One of the most tough-minded of biochemists, the late Lawrence J. Henderson, demonstrated the fact that the very distribution of the chemical elements on this planet was as if directed toward life, as if life were the object of blind natural processes. From this standpoint, the potentiality of entering into those unstable combinations which constitute life is an essential aspect of matter; and the once rigid dividing line between matter and life has disappeared.

With these biological interpretations have grown up an increased respect for all living organisms and increased tenderness for human creatures in particular. A desire to alleviate the sufferings of men, to wipe out disease, to eliminate unnecessary death, to sustain health and prolong life, has been the guiding motive of a vast amount of biotechnic research: anesthetics, aseptic surgery, dietetics have all registered enormous gains during the past century. In the application of medical insight to mental illness, Freud and his successors have gone even further: they have demonstrated that love is the very principle of all integration — biological, psychological, social. Without erotic love, without parental love, without brotherly love, the destructive impulses that have been engendered by man's struggle to survive might gain the upper hand. Originally, the care of the sick and the outcast was one of the chief functions of the Christian church, with its doctrine of universal love: today the doctrine of love has become one of the most practical concerns of those devoted to the care of the ill and the mentally disrupted.

In biology, medicine, and psychology, the maintenance and amelioration of man's life is one of the main purposes of scientific activity.

Even in the biological sciences, the knowledge that is available for the development of human life may be misapplied and corrupted: that almost goes without saying. A prejudice against natural processes, abetted by scientific pride, may cause physicians to dissuade mothers from nursing their young, or the technique of contraception may lead to the wholesale practice of sterility. But on the whole, the advance of knowledge in these fields has been accompanied by increasing tenderness, increasing sensitivity, increasing practical regard for maintaining the balances of nature that help sustain, not only human life itself, but all man's millions of co-partners and helpers in the animal and vegetable world. All creatures live by complicated partnerships; but in man, the dominant creature in the hierarchy of living organisms, the circle of his responsible control and conscious co-operation has widened, and without the counter-balancing development of love and understanding his powers of annihilation would now be boundless.

Part of our technics (not the least part), part of our science (also not the least part), are deliberately on the side of life. When we give ourselves to the control of the destructive processes that the age of atomic disintegration has released, we must summon up the aid of this powerful ally. Biotechnics alone will not be enough to offset destruction. But if we are to find a substitute gratification for our present infantile worship of the machine, we shall perhaps find it in the further application of the biological sciences to the arts of life. Without that counterweight, our political and moral devices might prove too feeble to move the world.

BACKGROUND OF MORAL DISINTEGRATION

Had the atomic bomb been conceived in the year 1300, the scientist who released this thought would have been imprisoned and the opportunities for working would have been denied him. This is not a wishful judgment; it is on record that Roger Bacon, who merely dreamed of automobiles and flying machines, was treated in precisely this fashion. Without exception modern thinkers have sided with Bacon against his ecclesiastical superiors; but in its distrust for the kind of thinking the experimental Bacon introduced, it is possible that the conservatism of the Christian church was more realistic than the sublime faith of the believers in progress, from Glanvill to H. G. Wells, that the untrammeled applications of science would automatically bring about a heaven upon earth. We can now see that the end of this automatic development may not be heaven but hell. Christianity, which had witnessed the disintegration of one civilization, knew something about the pride and destructiveness of man which modern man, precisely because of his pride and destructiveness, has resented being told. This knowledge we must now be humble enough to face.

If, from the standpoint of human safety, the thirteenth century might have been the best time for inventing the atomic bomb, the eighteenth century was perhaps the last moment in modern history when there still existed sufficient restraint, sufficient self-discipline, to ensure temporary safety. Even then, human insolence would have made the secret of atomic disintegration an incalculably dangerous toy to place in man's apelike hands. But certainly the invention of the bomb at the very climax of the Second World War raised its potential of destructiveness: for atomic disintegration has been preceded by a fateful moral disintegration.

We Americans, thinking of our momentary safety, may congratulate ourselves on the foresight, the intelligence, the scientific penetration, and the international co-operation that put this illimitable power in our own hands, rather than in those of our enemies.* But we must sober ourselves by recalling one fact: in the act of fighting the war we have already succumbed to our enemies' principles. We have used our invention with criminal levity, with childish impatience. Let us review the events that made this frightening transformation possible.

In the eighteenth century, as A. J. Toynbee has demonstrated, wars were fought with limited means for equally limited objectives. War brought suffering and death; but both the means and the ends of fighting were under human control. This was the result of a long effort to reduce the area of violence, broken by such mass horrors as the Albigensian Crusades and the Thirty Years' War. As a result, even such uneven contests as those between Louis XIV and the Netherlands did not result in the swift, overwhelming defeat of the Dutch; still less did it result in the elimination of the Dutch as a nation. Military power, though used for irrational political purposes, was still subject to moral control. Nobody held the fallacious notion that war itself was so bad it could excuse any degree of violence or butchery. Law had not yet, in Henry Adams's words, disappeared as theory or *a priori* principle.

These hard won conventions remained in operation until the Civil War. That was an early contest between democracy and a proto-fascism which rested on slavery, racism, and

* This of course refers to the situation in 1945, when this essay was written. [*Editors' note.*]

belief in the finality of military power. Sherman's march through Georgia was an attack, not only upon armies, but upon the enemy's ability to make war: it was the first large-scale application of totalitarian warfare in recent times. As with our use of the atomic bomb, this evil was perpetrated by the side that justifiably boasted the preponderance of moral good in its purposes. Though the Civil War was fought for a good end, part of the process by which victory was achieved was a bad process. The total demoralization of life in the South visited penalties upon the whole country from which we have not yet recovered. Not the least penalty was the insolence and self-righteousness exhibited by the victor: the little men who took over after Lincoln's death lacked both his imagination and his magnanimity. There are obvious parallels to this situation today.

Despite this grim episode, the attempts to restrict the savage possibilities of warfare, which mechanical invention had brought with it, continued right up to the First World War. Before that war broke out, men's consciences had become extremely sensitive to violence in any form, despite its sporadic outbreaks in pogroms, lockouts, and strikes. Accordingly, when a German military officer knocked into the gutter a lame cobbler who did not make way for him, in the little town of Zabern, the incident was reported throughout the world; and the public's reaction to this exhibition of military ruthlessness was overwhelming: so overwhelming that the German Reichstag itself dared to censure the German army for this conduct of one of its members. Which, indeed, is more incredible to our case-hardened consciences today — this universal reaction to a *single* act of violence that did not involve either torture or death, or the fact that even an autocratic government was still sufficiently under the sway of public opinion to give heed to the protest?

One must ponder well this Zabern incident to realize the

gap which separates the moral sensitiveness of even 1915 from that of 1945. For what was the chief reason for the United States' entrance into the First World War? It was essentially the practice of unrestricted submarine warfare, which the Germans opened by the sinking of the *Lusitania* in 1915. The world gasped with horror at this savage lack of restraint. It gasped, not alone at the loss of life, but at the abandonment of rules and limitations. The transformation of warfare, from acts of violence between opposing armies to unlimited terrorism and total destruction of the enemy nation, was now in full swing. The open enslavement of Belgian workers, the Zeppelin raids on England, were of the same order: likewise the attempt on the part of the English to bring the German armies to terms by cutting off the food supply of the entire homeland.

What has happened during the last thirty years? Nothing less than the dropping of the very principle of restriction. We have dehumanized ourselves and no longer accept any limitations, inner or outer, upon our will-to-annihilation. Within fifteen brief years every restriction has been removed: first in theory by our fascist enemies, then in practice by the same enemies, but finally *by ourselves* on an even more destructive scale. The fascist theory of total warfare was first put forth by the Italian General Douhet — volubly parroted by Major Seversky and others in the United States. The believers in this theory held that wars could be won by unlimited aerial attack upon the civilian population. The demolition of Warsaw and the center of Rotterdam brought this theory into action. Instead of recoiling against it and concentrating our whole might on the fighting area, we imitated our enemies. By the practice of obliteration bombing (alias strategic bombing) we lost any edge of moral superiority we originally held over the enemy with regard to our *methods* of fighting. (Our *ends* were still measurably more human.) This general moral disintegration paved the way for the use of the atomic bomb.

Nihilism had set up a chain-reaction in the human mind: by a succession of bombardments our last inhibitions were removed.

This change did not come about overnight, nor without considerable reluctance, even on the part of military commanders. The question as to whether it was morally defensible to achieve victory over Japan by wholesale destruction from the air was still debated in Washington as late as the spring of 1942: it was not yet a closed question. When the American Air Force first operated in Europe, it boasted of the accuracy of its so-called pinpoint bombing. It did not take long for the observer to realize that this was an empty boast. The excellence of the Norden bombsight was considerably abated by poor visibility, by flak, by inability to find the target, and by false identification of the target: the number of neutral or friendly civilians killed by our bombers — to say nothing of our own combat troops — runs into thousands, on the basis of scattered newspaper reports alone.*

Long before the war came to an end in Europe the Army had abandoned all pretense of bombing military targets alone: we resorted to devastation and terror on the largest scale possible. All our carefully built up inhibitions against unrestricted warfare had broken down. We concealed our abdication by smugly clinging to the letter of the Hague conventions with regard to the feeding of enemy prisoners of war —

---

* The report of the United States Civilian Survey Board, released October 31, 1945, on the effects of strategic bombing in Europe establishes the following facts: 1. Only twenty per cent of our missiles fell on their targets. (So much for the air arm as a weapon of precision.) 2. We did not severely damage Germany's industrial production until her air forces had been completely reduced. (Indeed, according to German figures, German production rose higher in 1944 than at any other time.) 3. The most decisive blow struck against Germany by air was the attrition of its fighter planes by our own planes at the rate of over 1000 a month at the beginning of 1944. The last item undermines the whole theory that our success in reducing Germany was due to strategic bombing: for *even in the air* it was due, rather, to the deployment of our forces, in an orthodox military manner, against the enemy's forces, not against cities, industries, and civilians.

even though at the moment our Allies were actually starving at the very gates of the camps where such prisoners were fulsomely fed. Despite our army's readiness to kill civilians by the tens of thousands in air attacks, we refused to reduce the diets of prisoners of war by even a few hundred calories in order to alleviate general starvation. With utmost punctilio we remained faithful to a minor convention of recent date, whilst we ruthlessly abandoned a far older and far more sacred convention. People who think in this fashion simply cannot be trusted. But it is precisely people who do think in this fashion who have the political and military disposition of the atomic bomb.

A. E.'s dictum, that man becomes the image of the thing he hates, was fully borne out in World War II. While the prewar fears that resistance to fascism would turn Britain or the United States into fascist countries have been proved an empty bugaboo with respect to their internal affairs, those fears have proved correct with regard to the practice of war itself. Now our methods of fighting have become totalitarian: that is, we have placed no limits upon our capacity to exterminate or destroy. Morality has become police: a mere tool of the state. In the act of grappling with fascism, the enemy has forced into our hands his most dangerous weapon, his moral nihilism. *That nihilism is the social counterpart of the atomic bomb.*

Though the transformations I have described have been swift, they have been accomplished, apparently, without any great moral shock: it needed the dramatic destructiveness of the atomic bomb itself to bring home the extent of our danger and our demoralization. Many " good " people, many " innocent " people, accept as commonplace acts which even thirty years ago would have been regarded as examples of unbelievable barbarism: they accept these acts as if no alternative were conceivable. We swallow as daily food, we good people, practices that would, a generation ago, have nauseated us almost beyond recovery if done only once in a lifetime.

We have, indeed, reason to be proud of the scientific genius that penetrated the secrets of matter's constitution and devised the means of disintegrating the atom. On this plane, modern man has achieved the ultimate miracle in physics, far beyond the wildest dreams of the medieval alchemist. During the century that opened with Faraday's researches in electricity, we have endowed mankind with godlike powers; but unfortunately we have not at the same time become godlike men. The ultimate physical means of disintegration have been discovered at a moment when our moral nihilism has brought us down to the level of Genghis Khan, or, if that is possible, somewhat lower. Even before the atomic bomb had been used, we had accepted, as a normal instrument of warfare, the practice of exterminating civilians. As with the Nazis, our lack of a sense of guilt was almost as great a sin as the sin itself.

Because the lives of their sons and husbands were at stake, many Americans, perhaps a majority, quickly found a way to justify the use of the atomic bomb; that first impulse was a natural one. But Mr. Truman and Mr. Churchill, who had taken upon themselves the decision to exploit this new invention without specific warning, sought also to pacify their fellow citizens' consciences. The very glibness of their words proved their unfitness to make such a grave decision. Our leaders pointed out that the use of the bomb reduced our possible military losses, perhaps to the extent of a million and a half lives. For a while, the alleged humanity of atomic bombing was stressed by official publicists. As to the first point, we have now learned that the enemy was actively suing for peace before the bomb was employed. We used the bomb when we were neither in military extremity nor even in a stalemate. As for the instantaneous death of the civilians bombed, which put the method almost in the realm of mercy killing, our comfort is a little abated by the reports of the shocked, the maimed, the burned, who were not quite exter-

minated. But when once success becomes the sole justification
of the means, there are no conceivable limits to human devil-
try. The history of the Catholic Inquisition proves that fact.

Do not blame the institution of war for this ultimate mis-
chief. It is not the rising tide of physical destructiveness that
has caused war to overflow our moral levees: rather, it is our
complete unreadiness to build higher and stronger levees that
has kept us from containing these forces. We ourselves have
breached the dykes that held back barbarism. There is no
moral code in existence that could excuse the indiscriminate
and wholesale slaughter of men, women, and children — no
matter how instantaneous or how painless that butchery
might be.

The wantonness of our apologetics has not been diminished
by the fact that Japan's surrender took place nine days after
the first bomb was used. While one may doubt that the use
of the atomic bomb alone shortened the war, other forms of
obliteration bombing, equally great in scale, surely hastened
the day. But the very success of the methods only increases
their menace. In any short term view, wholesale extermination pays higher dividends to the successful user of the method
than any other form of warfare. That in itself is a powerful,
almost irresistible temptation to its further use.

On a long-term view, the results of our success are less en-
trancing: we have widened the province of fear, and instead
of a local anxiety we have produced a universal one. The
unrestrained use of terrorism and extermination reacts upon
the user as well as the victim: if it does not cause revulsion, it
must deepen his debasement. Our victory will be a deceptive
one, if the present absence of inhibitions shortens the life-span
of the human race. For mark this: the ultimate weapon of
annihilation has been put in the hands of practicing nihilists,
ourselves. Once we become theoretical nihilists, too, as we
must when we attempt to justify our methods, then both the
degradation and the danger will be multiplied. At that mo-

ment the last step in the process described by Henry Adams will take place: disintegration will overcome integration.

NIHILISM IN PRACTICE

There was once a piece of parlor casuistry which went this way: If you could acquire a million dollars by pressing a button that would kill, without pain, a man on the other side of the world, would you press it? We have found such a button and to win, not a million dollars, but a war, we have used it. In two raids, one with incendiary bombs on Tokyo, and one with an atomic bomb on Hiroshima, we killed on a modest estimate more human beings than were killed in England by Germany's continued bombing over a period of six years.

This quantitative change has proved to be a qualitative one. By increasing our own capacity for annihilation we have, paradoxically, lessened our sense of horror. Here we are faced with one further result of modern technics: even our own forces no longer make visible contact with the enemy. This process began with the invention of long-range weapons long ago; but it has now reached its limit with stratosphere flying, the rocket bomb, and the atomic bomb. The ideological insulation of the technician from normal human considerations perhaps reaches its height in the training and practice of military aviators.

The consequences of this insulation are extremely treacherous. Attack from the air upon cities is usually made from such a height that only the threat of flak reminds the airman of the presence of human beings below. When he sees flame or watches explosions he beholds them — as Mussolini's son did in the war on Abyssinia — as esthetic spectacles, not as scenes of infernal torture and pain. Unlike the infantryman, who eventually confronts his victims, the aviator is deliberately cushioned from this human shock, in the interests of preserving his mental balance. Suppose our flyers had been compelled to check in each Japanese they killed at the door of an extermination chamber. Could they have killed as many as fifty visible civilians without suffering a mental breakdown?*

In this merciless form of warfare we have justified our acts, as President Truman justified the use of the atomic bomb, on the ground that the Japanese themselves have been a cruel foe. No doubt they have been so; their acts are on record: not merely our own, but countless thousands of Chinese dead testify to this. But if evil is to be retaliated by equal evil, what should prevent us from imitating the practices of the German extermination camps? For every rule of war the Japanese broke against us on the scale of hundreds, we have broken an equally valid rule on the scale of thousands.

To understand what we have done, let us ask what we ourselves would now feel had we been subject to the same treatment that we meted out to the Japanese. Would we not have reached new heights of moral indignation over our enemy's barbarism? Then let us ask ourselves one further question: What kind of people were we ourselves in process of becoming as the war mounted to its climax? Were we actually as innocent as we felt we were? Or had we merely hardened our hearts to the point at which we were capable of committing the unpardonable sin?

These are harsh words to address to a people who hated the idea of war and entered this one only at the extreme provocation of their enemies. They are even harsher words to address to a people who, in the moment of victory, naturally feel a grateful release: people who have keyed themselves to high-

* The rocket-bomb and the automatic, remote-controlled plane will complete this development. The airman, to his honor, risks his own life: if we permit war to exist, as a result of our selfishness and feeblemindedness in not creating an effective world organization, the principal operatives in our next war will be screened from all contact with the enemy: safe until they are annihilated by the same means of long-distance attack. Such a war might well begin — and end — without the victims' being able to identify the enemy, or even to identify the direction from which the bombardment came.

speed production and battle strain, and who have a natural desire to relax. Finally, these are terrible questions to ask men in combat whose lives have been spared by the method of wholesale annihilation we have practiced on the Japanese. In victory itself most of us are likely to find sufficient justification for our manner of winning it. Is this, then, the moment for drastic self-examination and self-criticism?

Yes; this is the moment for self-criticism. For it is precisely at the hour of our greatest success that we must beware the terrible sin of *hybris*, or untrammeled pride, which the wise Greeks knew, even before the Christian theologians, was the chief source of man's moral undoing. We are men and we have erred. In the very act of fighting the enemy we have let his evil become our good: a sinister transvaluation of values. Let us be strong enough to acknowledge our sins; let us be prompt to repent of them before they become habits. All the errors men made before the war, from Munich to Pearl Harbor, continue to fester because those who committed them have lacked the grace to say openly, " I was wrong." And so with this almost universal relapse into barbarism. Unless we can arouse our imaginations sufficiently to picture the consequences of our acts and to appraise rigorously their actual character, there is no further enormity that we might not, as a people, be ready to commit.

For mark this: if we can use one atomic bomb, we can use two and have done so. If two, then twenty: if twenty, then enough to wreck the world. Once we have lost the principle of control, once we have deadened our moral responses and released our inhibitions, we have lost everything. This is one of the facts that makes the present situation so serious. Modern technics, so far from helping to create a race of enlightened supermen, as Mr. H. G. Wells sentimentally dreamed, has produced a race of moral robots.

All of Henry Adams's predictions have come true. Explosives have now reached cosmic violence and, within the international sphere, law, as *a priori* principle, has disappeared. Unless our moral recoil becomes equally violent, there is nothing to prevent disintegration from overcoming integration. This may well take place at the very moment when we are most sure of our own good purposes, our moral sobriety, and our ultimate beneficence.

THE NEED FOR CHECKS AND BALANCES

The moral recoil against the atomic bomb has already begun to take place. Horror and fear may restore us to moral sanity. Even those who apologize for its use realize that it is a double-edged weapon. If the recoil goes far enough, it may set in action the human forces and impulses that will save us. But if we cushion the recoil with specious excuses and self-justifications, if we are reluctant to respond to the challenge of our own actions with sufficient promptness and sufficient zeal, mankind may be lost. Since we have the honor of possessing, for a brief time, the technological secrets of smashing the atom on a sufficiently large scale, the duty of taking the necessary political initiatives remains ours.

Perhaps the hardest thing for us Americans to realize is that we are no longer confronted by external enemies: the most dangerous enemy we face lies within us. The high religions have always acknowledged this enemy, in the human heart itself, and modern psychology has unearthed the same foe. In the depth of man's unconscious life lie the forces of destruction he projects outside himself and externalizes. As an infant he cherishes illusions of omnipotence, and the actual achievement of physical omnipotence may cause him to relapse into infantile modes of behavior. The history of every great concentration of imperial power, from Nebuchadnezzar to Alexander, from Ivan the Terrible to Hitler, bears witness to this threat of regression. " Absolute power corrupts absolutely."

To grapple with the enemy within, we must rapidly reconnoiter and reorganize our personal conduct: that is the first step toward adequate measures in the political and economic fields. Unfortunately, we find ourselves as unprepared for this effort as we Americans were unprepared for war in 1940, when our army was drilling with wooden rifles and wagons labeled as guns. But it may help us to accomplish the profound and rapid transformation that lies ahead, if we recall the way in which a peace-loving, somewhat self-indulgent people, used to their securities and comforts, actually met the situation. What accomplished the change? Two things: self-imposed coercion and external danger. The danger justified the coercion and the coercion made it possible to face the danger. In actual battle, danger produced the effect of a wholesale conversion.

Even in the factory, still more on the battlefield, men learned to displace their individual feelings and their individual purposes, to meet the common need. Easygoing men learned to give orders; irresponsible men learned to accept weighty responsibilities; soft men learned to harden themselves to carry burdens and to perform acts that nothing in their civilian experience had fitted them for. In 1940 our country was full of cagey defeatists who would have been as easy a pushover for the fascists as the French were. By 1943 we had produced millions of highly disciplined, excellently trained men and women who were equal to the most exacting ordeals of war. The outward pressure and discipline produced an inner change.

The process that began in the training camp was completed in the field, in the air, on the sea. In the presence of danger, men learned that *the price of survival was unconditional cooperation.* " We lived only by helping one another." " You stood by the other guy and some day he might be there to help you." Those are the commonest thoughts our fighting men have brought back: it was the secret of both survival and victory. Danger made the common soldier and sailor live from day to day as only saints had lived under less terrible conditions. No one used the word love; but the fighting men kept going under fire only because they loved one another: because they loved one another more than they loved life itself. There were exceptions; there were breakdowns: but the rule survives them.

The incalculable powers of the atomic bomb have put the whole world in a situation more desperate and dangerous than that on any battlefield. The consciousness of this fact has fortunately been widespread; it tempered our exultation, even in America, over our provisional conquest of atomic energy. In warfare, we have now carried the will-to-annihilation to its logical limits. Now mankind must rapidly learn, after the pattern of the camp and the battlefield, how to unite effectively to master this danger. No nation, no group of nations, is powerful enough to stand alone: none is sufficiently disciplined and moralized to be trusted. *Today unconditional co-operation is the price of mankind's survival. If we are sluggish in our response to this situation we may forfeit the immense human blessing that the very danger, a danger on a cosmic scale, carries with it.*

* * *

DEDICATION TO LIFE

Even under the limitations of his present development, modern man possesses enough life-furthering impulses and life-directed goals to save himself. But only on one condition: that a change in attitude overcomes his inertia and makes these impulses and goals operative. Man cannot save himself without first healing his split personality, without giving up his current habit of pursuing at the same time two different and incompatible goals. Power must become the willing servant of love.

No new principles of morality, no new devices of politics, need be invoked in order to achieve this psychological change, much though we might welcome them were they already at hand. What we need rather is the dynamic capacity to apply old principles and old devices to the situation we now face: to apply them and keep them vigorously in operation, even when the first threat of danger has seemed to subside. To effect this change on the world-wide scale our very technology demands, each individual must dedicate himself to his own self-improvement. It is the continued rule of the complacent and the unawakened ones — most of our present leaders in politics, business, and education — that we must fear, rather than the immediate outbreak of the more disintegrated and destructive types our civilization also produces. As in the 1930's the blindness of the first paves the way for the sadistic exploits of the second.

Since our first problem is the problem of control, let us begin with those elements of control which are still operative within the dominant pattern of our civilization; and first of all, let us consider the sciences themselves, which have developed, within their own fields, an adequate technique of control. The basis for this is the co-operative sharing of knowledge and the institution of the experimental method, whereby the findings of any particular man or group can be subjected to independent verification. This technique itself is a moralizing practice. Within the field of nature it has caused men to replace their random guesses or their untutored prejudices with instruments of measure and order from whose finding there is no appeal, except by a resort to similar methods. The humility of the scientist in the face of observed fact is the equivalent of " Thy will be done." The method of science, in other words, neutralizes man's local biases and partialities; it normalizes his rationality.

The world-wide diffusion of the scientific technique has fostered co-operation and mutual confidence among those capable of employing it. As far as they go, these controls are useful; but it would be presumptuous to think that the scientific method replaces other means of control: as presumptuous and unwise as the statement of a distinguished historian, as late as 1930, that science had forever removed the possibility of a recurrence of barbarism. The techniques of science only apply to the method, not to the end; they control the process of research, not the direction of research; and they discipline a fragment of the human personality, not the whole personality, many parts of which are untouched by this method and immune to its processes.

Indeed, the very over-emphasis of a method that displaces human wishes and desires in the pursuit of truth may create a compensatory willfulness in other aspects of the personality. In the evolution of science and technics to the dangerous state they have now reached, the scientist himself has often shown an incapacity for both self-criticism and self-control. Holding himself strictly responsible for processes, he has been incurious about the ultimate results of his work. Outside his own narrow realm, he may be a barbarian, and to the extent that he is concerned only with that narrow realm he is in fact a barbarian. Even in the social sciences, where the very subject matter should erect a safeguard against dehumanized thinking, the adoption of a more exact methodology has often been accompanied by a loss of direction and purpose, on the false assumption that true science has no human concerns.

Now, the emergency that confronts mankind demands that there should be a change in the direction of research itself. Until man's personal disciplines and social controls are capable of mastering the immense forces he now commands and putting them to wise use, he must desist from aggravating the danger by fostering further effort along the lines that have brought on the present crisis. Here our institutions of learning, our engines of research, must govern their apportionment of budgets and their selection of staff on a principle not hitherto generally respected except perhaps in Soviet Russia:

the principle of social need. Such an effort would multiply the number of anthropologists, sociologists, and psychologists, while it would diminish their opposite numbers in the physical sciences: it would endow schools of the humanities and curtail schools of technology.*

There is, of course, no magic in such a change unless it be accompanied by a new sense of urgency and responsibility, and a fresh capacity for distinguishing between the trivial and the essential. But this effort would be at least a deliberate attempt to rectify our one-sided preoccupation with mechanical invention and purely material improvements. In the end, a balance would be established; and the physical sciences themselves would probably benefit by this curb on their random productivity and by the opportunity for assimilating their own headlong advances.

Men act long before institutions move. The change I am advocating here has already taken place, in token form, through the redirection of effort by individual mathematicians and physicists. The humanistic studies of the mathematician, A. N. Whitehead, with his criticism of the mechanical world picture itself, were typical acts of reorientation. As if in a self-preservative effort to guard against the life-threatening knowledge that physics possessed, even before the atomic bomb was devised, men as eminent in physics as Erwin Schroedinger, as able as L. L. Whyte, have sought, as physicists, to ally their own findings to biology. All over the world such men are attempting to create a body of unified science, which would not alone adequately describe physical nature, but give their due primacy to life and mind and spirit. The quiet researches in optics of Professor Adelbert Ames at Dartmouth College have re-instated value and purpose at the most primitive level of physiological activity — that of supposedly pure sensation. Such work in many different fields

* I do not suggest that any of our existing schools of humanities, despite many superficial changes now taking place, will meet our need. — L. M.

lays the groundwork for a new age, not a new Age of Technics, but a new Age of Man, fortified by a technics that is under the control of man and is directed to man's survival and development. This age is still waiting for its new Bacon, who will re-write the *Advancement of Learning* with the human elements, which Bacon did not in fact exclude, in a dominant rather than a subordinate position.

But the reorientation of the sciences touches only one aspect of the human personality. The change that will make world organization effective must operate on many different levels of the personality; and to put all our trust in science would be to show that we have not learned as much about the human personality as the psychologist and the sociologist have already demonstrated. Perhaps the most we can ask of the scientist today is that he transfer his capacity for self-abnegation, his well-trained inhibitions, his rigorous respect for controls, to wider areas of knowing and doing. His knowledge must be oriented toward life; for only life is sacred. Here his insight and his example will have a powerful effect upon his contemporaries; for the mass of mankind today his authority is as absolute and as awful as that of a primitive medicine man.

Not the least important force we must mobilize, in the interests of survival, is an ancient one: that of religion. Both Benjamin Kidd a generation ago, and Henri Bergson in our own time, interpreted religion as a self-preservative effort, on the part of life, to guard man against the discouraging effects of his own achievements in knowledge. There is a profound truth in these interpretations. Though most of the classic religions have dwelled on the familiar facts of man's limitations and frustrations, centered in the ultimate mystery of death, they have all guarded life itself as zealously as the vestals guarded fire. Hinduism, Confucianism, Buddhism, Judaism, Christianity, even Mohammedanism, have sought to curb man's impulses to destruction and disintegration: each of them interdicts random killing, each of them encourages procreation, each of them has sought to foster love.

In this moment of common peril, we should do well to overlook the hypocrisies and failures of the orthodox: their very superstitions have nevertheless kept the ignorant, the willful, and the destructive under some limited sense of order and some minimum system of control. If the symbols of religion do not always stand up under rational examination, if their myths are more mysterious than the mysteries they would explain, that is not necessarily a proof of their inability to penetrate and control the irrational elements in man. Religion's function, in fact, is to redress man's pride in his intellect, to reduce his conceit and his complacence, so that he will be better fortified to face the ordeal of reality. Mankind is afloat on a frail life-raft. Religion understands the monsters of the deep and the storms that come up in the night.

Religion reminds man of his creatureliness and his creativeness, his impotence and his power, his cosmic littleness and his cosmic preciousness — for the tiny spark of consciousness man carries in his soul may be, up to now, the final event toward which the so-called physical universe has moved. Religion's cosmic time sense, achieved long before astronomy sustained the intuition with exact calculations, is a brake against the possibility that man might sacrifice his own long future to some temporary gratification or some temporary triumph. Here is a latent power for man's self-preservation: on the whole, theologians have made a more prompt response to the atomic bomb than any other group except the atomic physicists themselves, though they have still to show the capacity for unified effort that will make a wider renewal possible.

Morality is Sancho Panza to religion's Don Quixote; for morality develops out of the customs of the tribe and those customs, too, are usually life-preservative ones, though they may clash with those of other tribes. Modern man, proud of his fearless investigation of every part of the universe, conscious of his increasing powers to control his circumstances, has shown something less than forbearance to those primitive cultures whose daily acts are limited by taboos. But in throwing off the irrational object of most taboos, modern man has also forfeited the very habit of inhibition that the taboo imposed. He has thus forgotten one of the most essential secrets of man's advance: the practice of restraint. Whereas the older midbrain is the seat of man's instinctual energies and his explosive emotions, the newer forebrain, which takes care of his higher behavior, is also the seat of his inhibitions. Without the development of these inhibitions man's untempered curiosity might, long before this, have proved suicidal.

In little matters, modern man acknowledges taboos: he does not spit in a subway car, blow his nose in public without using a handkerchief, or enter a house with a quarantine notice posted on its door. But in general, his plan of life has resulted, not in exchanging taboos for rational restraints, but in exchanging taboos for equally irrational habits of relaxation. For the last two hundred years a long succession of thinkers, from Diderot and Rousseau onward, have urged man to throw off his ancient taboos: to act on his impulses, yield to his desires, abandon measure in his gratifications. If man were wholly rational and wholly good, these counsels would perhaps have been profitable: but Dostoevsky, who understood the demonic in man, pointed out long ago the dangers of this moral nihilism; and in our day those dangers have assumed cosmic dimensions.

Morality, in the elementary form of accepted inhibitions, is the first step toward the conscious control of the powers man now commands: without this lowest form of morality, engrained in habit, no higher form can be practiced. What Irving Babbitt called the inner check — the vital restraint — is essential to our survival. Promptly we must reverse Blake's dictum — we must bless braces and damn relaxes.

This moral tightening of the bit comes very hard to modern man; for it is no exaggeration to say that he has attempted in the past generation to live by the pleasure principle: he has tried to establish a regime of limitless gratifications without accepting deprivations or penalties. The very quantification of life through machine production has lifted many natural limits that once prevailed. So self-indulgent have we become that even a temporary shortage of cigarettes in America evoked a response far more irrational in character than any religious taboo on smoking would be: in the midst of a biting blizzard, crowds waited in line for a whole hour in order to purchase their quota of cigarettes. The indecent haste with which the American government threw off the rationing of foods after the Japanese surrender, at a time when the rest of the war-battered world was close to starvation, is an indication of a popular unwillingness to exercise self-control: an unwillingness most prevalent in the very circles that exercise most political influence.

Morally, such people are as unfit for the control of atomic power as a chronic alcoholic would be for the inheritance of a vast stock of whiskey. Those who have lost respect for taboos of any kind are most in need of their self-preservative principle.

Now, experience demands that we should recognize the place of negative stimuli in human development. Pains, abstentions, renunciations, inhibitions, are perhaps as essential for human development as more positive nurture. During the war, fighting men learned this lesson; it gave them power to confront danger and surmount it; and where civilians were placed under the same stresses, as in cities that endured aerial bombardment, they learned the same hard lessons. The imaginative widening of this experience among people who are still unchastened is an essential measure. To recover the very habit of restraint, to subject every act to measure, to place limits even on goods that may be offered in limitless quantities — this is the communal response we must make to the challenge of both physical and moral disintegration. The very processes of democracy, which it is so essential to extend to world organization, demand a high degree of conscious moderation. That is possibly why the most restrained of peoples, the English, are also the best exemplars of democratic processes. Every civilian must master, as the price of society's survival, the lesson that military organization teaches the soldier: group survival requires the acceptance of sacrifice.

In thirty years of public writing, I have perhaps never put forth proposals more shocking and more inacceptable than the present ones: I can remember how I myself was shocked by them, more than twenty years ago, when I first encountered similar ideas in Irving Babbitt's *Democracy and Leadership*. Our mechanistic folkways are at war with these assumptions and conclusions. In every Western nation, the devices of publicity are constantly used to break down our inhibitions in order to make us more susceptible to the allurements of the advertiser: narcotics, stimulants, aphrodisiacs in large quantities, both in the form of symbols and the form of material goods, all conspire to this end. The goal of the advertiser is to make the consumer say Yes to his every suggestion. Under the pressure of a totalitarian ideology, the breakdown of inhibitions became absolute in fascist countries: there was no conceivable fiendishness which the Nazis did not practice in their extermination camps. Along that road, we ourselves have gone no short distance; and if we are nearer hell than we had dreamed, it is partly because we thought that by abandoning inhibitions we were approaching Adam's ancient paradise.

The restoration of rational inhibitions and purposeful sacrifices is now one of the conditions for human survival. Men must institute these practices in their daily routines before nations will collectively follow their example. Our capacity for restraint must be proportional to the power we now command.

On no other terms will we be able to control the malign forces that exist, not so much in the atomic bomb itself, but in the human soul: forces whose eruption out of the unconscious has already brought this otherwise highly disciplined and highly co-operative civilization to an advanced stage of visible disintegration — visible in terms of the hundreds of cities ruined, the countrysides that have been devastated, the millions of souls that have been starved and tortured, maimed and killed. If our morality is not adequate, if our daily habits are not informed by rational purposes, if our inhibitions are not, when necessary, inviolable, the means that will validate our political controls will be lacking. Every institutional change will be insufficient unless we bring to it a fully awakened and constantly renewed personality. Love must transform aggression into sacrifice; and sacrifice must put aggression at the service of love.

Each of us must remember his humanness: it takes precedence over our race, our economic class, our politics, our religion, or our nationality. Only to the extent that the nations cultivate this humanness, becoming members one of another, can our civilization achieve peace and security, to say nothing of the well-being and creativeness that will eventually issue forth from them. If we do not put humanity, in every sense of this word, before all petty and limited ends, nothing can be saved.

If man is to survive on a high level, not like the diminished primitive hordes Mr. H. G. Wells pictured, our reaction to this challenge must be unqualified and universal. Every day, and every hour, every minute — I quote once again — we must walk around ourselves and watch ourselves and see that our images are seemly ones. No habits must be uncriticized; no values must remain unexamined; no institutional procedures must be regarded as sacred; no life-denying goals must remain unchallenged. It is not this or that group, elected or self-elected, that must carry the burden of mankind's salvation.

Every individual person must first mobilize himself to meet the danger, with a more unconditional acceptance of responsibilities and sacrifices than even the British did when they stood alone, facing imminent destruction, in the summer of 1940. Our best will hardly be enough to guarantee survival. Less than our best will be treason to humanity.

POSTSCRIPT: AFTER NINE YEARS

[*After writing this essay in August 1945, Lewis Mumford continued to speak out on the subject of the atom bomb; in the* New York Times *of March 28, 1954, he published the following letter about the hydrogen bomb and its problems:*]

The power of the hydrogen bomb has, it is plain, given pause even to the leaders of our government. Their very hesitation to give away the facts in itself gives away the facts. Under what mandate, then, do they continue to hold as secret the results we may expect from the use of weapons of extermination — not merely on our own cities and people but on all living organisms; not merely on our present lives but on the lives of countless generations to come?

Are our leaders afraid that when the truth is known our devotion to the perfection of scientific weapons of total destruction and extermination will turn out to be a profoundly irrational one: repulsive to morality, dangerous to national security, inimical to life?

Do they suspect that the American people are still sane enough to halt the blind automatism that continues, in the face of Soviet Russia's equal scientific powers, to produce these fatal weapons?

Do they fear that their fellow-countrymen may well doubt the usefulness of instruments which, under the guise of deterring an aggressor or insuring a cheap victory, might incidentally destroy the whole fabric of civilization and threaten the very existence of the human race?

Our secret weapons of extermination have been produced

under conditions that have favored irresponsible censorship and short-sighted political and military judgments. Under the protection of secrecy a succession of fatal errors has been made, primarily as the result (since 1942) of our accepting total extermination as a method of warfare. These errors have been compounded by our counting upon such dehumanized methods to preserve peace and security.

In turn, our very need for secrecy, in an abortive effort to monopolize technical and scientific knowledge, has produced pathological symptoms in the whole body politic: fear, suspicion, non-cooperation, hostility to critical judgment, above all delusions of power based on fantasies of unlimited extermination, as the only possible answer to the political threat of Soviet Russia. But demoralized men cannot be counted upon to control such automatic instruments of demoralization.

At a fatal moment our self-induced fears may produce the incalculable and irretrievable holocaust our own weapons have given us reason to dread. Only courage and intelligence of the highest order, backed by open discussion, will give us the strength to turn back from the suicidal path we have blindly followed since 1942.

Are there not enough Americans still possessed of their sanity to call a stop to these irrational decisions, which are automatically bringing us close to a total catastrophe?

There are many alternative courses to the policy to which we have committed ourselves, practically without debate. The worst of all these alternatives, submission to Communist totalitarianism, would still be far wiser than the final destruction of civilization.

As for the best of these alternatives, a policy of working firmly toward justice and co-operation, and free intercourse with all other peoples, in the faith that love begets love as surely as hatred begets hatred — this would, in all probability, be the one instrument capable of piercing the strong political armour of our present enemies.

Once the facts of our policy of total extermination are publicly canvassed, and the final outcome, mass suicide, is faced, I believe that the American people are still sane enough to come to a wiser decision than our government has yet made. They will realize that retaliation is not protection; that total extermination of both sides is not victory; that a constant state of morbid fear, suspicion, and hatred is not security; that, in short, what seems like unlimited power has become impotence.

In the name of sanity let our government now pause and seek the counsel of sane men: men who have not participated in the errors we have made and are not committed, out of pride, to defending them. Let us cease all further experiments with even more horrifying weapons of destruction, lest our own self-induced fears further upset our mental balance.

Let us all, as responsible citizens, not the cowed subjects of an all-wise state, weigh the alternatives and canvass new lines of approach to the problems of power and peace.

Let us deal with our own massive sins and errors as a step toward establishing firm relations of confidence with the rest of mankind. And let us, first of all, have the courage to speak up on behalf of humanity, on behalf of civilization, on behalf of life itself against the methodology of barbarism to which we are now committed.

If as a nation we have become mad it is time for the world to take note of that madness. If we are still humane and sane, then it is time for the powerful voice of sanity to be heard once more in our land.

Re-birth of the Family

Life succeeds only in an environment of life.

Among the family papers of a neighbor of mine is a biography of his great-grandfather; the notebook still remains in the house the old man lived in, though since that time the family itself has divided and moved away. " My dear Brother," this family book begins, " I have long wished that our children and those who shall come after them might have some knowledge of those traits in the character of our honoured and dear Father, which we remember with so much pleasure, and which in some respect distinguished him from others."

This book is a happy attempt to understand and appreciate a personality, to define the values he lived by and to pass them on. In purpose and belief, it is just the opposite of those sordid debunking biographies that were fashionable in the 1920's, following Lytton Strachey's *Eminent Victorians*. And at the end, this story carries an account of the military enlistment and eventual death of the writer's own son, not yet nineteen years of age, in the Civil War. A noble record, a beautiful book, this country biography: it gives the reader a faithful picture of a family that has lived and left its mark on life.

In that simple introduction, of brother writing to brother, is the spirit of an older text: Let us now praise famous men and our fathers that begat us. This impulse is the very essence of both history and biography, or at least of any that deserve the name. The fact that such family papers are no longer produced, sometimes no longer kept and treasured, shows more than any other single fact what has happened to the very principle of family continuity in our society. Even the family Bible, with its record of births, christenings, notable events, honors, and deaths, has disappeared. If any records of family life remain, they are only those of the scattered individuals: one must search for them in the bureau that registers births, in the files of a physician or an insurance office.

In political oratory, as in pious sermons, nothing is more common than fulsome praise of the family, as the kernel of all our other social institutions. The praise is as just as it is hollow; for in the act of abandoning farmsteads for cities, and family businesses for impersonal corporate organizations that command large quantities of capital, we have permitted the economic basis of the family to be sapped.

This drift began as far back as the sixteenth century. Thomas Mann has painted a picture of later family dissolution in *Buddenbrooks;* but what he pictures as a weakening or diversion of practical judgment and economic grasp was much more than that: it was a vital and social failure to provide for the continuity and higher nurture of the human stock. Life drained away from the institution that guarded life: the grave events that are centred in the family, courtship and marriage and birth and education and death, ceased to be the main core of human interest. Except among the poor, except in the quiet villages: for the poor are, in a sense, the " pagans " of our civilization, who cling in defeat and sorrow to the old homely ways.

Family events that once had social dignity and all manner of æsthetic enrichment have now been reduced to purely physical processes, presided over by paid specialists. Certain vestiges of older ties are perhaps still kept up for the young, as in the celebration of birthdays; but the sense of the family unit and of family unity has been largely lost. Divorce is all too easy because the original knitting together has never been performed. In modern marriage the partners too often remain isolate atoms that resent the very suggestion that they might lose their identity in the family molecule. Each one is for himself, whereas the very essence of the family is: all for one and one for all. That had its bad side, of course, in the ancient blood feud; but even that narrow perversion of family unity still points to the essential social fact: the loyalty of kindred.

For a family to maintain its sense of itself, it must have a permanent headquarters, a permanent gathering place. It must provide opportunities for the old and the young to meet and mix and to encounter life together. That solidity requires land and economic foundations: at least enough land for a house, at least enough economic support to keep the house in order. In the swift exodus from the open country, which began in England in the eighteenth century and by the end of the nineteenth century was world-wide, the ancient soil of the family was deserted. Speculators built mean little houses, and expected cannily to get them back when the interest on the mortgages was not forthcoming; banks and insurance companies invested in farms, and, when hard times came, seized them, reducing the owner to a tenant or ousting him altogether. Under current financial conditions the dwelling house was a liability, home-ownership was a form of *in*security. The gullible grasped at the shadow of ownership and family independence; but society had removed the substance.

In the rush to the cities, tenements were built not only to house the childless, but to provide quarters, cramped and dark, for those who were founding families. Economic conditions, crises, depressions, low wages, high land values — all these things mocked at the security of the family. Who could afford to bring children into the world, when that world denied by every act that children were valuable or families important? Prudence dictated sterilization: fewer children to the intelligent and the provident. The churches, particularly the Roman Catholic Church, might sternly resist birth control; but the statistics of population, in Catholic countries hardly less than Protestant countries, showed how scant was their success.

Except in rural areas, where traditions die hard and life itself is uncowed, the family has remained as a vestigial institution. Among the landed aristocracy in England or the peasants in France and China, for example, the family still kept its roots in the soil, tough and unshaken; but elsewhere, and above all in the big cities, the family steadily failed, dwindling as a biological unit, losing all authority as a focus of loyalties and sentiments.

One proof of this ultimate retrogression is final. In America, in population centers of over 100,000 inhabitants, the typical family did not bear enough children to reproduce itself or keep up the population of the city without an influx of outsiders. When one opens the family cupboard one discovers only the skeleton. Plainly, it takes families of more than 3.2 people to reproduce the human race; even families of 4.0 people cannot fulfil their bare biological function of ensuring survival, since disease and untimely death reduce the number of those who would finally mate.

The disruption of the family has been associated with various conditions that we have permitted, in the absence of sounder values, to be unqualified in their operations.

The first was the ruthless destruction of the household arts and crafts, on the assumption that the equivalent can be purchased at a shop; and if the manufactured product is not better, it will at least provide profit to the manufacturer and his investors, instead of being merely a personal satisfaction to the members of the household. Often this change is described as laborsaving — forgetful of the fact that no person who practises an art with skill and pleasure really wants his labor saved: he wants it used.

Not merely have laborious operations, like soap-making and wool-carding and washing clothes, disappeared in good part from even the rural home, but all the arts that gave distinction to the housewife — the preserving of fruits and vegetables, the baking of cakes, the curing of bacon and hams — have been taken over for large-scale production. Even in the country, the insistent chain-store baker hammers at the door twice a week, trying to persuade my wife that her own skill is worthless, and that, if she buys his cakes, she will have more time for herself. But more time for what? For polishing the nails? Or for finding a frivolous occupation to take the place of one performed with intelligent art and smiling dignity; one capable of giving to maker and eater the sense of communion that comes through sharing and appreciating any art.

In like fashion the enterprising business man has sought to discredit and outmode all the other crafts that once provided education and sane activity to the inhabitants of a household, or to the local craftsmen who contributed their special skill to its well-being. The result is that the modern urban household has become an intensely specialized institution for the speedy accomplishment of certain minimum physiological activities: eating, bathing, defecation, copulation, and sleep. Eating is the only one of these that requires even the partial co-operation of all the members of the household. Even here, in the big cities, a hurried breakfast is followed by a lunch outside the household. The family meets as a unit — if at all — at night; and the more prosperous the family, the less often will it meet. As for intercourse between various branches of a family, that has become perfunctory; for where, except in the open country, are there still homes among the middle classes with as much as a single extra bedroom?

In consequence, family life has been trivialized and impoverished; emptied of real social content and of the constant æsthetic and personal values it once had. To be just a housewife is to have, in the metropolitan scheme of values, no real place in life. From the standpoint of current fashion, it is more important to write a dishonest piece of publicity or a bad poem, to spend eight hours hammering at a typewriter or sewing in a dressmaking factory, or even to stand all day at a counter in a dry-goods store than to make a bed properly, diaper a baby neatly, or grow a beautiful stalk of snapdragons.

Even the daughters of the rich, who have no need for money, compete with their more necessitous sisters for jobs, so vacant do their lives seem to them, except in relation to that which alone seems to engross their interests or encompass their appetites — business success, or at least business: " real life." Instead of taking advantage of the machine to endow themselves more richly with those goods the home might specially provide, our women, young and old, have done precisely the opposite. They have not gone in for children and the skills and arts needed to educate children; they have not husbanded their energies for nurture and for passionate play. Even when they dress artfully for sexual appeal they postpone too easily the actual encounter. Obviously if modern women had the faintest notion of acting as amorously as they look, they would not smear their lips with colour whose contour and outline would be spoiled by other than a peckish kiss.

No: business demands that woman adopt the smooth role; that is to say, the role of a neuter. At her best, woman brings some faint perfume of sexuality into office and factory, lightening, if only by a show of her ankle or a glimpse of her breasts, the dry routine of machine-tending. At her worst, however, she practices the really debilitating vice of carrying back into the home the efficient neutrality of the office. She is impersonal with her children, cool or slightly abstracted with her mate, too exhausted by her preoccupation with the life of industry to mind the real industry of life.

All this applies almost as much to the leisured sister of the upper suburban middle classes, who makes a business of golf or bridge, or of clubs and causes, as it does to the actual working woman. An odor of anxious antisepsis hangs even over her love-making. The only mortal error for which she feels responsible, as either an easy-going bachelor or a certificated wife, is that of being " caught " — in other words, the unfor-givable sin of finding a baby growing in her womb.

There is one rough way of gauging the relative importance of an institution; and that is to observe the amount of time given to it. Though the household may remain in constant use twenty-four hours a day, the amount of time and energy given to family life, as active partnership and intercourse be-tween parents and children, is probably in middle-class house-holds less than that given to the motion pictures or the beauty parlor. If I exaggerate here, I only emphasize a truth.

People have thoughtlessly come to accept this routine as a quite normal one; " everyone lives in that way." Many even value it as a mark of a civilized life. For the great mass of urban families there is as yet no other possibility; the nearest they come to a common way of life together is in the Sun-day motor ride, most of which is spent in the constriction of a car, in the benumbed state that has become so constant that motorists are not even aware of its existence. An eight-hour day in the factory or the office actually permits a man to see less of his wife and children today than a twelve-hour day did when he spent most of it in his own workshop or on his own farm.

At the end of a day of intense toil, perhaps mechanized and speeded up, the husband is tired; so, often, is the wife, espe-cially if she have outside work to do, as well as household duties. Since the school accepts the hours and schedules of the business machine as a natural pattern for its own efforts, the children are in the same fix: either taking part in school routines or chained to homework when they escape the actual confines of the school. On one day out of seven there is a chance for a common life. That is how much our civilization, during the past fifty years, has come to value the family.

What is true of the apportionment of hours holds elsewhere. Family life, in the most elementary sense of biological repro-duction, is deficient; and even in the more prolific rural areas, it has come down in the United States to a rate that will produce only stability. While a thousand useful machines and futile gadgets have been poured forth by industry during the past century, the physical utilities needed to raise a family are poorer in the biggest cities to-day than they were in an eighteenth-century village.

For what does a family need? Open plumbing? Glassed-in shower-baths? Hot and cold water? Air-conditioned heating systems? All these things might be useful, in one degree or another, provided the primary needs of family living were satisfied. But these utilities do not cover the essential family needs; quite the contrary, they claim for themselves the money that should go *directly* into those needs.

The family's basic need is for space; garden space and house space. Space for living: commodious rooms, well equipped for rest, relaxation, conversation, social intercourse; space for infants to toddle in and for runabout children to romp in; space for solitude as well as for sociability, the boudoir or " sulking " room, and the quiet study for reading and writing; space for storage, so neither physically nor spiritually will the family have to live from hand to mouth; space to store clothes and playthings; space to keep pictures safely; space to keep all manner of records, photographs, papers, diaries, drawings, so that the past will not become too shadowy; space for growing things, with a soil capable of yielding good measures of flowers, fruits, vegetables. And space is precisely what is lacking; we have been trained to do without it; our very housing authorities, fatuously thinking that they are improving conditions, boast of establishing first-class mechanical equipment in the midst of fourth-class living space.

Life succeeds only in an environment of life. The sterile felicity of the urban apartment house — even a model apartment house, with open areas around it and plenty of sunlight — is not, can never be, a substitute for living space. Here again we have reversed the order of human needs. As the number of mechanical utilities has increased within the house, its space has shrunken. So in some of our desperate efforts to repair the evils of old slums we have created new ones. One would think that the designers of our metropolitan housing projects hated the family; and without being conscious of the bias, they probably do. How otherwise could they be so ignorant of its requirements, so unable imaginatively to interpret them?

Culture of the Family

Be fruitful, not prudent: increase and multiply your children, not the ciphers in your bank account.

Only those fortunate enough to have had the experience of mating and raising a family under conditions that favor this occupation have any real conception of what is missing at the very core of our civilization. Most people have experienced love and parenthood, alas! under conditions that thwart them at every step: the middle classes no less than the poor. The family can flourish only by the process of continuously living in an environment which itself bears the impress of that life, favors it, responds to it, elevates it. For the family does not merely symbolize human continuity: it *is* that continuity.

It is first in the eager love of mates that the tamest personal life quickens into a fierce ecstasy: an ecstasy whose ebbing and renewal, in the long process of marriage, is one of the perpetual miracles of life. All good things take time to develop; and marriage, the best gift to lovers, requires more time for its development and completion than any other good thing. Auguste Comte well said that a lifetime was not too long for two lovers to get acquainted in.

In time, the links multiply. In the birth of their child, the man and wife perhaps first face death together; and the woman's is the braver part; for she is the soldier of marriage, and man the civilian. In the care of their children, parents relive imaginatively their own youth, in the very act of deepening all their responsibilities as adults: honey from the body of the lion! The cares, the anxieties, the sacrifices, the tensions and tribulations of parenthood hold a couple together no less than their heady joy in each other's body, their tender feelings toward all the little significant things, the clear ring of a laugh, the unconscious lift of the head, or the sobriety of a reassuring hand. Marriage may hold many joys; but it is only in suffering that has been shared that the ultimate limits of love are reached and tested.

To build a house: to plant a tree: to beget a child — these are the steps that make all the more social tasks of creation possible. Through these acts the past relives itself, starting afresh, as if love had never awakened before; and so, the future replenishes itself with hope and expectation. Even to watch a garden grow from day to day, especially if one has planted it and cared for it, deepens one's solid inner faith for living. And still more a child, or a brood of children.

The basic standards of the past century were false. The family is more important than the factory: life only avails, not the means of living. And if the family is more important, it must claim greater weight in all our calculations and time-schedules, and activities and social plans. We must arrange wages and hours and seasons of work in order to fit the needs of the family; the family budget must take precedence over all other budgets, modify them, and make them conform to its needs. Our methods of financing and building houses, our methods of designing communities and organizing cities, must all meet the demands of the family: give it a foundation and ensure its continuity. In the course of regrouping these institutions and activities, much that was important in an age devoted to money and power will drop out, as senseless and sterile.

For unless our biological and social foundations are sound, the superstructure will be a mere makeshift, no matter how solid it may seem. The love of lovers, the nurture of parents and children together: these are fundamental things; and to bring more abundant life into the world is the only guarantee we have that our civilization will renew itself and endure. Life and more life! Life before the means of living! A higher and better life in the home, in order to offset the deprivations and sacrifices that these perilous times will inflict on all of us. Our homes and our communities must, even as physical structures, express the central importance of the family; they must be built on a human scale, and wear a friendly face. They must be designed out of love, not merely out of economy; and they must be designed to make love possible.

There have been doubtless people in every age who have no vocation for family life; and of course they will remain in ours. Some of these will always devote themselves — and properly — to specialized careers; they will want to live alone, in apartments or dormitories or college halls. Even if they marry, such people will do well to avoid having children. But for more normal men and women, in the days to come, the family will be a reality of incomparably higher importance than it has been for the last century. It will not merely hold them: it will mean more to them. And why should it not? For once our modern age has re-oriented itself, it will bring to the culture of the family a wealth of scientific and imaginative interests that our ancestors did not possess.

On the physical side of family culture modern communities have already, in the very face of sterility, worked marvels. Our survival rate has kept up even though the birth rate has dropped; indeed our achievement here, particularly in the prevention of infant and child mortality, surpasses every other race and country for which there is a trace of a record. We have no need for that shameless animal fecundity of which the race boasted in the past. Nor need women submit to that exhaustion and early death that so often overtook them in the past, when they produced, possibly, twelve babies in as many years. At the end of that time they often yielded their own life in childbirth without having given to the world any larger number of survivors than their more artfully sterile sisters today.

There is no doubt, in America, of the superior physical health of children who have been bred carefully, in families that possess both economic means and affectionate intelligence. Their moral and æsthetic and social life, however, is not so indisputably in advance of past periods; even the utmost efforts of deliberate education, in well equipped schools, have only succeeded in part in offsetting the debilitating effects of our too mechanized environment and our too impassive routine.

The household has become a new focus for contact with the outside world: the radio, the telephone (presently television), reduce the isolation of the home. The wide world is now but a neighboring village. But this development has been too much on the passive side: the family receives but it does not as yet give. The gramophone is highly to be prized, but it is not a substitute for the part singing of madrigals that intensified the life of the Elizabethan household in England.

The culture of the family requires time, patience, and fuller participation by all its members; and for its personal sustenance, interest must be awakened on its spiritual side: its history and biography. The antiquarian search for a family tree is too often the lowest snobbism; but the actual planting and cultivating of the family tree is a different matter. That is worthy of everyone's highest skill and immediate attention.

Every nation has a great advantage over the people who lived even a hundred and fifty years ago. In contrast to them, we are nations of literates: reading and writing are our minimum accomplishments. So for us the widespread keeping of family records is at least mechanically an easy job: spiritually it will require immense effort, before we pour into the work all the love and skill that it demands. The writing of journals, psychological records, and family histories beginning with the here and now should be one of the most grateful tasks for parents: the gathering of souvenirs, memorabilia, drawings, the recording of anecdotes and stories — all these things will build up that past which will form a bridge, over the most turbid autumnal torrent, to a firmer, finer future.

Some of our young people will die before their time, fighting barbarian forces or combating famine and plague. Those who survive them in the family will bear the loss more easily if they do not vanish completely, leaving behind only a few fading photographs. The richer the record, the fewer of them will die. That is the consolation of the writer and the artist when he faces death: let it also be the consolation of parents and children. Life becomes precious again in the family: let us therefore live and relive its best moments — first in action, then in memory.

There are other grounds for creating a book of the family, scientific no less than sentimental. The completer the records of a personal life, the easier it is to retrace mistaken paths, or to put together dispersed fragments. At critical moments in life, before a marriage or a new departure in one's vocation, it is good to go back into the past, in order to have a running start for the leap one must take.

There is nothing that gives depth to life more than such a conscious piling up of experience; nothing that serves as a better guide, in periods of tension and crisis, than a renewal of these sources of one's personal growth. Half of those buried experiences the psychoanalyst seeks to spade up from the compost of rotted memories might be available, in surer form, from the records of the family book. Those are the true confessions that would replace the tawdry magazines devoted to this theme. Such books would of course vary from the most bare and simple annals, done conscientiously but stupidly — and nevertheless valuable in their own degree — to the truly imaginative record in which the novelist and the psychologist would blend their skills to a new task in biography.

The plea that there is no time for such observation and such record cannot be defended. There is always time for what we think worth doing. People today find time for frequent visits to the motion pictures, endless repetitions of radio broadcasts, and interminable hours of wheeling along glib highways. They are well equipped and ready for any kind of passive, semi-automatic activity, provided it makes no serious demands on them. Our time is our own, to use well or ill. If people were concerned with their personal relations, their love relations, and their family relations as seriously as they are concerned with a more mechanized routine, they would have plenty of time for it. What has been lacking is interest. For the majority of the passing generation domestic life was just not living.

Yet was it not absurd that our children should grow up without ever knowing their parents even in retrospect? That parents should often involve themselves in heavy labor on behalf of their children, without having the opportunity to participate as sympathetic observers in their growth? The parents themselves miss those precious moments when growth reveals itself in a gesture, an act, or a sudden word; and the child in turn misses the feeling of stability he needs through the mere upright presence of those whom he loves and respects. This task of watchful intercourse cannot be entirely transferred to teachers, though of course there must be something of the parent in every good teacher, as there is something of the teacher in every competent parent.

I recall the confession of a young German girl who had lived through the desperate inflation period in Germany. Her parents had been rich; and she scarcely knew them in their period of prosperity, since her time was spent with governesses, tutors, chauffeurs. As a result of the inflation they lost their fortune; and instead of living in a luxurious house, with a greenhouse that provided flowers, they moved to a cottage near the country, and they used to go out as a family for walks afield over the weekend, picking wild flowers by the roadside. She looked back to that period as the most enjoyable one in her life: one that gave her for the first time what she as a child had desired — two interested and amusing parents.

Need I add what happened when " prosperity " came back? As soon as money returned, the real goods of life diminished. Her parents, despite their own obvious pleasure in this simple existence, dropped back into the routine of fashionable society.

Here, then, is the very core of a fresh culture: the cultivation of the family. Biological cultivation; care and responsibility in mating; development of the erotic ritual; rational spacing of births; and finally a new joy in fecundity itself, even if the coming of an extra child means the curtailment of some familiar mechanical luxury. The times in which we live will require the strictest asceticism in the purchase of a hundred oddments we once thought essential: even those who can afford motor cars will have to watch their petrol. But in compensation, every family that is conscious of itself as a family, conscious of its unity and its destiny, will have an opportunity to enjoy the wealth of the poor: children.

Social cultivation of the family springs out of this biological root. The old arts of the household, from cooking to good manners, and the new arts of the household, including the exquisite nurture and observation of the young — these arts will stimulate vital interests and beget more durable joys. They will utilize everyone's emotional and intellectual capacities, up to the limits of his growth. The family book and the personal record will accompany this nurture; and so people will hand on, first from day to day, and then from generation to generation, the oldest and toughest of human traditions — and the youngest and dearest.

The great capacity of the Jews and the Chinese, above all other peoples, to survive the cancerous attacks of dehumanized power has derived from their sense of the family: their loyalty to the generations behind them and those yet to come. If we recover that sense nothing will shake us; no disaster that may in the meanwhile lie in wait for us will cause us to lose our faith in what is still to come. Except where commercial farming and high finance have displaced rural life with one-crop farms, and left behind a sour and sapless life, the open country still holds the germ of a more vital economy. More than half our people are still within reach of mother earth; and already the growth of our cities during the last decade shows a slowing up.

We have enough people on the land, and enough of the tradition of the family vaguely left, to form the core of a new economy to displace the now discredited economy of paper profits, paper joys, and paper wealth. Out on the pastures and the prairies, in the cornland and the grassland and the wheatland and the vineland, life still holds its own: the cows with their calves, the mares with their foals, and mothers with their children.

Be fruitful, not prudent: increase and multiply your children, not the ciphers in your bank account. Those are the sane words for our time. The girls and boys who marry young will taste young love's first tartness, and have that for contrast with the richer, juicier years of old experience. The young people who dare to have a child, though they must use a basket for a crib, will have a better reward than if they save their dollars for a swell layette and crib and carriage — and miss the baby. Those who have no old home to look back to may have it still in the home that their children and their grandchildren will look back to. Life will go on through the dark days and the scrimping days because the real demands of life are simple and direct — much more direct and simple than those who see only the complicated scaffolding of our power civilization have dared to dream. When one removes that heavy scantling, the outlines of life's structure itself are plain.

The culture of the family will be our first great simplification of life, our first act of restoring faith for the living. He who has dropped a seed into a garden or into a woman's womb is ready to fight for the right of that seed to grow and fulfill itself. He who has stood by it and nurtured it is himself in the line of growth. Many other conditions are necessary for the good life; but this bottoms them all.

The " New Man " and the " New Woman "

For both man and woman the utilitarian ideal was an anti-biological one; but in woman the results were more conspicuously disastrous.

In literature the utilitarian man has had many incarnations and since he is an ideal type, it is perhaps in fiction that we should examine him. Dickens in *Hard Times* was perhaps the first to define him in his gaunt, unrelieved outlines: his classic portraits of Gradgrind and Bounderby, the educator and the businessman, have the merit of portraying both the spiritual and the temporal aspects of this new personality. What were their fundamental principles and their aspirations? What figure emerged as the fulfillment of at least three centuries of indoctrination, inventive effort, and organization?

First, the utilitarian man believed in work: for him activity was not rhythmically counterbalanced by passivity, and experiment with contemplation: but a high pitch of continued busy-ness was a mark of the truly happy and successful man. He confused use with profit, profit with well-being, and well-being with the maximum consumption of goods: the good life consisted in whatever contributed to the process of industrial production. All that mattered must be expressed in terms of work or directly or indirectly contribute to efficiency in work: the business office, the factory, the mill, the mine were the real seats of living, and those who preferred to hunt on the moors, to fish in a shady pool, to make love on a hilltop, or to paint pictures in a studio were mere triflers with life.

So much of the utilitarian man's libido poured into work that his sexual impulses were depleted of energy by his daily routine: the factory performed the same office in the new economy that relentless athletics was supposed to achieve in the boy's boarding school. But this fact increased the need for sexual surrogates, for sublimations that should lend themselves to utilitarian effort. The asceticism of industry was counterbalanced by a religion of comfort: and a good part of industrial effort turned itself to the provision of comforts. In the end, this led to the perversion of the utilitarian ideal itself: witness the American motor car whose technical backwardness during the nineteen-thirties was duly concealed under more luxurious provisions of cigarette lighters, upholstery, and brightwork.

The insufficiency of the utilitarian ideal, in its final manifestations, was the constant theme of Sinclair Lewis' early novels; and the ritual of Babbitt's waking life, with its succession of slick gadgets and over-advertised felicities, points to the ultimate horror of a world in which Edward Bellamy's dream should be fulfilled, and the common man have by right what the Babbitts achieve for themselves and their kind by lucky enterprise and shrewd effort. But in Babbitt, pragmatic perfectionism is already besmudged: he lacks the austerity of Gradgrind and the ruthlessness of Bounderby; into the image of the New Man go expensive imitations, like the furniture in Babbitt's parlor, of the showy luxuries and the bodily satisfactions of the baroque period: the country club, golf and tennis, the customs of over-eating and over-drinking, a half-hearted dabbling in sexual adventure — what are these but the resurrection of impulses that had been excluded from the utilitarian scheme? And which is worse — utilitarianism naked and unrelieved, wholly concentrated upon invention, practical effort, money gains, or a utilitarianism debased and de-energized by stimulating so much of the libido as will promote the sale of cosmetics, hair-waving machines, and night-club entertainment? Obviously Bounderby was more alive than Babbitt, and got more fun out of his sordid but hearty appetites.

When one turns to the New Woman, the results are perhaps even more distressing: in fitting herself for her utilitarian role she not merely forewent domesticity but gave to inanimate objects, like typewriters and filing cases, some of the fierce devotion she had traditionally expended on the family. In literature, the New Woman appeared about a generation after the New Man: she was the Nora of the *Doll's House,* and the succession of businesslike heroines that Shaw created in the nineties — women who take over the masculine role under the conviction that only thus could they earn the right to a complete and independent development. The improvement of contraceptive practice during the nineteenth century put a premium on woman's sterility: that was one source of her independence as a worker, boldly entering the shop, the office, the university, and of her dethronement as a complete personality. What was left was only tepid love — and that is what she offered to man. She was ready to give her body to a man more freely than ever before, on condition that it should not alter her life or make any deep-seated difference to either of them. When she bore children, she demanded a similar detachment from them.

For both man and woman the utilitarian ideal was an antibiological one; but in woman the results were more conspicuously disastrous, and they ramified through every corner of modern civilization. Of what use was it to open up the masculine world to woman, if woman closed her own world to man, and thus failed to turn his energies into more vital channels than they followed by way of the machine? Man's efficiency and woman's freedom both suffered from this perversion of biological aims. If exceptional women once more ably came into their own in their special vocations, traditional or new — Florence Nightingale as nurse, George Eliot as novelist, Violet Paget as writer, Jane Harrison as archaeologist, Marie Curie as physicist, Mary Cassatt as painter, and Jane Addams as " Abbess of Hull House " — women as a class missed their true vocation by their mechanical mimesis of masculine ideals, and by their acceptance of the utilitarian environment as the real world. Woman lost interest, above all she lost confidence, in her own form of life-play.

Precisely those who thought of themselves as most advanced, like the wife of Havelock Ellis, were in fact the farthest in the rear, and the new life that they sought to exemplify and boldly preached was by nature sterile, self-defeating: so that the suicide of Hedda Gabler was the proper symbol of that false emancipation. Shaw's spinsterly influence here was almost as active as Rousseau's had been in the eighteenth century, and unfortunately his sanifying laughter was partly the product of his own emotional immaturity; for his serious efforts to de-emotionalize sexual attachment and to rationalize domesticity were achieved only by doing violence to love itself. In practice Shaw's Life-Force stopped short at procreation. By dissociating her love-life from her life-work the woman who followed Shaw became a seeker for power, like utilitarian man: seeking power through sex, she lacked the humility to surrender as either lover or parent — and so ultimately she deprived herself of even her sexual satisfaction.

Individuation and Socialization

> Good planning is an attempt to keep the whole environment
> in a state of dynamic equilibrium.

The modes of sociality and individuality are undergoing
radical changes. In the past, each of these attitudes stood for
a whole theory of society: they came before us as social and
political philosophies, clustered around the dogmas of private
property and individual liberty that had taken shape in the
eighteenth century. They were looked upon as alternatives.
Individualism was a theory that believed in the existence of
atomic individuals as a primary fact. It held that these individuals had an inherent right to possess property and enjoy
personal protection under the laws, and that no laws abrogat-
ing that species of personal freedom founded upon private
property were valid. Socialism, in all its diverse manifestations, regarded the community as a primary fact, and it
treated the welfare of the community as more important than
the claims of any atomic individual to special protection or
sustenance.

In actual practice, both these doctrines, during the last century, presented a sinister aspect. Masquerading under the
noble slogans of the rights of man, pretending to continue its
old war on despotic power, individualism established itself as
the claim of small groups of privileged people to exploit the
work of other men on the basis of a monopoly, partial or complete, of land, capital, credit, and the machinery of production. For the single despotism of the king, it substituted a
multitude of petty, and not so petty, despots: industrialists,
financiers, robber barons. "Socialism," on the other hand,
has meant in practice the unlimited capacity of the govern-

ment and the armed forces of the state to impose obedience and co-operation upon its subjects in time of war: pushed to its extreme, it becomes the state-deification of fascism and the unity of war-dictatorship. " Individualism " rested on the doctrine of the " free market " in which price exercises the functions of an almighty providence; " socialism " rested on the doctrine of the closed frontier, in which every human activity within, thought itself, is subjected to state monopoly. The inequalities of the first and the uniformities of the second were equally oppressive to a good society.

In the senses in which individualism and socialism have gained currency, both are mythological distortions of the underlying facts of community life: the processes of individuation and socialization. In actuality, these terms are alternatives only in the sense that north and south are alternatives. They indicate directions of motion, without giving any descriptive reference to the goal to be reached. No human society is conceivable in which, to some degree, both tendencies did not play an active part.

As concerns origins, the social theory is largely correct: society exists as a fact in nature, and without an underlying symbiosis no single member could survive. The more primitive the state of existence, the greater the influence of brute compulsion and irrational but coercive taboo. The separation of the individual from the generic is a social fact that occurs only in those socialized animals that have some extra-organic means of inheritance; otherwise individuality is a matter of accident and latent tendency. Only through a specific social heritage, beginning with the art of language, can individuation arise. The individual, left to himself, is not a source. Left to himself, indeed, he would starve, go mad.

As concerns emergents, however, the theory of individuation is a fact. When the apparatus of socialization becomes more adequate, through language, through the written word, through the division of labor, through the development of cities, special forms arise in the hitherto less differentiated mass. Each group, each community, each vocation, each habitat creates new patterns of individuality: by their inter-action in the close medium of the city, they provide endless permutations and combinations in all its members. The common environment provides an underlying unity: the city itself may become the cohesive symbol of that unity: but within that common environment all the differentiations of a true culture arise with a wealth of example hitherto un-explored. Through intermixture of stocks and races in the city, the biological inheritance, in turn, combines with the equally complicated facts of social inheritance: these facts are individuated from moment to moment as personal experience. For practical purposes one often forgets the fact of individua-tion: but by intercourse with a de-individuated person, whose full human inheritance has been ideologically castrated, one realizes the difference between the deadened oneness of totali-tarian doctrine and the vital and many-faceted product of a genuine community, in which social conflicts and cultural intermixtures play an active part.

Both individuation and socialization must be respected in the design of cities and their separate structures. Unfortu-nately, working under the false mythology of individualism, our modern capitalist societies have in the past assigned values to " individual effort " in precisely those departments where standardized practices and socialized controls are necessary. The right of an individual property owner to obtain by pur-chase or inheritance a parcel of land, and to use it entirely at his own pleasure under minor legal regulation, has been treated as sacrosanct; and the gains that have followed the col-lective procedures of science, the collective discoveries of technics, have been permitted to go, like ground rents, to lucky or rapacious individuals, when they should in fact have been kept in trust for the community. In a similar way, *laissez-faire* principles encouraged the individual prospecting for industrial sites, the individual parceling of ground, the individual owning and building of houses, although all of these are in essence collective functions which are preparatory to true individuation. Indeed, individuation cannot enter in a cultural sense until a good part of our activities are reduced to a mechanized or socialized routine: only by multiplying the functions of the spinal cord, making them automatic, can the higher functions of the brain be released. This is the essential truth underlying Aristotle's otherwise barbarous remark that a good polity must rest on slavery.

Under an equally mythological sort of socialization, whether undertaken in the interest of a ruling financial class or the power state, the reverse of this tendency has been practiced. The state attempts to impose uniformity and "socialization" in matters of education, intellectual culture, and political judgment where, within the common pattern of the civilization (which "enforces" itself), a wide span of individuations should be encouraged. Contrary to the prevailing doctrine, no special measures should be taken, other than the common processes of discovering and systematizing truth, to extirpate obsolete religions, discarded scientific doctrines, idiosyncrasies and aberrant beliefs: since it is sometimes by unexpected combinations in our social inheritance, or unorthodox re-interpretations of past beliefs, that important mutations are made. The tendencies making for human uniformity are indeed so deep, so abiding, that it is only by providing for free play in individuation that we can avoid the sessile habits, the dangerous encystments, of past civilizations.

Every community must attempt in its structure to reconcile stability and adaptation, standardization and flexibility, socialization and individuation. None of these qualities is a terminal point of objective: they are directions of movement and change. Good planning is an attempt to keep the whole environment in a state of dynamic equilibrium, in which discipline does not mean an even more vacuous death.

The great aristocracies of the past knew that the labor of a thousand serfs, the accumulations of vast congeries of buildings, with all necessary land for their support, might not be too extravagant a price to pay for the culture of a truly enlightened and disciplined individual: in the long run, the millions would profit. But because of the social inequality and the bitter injustice of these arrangements, such aristocracies but rarely produced a Plato. Today, with our vast accession of energies, with our abundant collective resources, we have the opportunity of upholding these principles, not for the sake of an oligarchy, but for the welfare of every member of the community. The base must be generic, equalized, standardized, communal; the emergent must be specific, unstandardized, individual, aristocratic: differentiated groups, differentiated individuals, differentiated regional and civic communities.

From a Money-Economy to a Life-Econmy

The higher the vital standard, the less can it be expressed adequately in terms of money.

In the pecuniary economy that developed during the last five hundred years, there was only one criterion of effort: profit. If more profit could be obtained by baking stones than by baking bread, stones would be baked, even though in fact people were starving. Scarcity and surplus, demand and supply, had reality not in relation to men's actual wants, but in relation to the market. Wants that could not be expressed in terms of the market remained unfulfilled, unless they were satisfied through an institutional life brought over from another period. Money was the symbol of power, and power was the chief end of man.

Under the pecuniary economy, wants that can be expressed in terms of a demand in the market kept on expanding: this was marked first by an increase in the variety of goods offered, and second by an increase in the amount created through mechanized production. In order to make the highly specialized division of labor possible, in an anonymous and undirected production for a world market, it was necessary that wants should keep on increasing: likewise that the rate of consumption should be hastened: by this means alone could production be geared higher and profits increased, or at least kept secure. Saturation of the market, with new production limited to legitimate replacements, would decrease the opportunities for profit and undermine the existence of the over-expanded plant: stability meant, in terms of profit, frustration; contraction meant bankruptcy.

Under this pecuniary economy, the civic and domestic

needs of the greater part of the population have never been satisfied through the ordinary processes of the market. Calicoes, knives, and watches might be cheaper, as they entered the channels of international trade and displaced increasingly the local products, by a price competition which often concealed the eventual inferiority of the goods: but the low wage levels which entered into the production of these cheapened goods made it impossible for any large mass of workers to make an adequate demand for dwellings and for the community equipment that goes with urban living.

This held true in the eighteenth and nineteenth centuries, with results that I have described in detail in earlier chapters: but the point is that it holds equally true today. *Without doubt the prime obstacle to urban decentralization is that a unit that consists of workers, without the middle class and rich groups that exist in a big city, is unable to support even the elementary civic equipment*, of roads, sewers, fire department, police service, and schools. At present it is only by remaining in metropolitan areas, where the taxes derived from the well-to-do districts can be partly applied to the working class quarters, that the worker can obtain even a modicum of the facilities for a good life.

This fact was discovered by the planners of Radburn, New Jersey, in attempting a rational organization of its municipal life and it was further demonstrated by Mr. Clarence Stein in a study made for the Resettlement Administration. It has been amply substantiated by the London County Council's efforts at municipal decentralization: Becontree, for example.

What effect did machine production, corporate economy, specialized division of labor, and concentration of output on a blind market of buyers have upon the provision of dwelling houses? Here again the total inadequacy of a pecuniary economy to satisfy the essential biological and social needs of a community has been completely demonstrated. As the standards of housing have risen, the opportunities for profit through their sale or rent have dropped. In a capitalist economy, this means that production has gone into other channels. Result: a quantitative shortage in dwelling space has been chronic in highly industrialized countries like England ever since the beginning of the nineteenth century, and in the more overcrowded industrial centers, like London, since the sixteenth century.

In order to make it possible for capital to enter this field at all, the qualitative standards have kept consistently below the level of decency available under the existing technology. The dwelling house, far more than the farm, has been the backward point of modern technics. Wage levels and incomes have borne simply no relation to the requirements for a decent dwelling. The failure of the pecuniary economy in this department is abysmal — all the more because rent is the largest single item in a family budget, rising from ten or fifteen per cent among the working classes of Holland to between twenty and thirty per cent for those in other countries. Rents that occupy more than twenty per cent of the total, especially on the lower income levels, mean a sharp curtailment of vital necessities at other points in the budget.

The failure of decent housing to obtain capital through competition in the market has led to widespread attempts to foster home-ownership among the workers; under the guise of offering security, those who have fostered this movement, including government agencies, have sought to burden the worker with risks: risks whose returns are not sufficient to attract the necessary capital from the more wary. This diversion of the worker's meager budget to housing not merely undermines his standard of life: it lessens his freedom of movement and, during a financial crisis or a local shutdown, often results in the complete loss of his entire investment — and the roof over his head as well.

Needless to say, this is no solution of the housing problem:

even apart from the fact that the building of individual houses is technically an extremely wasteful process. Except for the income groups well on the comfort level, the building of houses for profit has been carried on throughout the Western world only by debasements of design: systematic overcrowding of the land, and overpopulation of the interior quarters on the part of those who must eventually rent them. And so long as pecuniary canons remain uppermost, there is no prospect for a change.

What do all these facts signify? They signify that some of the most essential items in the construction and equipment of cities cannot be produced, on any terms, under a pecuniary economy; and that houses in particular can be built only by ignoring the positive standards, based on scientific data, that are appropriate in an advanced civilization. This discovery has been slowly sinking into the minds of thoughtful people for the last century; and in the realm of both city development and housing it has resulted in a series of measures that cannot be sanctioned in terms of private gain and pecuniary aggrandizement.

Housing, in fact, is the focal point in that change from a pecuniary to a biotechnic economy which has been slowly developing throughout the Western world, and which received a great impetus in the decade that followed the First World War. The older type of industrialism chose to meet the inadequacy of income to a genuine standard of life by maintaining low wage levels as long as possible and ignoring the possible existence of a positive standard of life. Whatever the worker could get along on, whatever a landlord could demand, in the main determined the rental levels and the standard of accommodation: even during periods of relative prosperity for the worker, housing remained a third choice in his expenditures. In Middletown, the Lynds discovered workers who owned automobiles of the latest model, whilst they bred their families in houses that lacked even bare sanitary conveniences. Even the worker, guided by advertising, sales talk, and emulation, followed fashions.

Under the biotechnic economy, these conditions are reversed. Instead of wages and income directing market demand, vital demand determines the level of income and directs production into socially useful channels. First we must erect a standard of living. In terms of housing, the minimum standards are set by objective criteria of air, water, sunlight, heat, privacy, and so forth, and further modified by those social provisions which tradition and current investigation prove to be necessary for the nurture of children and the education of responsible citizens. At any given period, in any given region, these standards should set a minimum level for wages: industries that cannot meet such a level must be looked upon as economically inefficient and socially defective, to be abolished or taken over by the community.

Where such standards have been set to a greater or less degree in publicly aided housing, one of two things must happen: either incomes in industry will rise to the necessary level, or the state will tax the larger incomes and make the reapportionment directly in the form of subsidies to the housing — money lent at low interest rates, subsidies to rents to make up the difference between the cost of the house and the worker's ability to pay, or outright grants. In the governmental housing that has been undertaken so widely throughout Europe, beginning with the first efforts in England and Belgium after the middle of the nineteenth century, one or all of these methods have been used. Inevitably. Had the capitalist discovered for himself a way to supply decent housing to a depauperate or indigent population at a profit to himself he would have followed it.

Now, in a pecuniary economy, production for sale and profit dominates: the surplus over current need goes back, apart from minimum expenditures for private display and public services, into further mechanical production. In a biotechnic economy, on the other hand, consumption and service must take precedence. Production must be directed, in greater amounts, into channels where a surplus of energy is made available, either for direct use in life, as house, as city, as regional habitat, or for storage against future vital uses. The benefits of automatic machinery, the economies of finely organized production, the displacement of labor, the surplusage of modern agriculture all mean — if they mean any human benefit — this release of energy for the direct service of life. Whereas under a pecuniary economy profit came through the expanded rôle of the machine, the biotechnic economy will be marked by a general contraction of the machine and, with balanced regional economies, a diminution of the importance of the world market, now to be reserved for surpluses and specialties.

But consumption itself, under a biotechnic economy, is not consumption anyhow, in any quantities, toward any purposes. Capitalism had no need to inquire into the quality or end of consumption: indeed its most ardent advocates during the period of intellectual formulation even defended the adulteration of foods and drugs in the competitive market, on the ground that to erect a standard of purity would be to do away with free competition. Under a biotechnic economy, consumption is directed toward the conservation and enhancement of life: a matter where qualitative standards are imperative. One uses the word life in no vague sense: one means the birth and nurture of children, the preservation of human health and well-being, the culture of the human personality, and the perfection of the natural and civic environment as the theater of all these activities. Here are substantial goals for consumption not envisaged in the abstract doctrine of increasing wants operating within an ever expanding circle of new inventions and multiplying productive mechanisms.

Against the wasteful duplication of mechanical equipment, the aimless productivity, the random expansiveness of production under pecuniary canons of success, a biotechnic economy erects rational goals: the best possible environment for human nurture and culture; the primacy of consumptive and creative activities over the instrumental processes; the denial of " success " embodied in the destructive facilities of war and the mounting certificates of debt which mark the prevalence of a pecuniary economy. But to normalize consumption is to erect a standard that *no single class*, whatever its expenditures, *possesses today*. That standard cannot be set down in terms of any arbitrary sum of money, like the five thousand dollars a year suggested by Bellamy: for it involves the use of a complicated civic equipment whose individual appropriation is beyond the scope of even wealthy individuals. And indeed, the higher the vital standard, the less can it be expressed adequately in terms of money, and the more remote it is from the operations of the market. Vital standards must be expressed in terms of leisure and health and biological activity and esthetic pleasure and social opportunity: that is, in terms of goods and environmental improvements in which machine production and all the devious and indirect processes that subserve such production have but a subordinate part.

In putting a vital standard first, we thereby make the dwelling house, the school, and the city the concrete, all-engrossing end of industrial and agricultural production. *The aim is not more goods for more people to buy, but more opportunities for them to live: hence only such increases in goods as are instrumental to " the best life possible."* Under such an economic order, communal choices become more important than individual choices, and more and more of the activities of the citizen's life are released from pecuniary constraint.

Until such standards are erected, planned production is merely a wishful abstraction, and none of the preparatory incidents of current production, however resourceful in a technical sense, can contribute more than a modicum of their possible benefits to the community. Fortunately, our civilization as a whole is now at a point technically where it is feasible to give the population as a whole that basis in good breeding and good nurture which has hitherto been the exclusive possession of aristocracies.

This, then, is the meaning of the change that has been slowly taking place in our civilization since the third quarter of the nineteenth century. The increase of collectivism, the rising of municipal and governmental housing, the expansion of co-operative consumers' and producers' associations, the destruction of slums and the building of superior types of community for the workers — all these are signs of the new biotechnic orientation. This change is so deep, so pervasive, that it can be witnessed even in places where the profit system, which is its antithesis, has reached a pinnacle. One can behold it, for example, in the budget of a great municipality like New York, which annually spends more on education than even on transportation or street cleaning; one may watch it at work in a country like England, which has been tearing down slums and planting new communities whose tiled roofs are deeply embedded in green trees and greensward. One saw it on a grand scale in Germany when, in five quick years after 1925, before the suicidal impulses of Nazism got the upper hand, one beheld in every department of life the outlines of a new human culture: a complete conception of the good life which put pre-Nazi Germany at the very forefront of modern civilization.

Whereas the pecuniary economy expanded the rôle of the machine, the biotechnic economy enlarges the rôle of the professional services: a greater proportion of the income and free energy go into the support of the artist, the scientist, the architect and technician, the teacher and physician, the singer, the musician, the actor. This shift has been going on steadily during the last generation: the tendency is statistically demonstrable. But its significance has not been generally grasped: for its result must be the transfer of interest from the subordinate mechanical arts to the direct arts of life. And it brings with it another possibility, indeed another necessity: the universal rebuilding of cities for the sake not merely of better conditions of living, but of a more purposive creation and utilization of the social heritage — such a life as men have occasionally had a glimpse of in Jerusalem, Athens, Florence, or Concord.

The New Mutation

The new polarizing element is the concept of the person: the last term in the development of the organic world and the human community.

The re-polarization of the existing creeds and ideologies and methodologies, which now function at cross-purposes, could take place only under one condition: through the appearance of a new concept of space and time, of cosmic evolution and human development.

Such a mutation of ideas has in fact been taking place during the last century, particularly during the last generation. One associates this dominating concept with the new insights into the nature of the organism and of the ecological processes in biology: with the exploration of the pre-rational and unconscious and self-determined elements in human behavior, which makes it possible to include art and religion in our total understanding of the nature and destiny of man. Finally, one associates the new concept with the emergence of a sociology and a philosophy capable of doing justice to every aspect of human life, the inner and the outer, the individuated and the associated, the symbolic and the practical; that understands both repetitive processes and singular moments, causal sequences and purposeful goals.

Now the new polarizing element is the concept of the person: the last term in the development of the organic world and the human community. Instead of taking as fundamental such a derivative concept as the physical universe, our thought now begins with the agent through whose history and development such a concept becomes possible. In other words, we begin with man himself, at the fullest point of his own development, his emergence into a person: with man as the interpreter of natural events, man as the conservator of meanings and values and patterns of life, with man as the transformer of nature, and with man, finally, as the projector and planner of new purposes, new destinies, not given in nature, man transcending his own creatureliness in his forecasts of further creativity. Even in the physical cosmos, considered by itself, the new astronomers and physicists tell us, creation may be a continuous process, perhaps the primordial one, while what we once regarded as the " real " world, with its stabilities and regularities, may be only a relatively inert residue — the detritus of this creative process.

At all events, only when we begin with the person can we fill out the blank spaces in our understanding left by the purely causal interpretations of science. Causal explanation endeavors to understand the complex by means of the simple; breaks up the whole to deal with the part; treats all events as determined sequences, as they in fact are — once they have taken place. Teleological explanation seeks to understand processes in terms of goals, the thread in terms of the pattern, the part by its dynamic relation to the whole. So, too, it interprets the past with reference to the future, the necessary in relation to the possible, the actual as revealed in the potential. From this new standpoint, we realize that facts are no more primary than values, that mechanical order is no more fundamental than pattern and purpose, and that we have not fully understood the cosmos until we have explored all the dimensions — visible and hidden, actual and potential — of the person.

Man's world, as we now conceive it, is a multi-dimensional one, both in time and space. To take full account of it, we must include both its subjective and objective aspects: not casting aside qualities or patterns or purposes because they are irrelevant when we wish to measure the speed of a falling stone or the motion of a planet. Into the person, the mechanical, the organic, the social all enter: from the person, creativity and divinity emerge. To interpret the whole, we must approach experience at various levels of abstraction and concretion; only by so doing can we even partly grasp its dense, inter-woven, many-layered complexity. Even in the physical sciences, from which so many essential attributes of organic life are eliminated, there is a molar aspect and a molecular one, an astronomic field and an atomic field: and between these extremes there are many levels of experience and consistent interpretation. When we begin with the person, which includes even the most elementary physical phenomena, we penetrate life at every level, and reject nothing that is given in human experience, even if it appears but once.

With this new orientation man now resumes the place that he voluntarily abdicated three centuries ago, when Western man overlooked his own creative properties and gave precedence to matter, motion, quantitative change. The order and continuity man finds in nature, he takes to himself, in order to further his own development. Likewise the variety and adventure, the creativeness and expressiveness he finds in himself, he reads back into nature, with new insights into events that remained meaningless when taken in isolation, cut off from their final destination. Through the new sense of the organic and the personal come the auxiliary notions of dynamic equilibrium and creative emergence. There is no phase of knowledge or practical activity that will not be affected by this re-establishment of the primacy of the person.

Such a polarizing idea, when it takes hold in a society, plays the part of the "organizer" in cell growth: it provides the spatial pattern and the temporal order through which every activity becomes interrelated in a new design. The idea of a physical world from which many of the higher operations of personality were excluded, which was the very basis of the scientific and industrial civilization of the past, was such a polarizer: the progressive dehumanization and annihilation of man in his conquest of the planet and his exploitation of power, was partly the result of this limited concept. In so far as the idea of the person does fuller justice to the order of nature and the condition of man, it may in the days to come offset the errors of the past and lay the basis for a worldwide integration of both thought and life. Our machines have become gigantic, powerful, self-operating, inimical to truly human standards and purposes: our men, devitalized by this very process, are now dwarfed, paralyzed, impotent. Only by restoring primacy to the person — and to the experiences and disciplines that go into the making of persons — can that fatal imbalance be overcome.

The new formulations of organism, community, and personality are now increasingly operative in many departments of life: in medicine and psychological guidance and education, in community development and regional planning, not least in technics, where an understanding of organisms has enabled the inventor to pass from the limited world of pure mechanics to that of organically conditioned mechanisms, such as the electronic calculating apparatus. In human beings a dynamic balance is the condition of health, poise, sanity; and faith in the creative processes, in the dynamics of emergence, in the values and purposes that transcend past achievements and past forms, is the pre-condition of all further growth.

Love and Integration

For social and personal integration we must develop the small life-promoting occasions for love as well as the grand ones.

Everyone realizes, at least in words, that only through a vast increase of effective love can the mischievous hostilities that now undermine our civilization be overcome. The means are plain enough but the method of application is lacking. Though love could bring regeneration, we have still to discover how to generate love: as with peace, those who call for it loudest often express it least. To make ourselves capable of loving, and ready to receive love, is the paramount problem of integration: indeed, the key to salvation.

Both in the individual personality and in a culture as a whole, the nature of disintegration is to release impulses of aggression and expressions of antagonism that were, during the period of development, sufficiently held in check to be innocuous, indeed, in some degree serviceable to the personality. The transformation of a benign personality into a belligerent one is one of the frequent aspects of senile decay: covered traditionally by humorous references. Though social phenomena are of a quite different order, a parallel deterioration, for parallel social causes, seems to operate there.

The transformation of hate and aggression into kindness, of destructiveness into life-furthering activities, depends upon our discovering the formative principle that prevails during the period of growth and development. Perhaps we can gain a clue to this by looking more attentively at the conditions that accompany senile breakdown. In that unfortunate state there is a curtailment of energies, a deterioration of organic functions, an undercurrent of frustration due to inadequate co-ordination, an increase of uncertainty and anxiety, and a steady shortening of the future; with this goes a shriveling of interest in activities that lie outside the visible present — such a withdrawal as will eventually reduce life to the body's concern with food and evacuation. So the withdrawal of love and the rise of aggression go hand in hand; for love is a capacity for embracing otherness, for widening the circle of interests in which the self may operate, for begetting new forms of life.

Integration proceeds by just the opposite route: a deliberate heightening of every organic function; a release of impulses from circumstances that irrationally thwarted them; richer and more complex patterns of activity; an esthetic heightening of anticipated realizations; a steady lengthening of the future; a faith in cosmic perspectives. Precisely out of this sense of abundance and fullness of life comes the readiness to embrace the divine. Instead of withdrawing from situations it cannot master in order to maintain mere bodily balance, love risks everything, even life itself, for the sake of a more complete engagement with that which lies outside it and beyond it. On this interpretation, the withdrawal of love is the deadliest sin against life; and the unrestricted giving of love and yielding to love are the only effectual means of redeeming its pains, frustrations, and miscarriages. Those who are impotent to love, from Hitler downward, must seek a negative counterpart in hatred and disintegration.

Charles Peirce approvingly quoted Henry James Senior on the final nature of love: " It is no doubt very tolerable finite or creaturely love to love one's own in another, to love another in conformity to one's self; but nothing can be in more flagrant contrast with creative Love, all whose tenderness *ex vi termini* must be reserved only for what intrinsically is most bitterly hostile and negative to itself." " Everybody can see that the statement of St John," Peirce goes on to say, " is the formula of an evolutionary philosophy, which teaches that growth comes only from love, from — I will not say self-*sacri-fice*, but from the ardent impulse to fulfill another's highest impulse."

To extend the domain of love, we must doubtless apply fresh psychological and personal insight toward promoting adventurous courtship, erotic fulfillment, marital harmony, parental nurture, neighborly aid and succor. But while the renewal of all these phases of love is vital to the more general spread of gracious and loving ways thoughout society, even this is not enough. Love is concerned, fundamentally, with the nurture of life at every occasion: it is the practice of be-stowing life on other creatures and receiving life from them. Love is egocentric and partial until it can also embrace all the dumb creatures who unconsciously participate in the wider scheme of life, until it bestows itself on those who will never thank one, because they are unconscious of our gift or because they are unborn; until it embraces those who would do one injury, prompting us to treat them with dignity and gener-osity, as warriors in reputedly more barbaric ages often treated the enemy.

So it follows that part of our love must be expressed by our relation to all living organisms and organic structures; some of our love must go to sea and river and soil, restraining care-less exploitation and pollution; the trees and wild creatures of the forest, the fish in the rivers, are as subject to our affection-ate care as the dogs or the cats who live in closer dependence on us. Consider the systematic wiping out of the natural landscape and the withdrawal from rural occupations and rural ways that took place during the past century: the spread of megalopolitan deserts undercuts love at its very base because it removes man's sense of active partnership and fellowship in the common processes of growth, which bind him to other organisms. When such habits prevail, love is reduced to a thin verbal precept, not a daily practice — a precept to be cynically disregarded on more intimate occasions as well.

For social and personal integration we must develop the small life-promoting occasions for love as well as the grand ones. Not a day, then, without nurturing or furthering life; without repairing some deficiency of love in our homes, our villages, our cities; without caring for a child, visiting the sick, tending a garden, or making at least some token payment of good manners on this common debt. But likewise not a day without some more smiling expression of the delights of love: generous evidence of what William Blake called " the lineaments of satisfied desire." Not just succor and service are the expression of love: beauty is its oldest witness.

Now beauty, as Plato taught, is the tangible proof of love: both in its incitement and its consummation. Beauty of movement and gesture; beauty of bodily form and costume and manner; beauty that leaps to life in dance or song; beauty as simple people know it in their daily life — the folk of Hawaii, Bali, Mexico, Brazil, or those little islands of farmers and fisherfolk that preserve their old dances and their old songs, full of disciplined passion, in the midst of the drably sophisticated society that envelops them. By all these means, when life is not reduced to a mechanical regimen, we make the love in our souls visible to others, courting their approval and their cooperation, moving them by way of art into a closer union.

When Erasmus came to England he was delighted to find that the Englishwomen of that day habitually saluted the newcomer with a kiss, out of affectionate courtesy; and what could have been a better proof of their sound erotic life? — a life that was to break forth, presently, into such a lyric poetry as only a woodland of mating birds might produce. " Come live with me and be my love! " Though one may not or can not usually carry out that invitation, it ought to hover over the threshold of all human meetings; and where social relations are healthy, and love itself has not become sick with denial, art may honestly serve as surrogate for love: the social blessing bestowed for the personal blessing withheld.

When love takes slow rise in a thousand tiny rivulets, con-
verging from every part of the landscape, even erotic passion
will cut a deeper channel, instead of breaking forth, as it now
too often does, like a flash flood that spreads ruin to the lovers
and in a short while leaves behind the same arid waste it had
suddenly overwhelmed. Love is not simply the insidious
potion, the almost morbid poison, Tristan and Iseult found it:
love, conscious and unconscious, is the daily food of all living
creatures — the means of living, the proof of their capacity to
live, the ultimate blessing of their life. The final criticism of
Western civilization, as it has developed these last four centuries, is that it has produced the sterile, loveless world of the
machine: hostile to life and now capable, if modern man's
compulsive irrationalities increase, of bringing all life to an end.
To open the way to love, by a score of daily acts, is the first
step toward integration: not salvation merely through orgasms, but the possibility of creative fulfillment through an
ever-widening partnership with life.

The Renewal of Life

The balanced person treats his own situation, however formidable or threatening, as the raw material he must master and
mold.

One phase of civilization does not replace another as a unit,
in the way that a guard assigned to sentry duty takes over its
post. For a while they mingle confusedly, until a moment
comes when one realizes that the entire scene has changed
and all the actors are different. So with the internal change
that will produce the new person. After a transition period
a critical point will come when it will be plain that the new
personality has at last matured and that those who wear a different mask look oddly antiquated and are " out of the picture." Though the object of this change is to make possible
a new drama of culture, no one who understands the social
process would pretend to write the lines or to describe, in any
detail, the action and plot; for it is part of the very nature of
the living drama that these things must be left to the actors.
If here and there I have ventured to anticipate the next moves,
it is only because the first steps have already been taken.

How shall one describe the balanced man and woman, considered as an ideal type? Let me begin with a negative description. He no longer belongs exclusively to a single culture, identifies himself with a single area of the earth, or
conceives himself as in possession, through his religion or his
science, of an exclusive key to truth; nor does he pride himself
on his race or his nationality, as if the accidents of birth were
in some way specially laudable: that democratic parody of
ancient feudal pride. His roots in his region, his family, his
neighborhood will be deep, and that depth itself will be a tie
with other men: but one part of his nature stays constantly in

touch with the larger world through both his religion and his politics, and remains open to its influences and its demands.

The balanced man has the mobility of the migratory worker of the nineteenth century without his rootlessness; he has the friendliness toward people of other cultures that we see most admirably in the native Hawaiian; and with the habits so engendered goes a lessening of his conceit over what is exclusively indigenous. With respect to his own region, he observes two rules: first he cultivates every part of it to its utmost, not merely because it is near and dear, but because it can thus contribute its specialties and individualities to other places and peoples; and second, when he finds his own region deficient in what is essential for full human growth, he reaches out, to the ends of the earth if need be, to bring into it what is missing — seeking the best and making it his own, as Emerson and Thoreau, in little Concord, reached out for the Hindu and Persian classics.

Into the balance of the new man, accordingly, will go elements that are not native to his race, his culture, his region, even if the place he identifies himself with be as large and multifarious as Europe. The savor of his own idiosyncrasy and individuality will be brought out, rather than lessened, by this inclusiveness. So in him the old divisions between townsman and countryman, between Greek and barbarian, between Christian and pagan, between native and outlander, between Western civilization and Eastern civilization, will be softened and in time effaced. Instead of the harsh and the coarse contrasts of the past, there will be rich fusions and blendings, with the strength and individuality that good hybrids so often show: this one-world intermixture will but carry further a process visible in the rise of most earlier civilizations.

The change that will produce the balanced man will perhaps occur first in the minds of the older generation: but it is the young who will have the audacity and courage to carry it through. In any event, the new person is, to begin with,

one who has honestly confronted his own life, has digested its
failures and been re-activated by his awareness of his sins, and
has re-oriented his purposes. If need be, he has made public
acknowledgment of such errors as involved any considerable
part of his community. What has gone wrong outside himself he accepts as part and parcel of what has gone wrong
within himself: but similarly, where in his own life he has had
a fresh vision of the good or has given form to truth or beauty,
he is eager to share it with his fellows.

The capital act of the new man is an assumption of responsibility: he does not transfer the blame for his personal mis-
fortunes to his parents, his elders, his associates, his circumstances; he refuses to make his own burden lighter by treating
himself as a victim of processes over which he could have no
control, even when he has innocently suffered, for he knows
that in the moral life future intentions are more significant
than past causes. On the map that science and objective investigation supply him, he superimposes his own plan of life.
So the balanced person treats his own situation, however formidable or threatening, as the raw material he must master and
mold. But his humility, born of self-awareness, has another
side to it: confidence in his own powers of creation.

Confidence in creation: a sense of the rich potentialities of
life and of endless alternatives, beyond those that the immediate moment or the immediate culture offers. Confidence in
creation, as opposed to the fixations, the rigidities, the narrow
alternatives of the existing economic systems and cultural
schemes: yes, here precisely is the deepest difference between
the new person and the old, who gave to external conditions
and external stimuli the initiative that living organisms and
above all living persons must keep for themselves. Those who
have this confidence are not afraid to break with the existing
patterns, however compulsive and authoritative they may
seem; and they are not afraid to make departures on radically
different lines, merely because they may meet with rebuff or

failure. Such confidence once existed in a high degree among the great industrialists who girdled the planet with railroad lines, steamships, ocean cables, and factories; and those whose task it is to build a new world on the ruins of our disintegrating civilization must have that faith in even fuller measure. The new person, because he has not feared to transform himself, is capable of facing the world in a similiar mood of adventurous amelioration.

Only those who have confronted the present crisis in all its dimensions will have the strength to repent of their own sins and those of their community, to confront and overcome the evils that threaten us, and to re-affirm the goods of the past that will serve as foundation for the goods of the future that we have still to create. For those who have undergone these changes, life is good and the expansion and intensification of life is good. To live actively through every organ and still remain whole; to identify oneself loyally with the community and yet to emerge from it, with free choices and new goals; to live fully in the moment and to possess in that moment all that eternity might bring; to re-create in one's consciousness the whole in which man lives and moves and has his being — these are essential parts of the new affirmation of life. The rest lies with God.

Without fullness of experience, length of days is nothing. When fullness of life has been achieved, shortness of days is nothing. That is perhaps why the young, before they have been frustrated and lamed, have usually so little fear of death: they live by intensities that the elderly have forgotten.

This experience of fulfillment through wholeness is the true answer to the brevity of man's days. The awakened person seeks to live so that any day might be good enough to be his last. By the actuarial tables he knows, perhaps, that his expectation of life at birth is almost three score and ten; but he knows something more precious than this: that there are moments of such poignant intensity and fullness, moments when every part of the personality is mobilized into a single act or a single intuition, that they outweigh the contents of a whole tame lifetime. Those moments embrace eternity; and if they are fleeting, it is because men remain finite creatures whose days are measured.

When these awakened personalities begin to multiply, the load of anxiety that hangs over the men of our present-day culture will perhaps begin to lift. Instead of gnawing dread, there will be a healthy sense of expectancy, of hope without self-deception, based upon the ability to formulate new plans and purposes: purposes which, because they grow out of a personal reorientation and renewal, will in time lead to the general replenishment of life. Such goals will not lose value through the changes that time and chance and the wills of other men will work on them, in the course of their realization; nor will the prospect of many delays and disappointments keep those who are awakened from putting them into action at the earliest opportunity. Nothing is unthinkable, nothing impossible to the balanced person, provided it arises out of the needs of life and is dedicated to life's further development.

Even in his most rational procedures, the balanced person allows a place for the irrational and the unpredictable: he knows that catastrophe and miracle are both possible. Instead of feeling frustrated by these uncontrollable elements, he counts upon them to quicken the adventure of life by their very unforeseeableness: they are but part of the cosmic weather whose daily challenge enlivens every activity.

Life is itself forever precarious and unstable, and in no manner does it promise a tame idyll or a static eutopia: the new person, no less than the old, will know bafflement, tragedy, sacrifice, and defeat, as well as fulfillment — but even in desperate situations he will be saved from despair by sharing Walt Whitman's consciousness that battles may be lost in the same spirit that they are won, and that a courageous effort consecrates an unhappy end. While the conditions he confronts are formidable, the initiative nevertheless remains with man, once he accepts his own responsibility as a guardian of life. With the knowledge man now possesses, he may control the knowledge that threatens to choke him; with the power he now commands he may control the power that would wipe him out; with the values he has created, he may replace a routine of life based upon a denial of values. Only treason to his own sense of the divine can rob the new person of his creativity.

Harsh days and bitter nights may still lie ahead for each of us in his own person, and for mankind as a whole, before we overcome the present forces of disintegration. But throughout the world, there is a faint glow of color on the topmost twigs, the glow of the swelling buds that announce, despite the frosts and storms to come, the approach of spring: signs of life, signs of integration, signs of a deeper faith for living and of an approaching general renewal of humanity. The day and the hour are at hand when our individual purposes and ideals, re-enforced by our neighbors', will unite in a new drama of life that will serve other men as it serves ourselves.

The way we must follow is untried and heavy with difficulty; it will test to the utmost our faith and our powers. But it is the way toward life, and those who follow it will prevail.

The Triumph Over Systems

The skepticism of systems is a basic thesis of this book, but it has another name: the affirmation of organic life.

Most ethical philosophies have sought to isolate and standardize the goods of life, and to make one or another set of purposes supreme. They have looked upon pleasure or social efficiency or duty, upon imperturbability or rationality or self-annihilation as the chief crown of a disciplined and cultivated spirit. This effort to whittle down valuable conduct to a single set of consistent principles and ideal ends does not do justice to the nature of life, with its paradoxes, its complicated processes, its internal conflicts, its sometimes unresolvable dilemmas.

In order to reduce life to a single clear intellectually consistent pattern, a system tends to neglect the varied factors that belong to life by reason of its complex organic needs and its ever-developing purposes: indeed, each historic ethical system, whether rational or utilitarian or transcendental, blandly overlooks the aspects of life that are covered by rival systems; and in practice each will accuse the other of inconsistency precisely at those imperative moments when common sense happily intervenes to save the system from defeat. This accounts for a general failure in every rigorously formulated system to meet all of life's diverse and contradictory occasions. Hedonism is of no use in a shipwreck. There is a time to laugh and a time to weep, as The Preacher reminds us; but the pessimists forget the first clause and the optimists the second.

The fallacy of systems is a very general one; and we can follow its ethical consequences best, perhaps, in education.

The moral becomes equally plain, whether we consider a fictional or an autobiographic account. One thinks, for example, of Sir Austin Feverel's system in Meredith's *The Ordeal of Richard Feverel*. Full of reasoned contempt for the ordinary educational procedures of his culture, Sir Austin contrives a watchful private system, designed to avoid current errors and to produce a spirited, intellectually sound, thoroughly awakened, finely disciplined young man. But the system-maker had not reckoned upon the fact that a young man, so trained, might, as the very proof of the education, fall in love with a young girl not duly accounted for in the system and elope with her in marriage; and that when the system intervenes in this marriage in order to carry out its own purposes, it would bring on a far more harrowing tragedy than any purely conventional mode of education, less confident of its high intentions, less set on its special ends, would have produced.

Or take an even better case, none the worse for being real: the childhood of Mary Everest, that extraordinary woman who eventually became the wife and helpmate of the great logician, George Boole. Mary's father was the devoted disciple of Hahnemann, the philosopher of homeopathic medicine; and he applied Hahnemann's principles, not merely to illness, but to the whole regimen of life. Following strictly the master's belief in cold baths and long walks before breakfast, the system-bound father practiced upon his children a form of daily torture that drove Mary Everest into a state of blank unfeelingness and irresponsiveness. She hated every item in the strict routine; and her whole affectional and sentimental life as a young girl, in relation to her parents, was warped by it. The resentment she felt against this inflexibility and this arbitrary disregard of natural disposition is indeed still evident in the account she wrote at the end of a long life.

Believing blindly in the system, Mary Everest's father never observed what was happening to his beloved children in actual life: for the sake of carrying through the doctrine, he disregarded the testimony of life and took no note of scores of indications in his children's conduct and health that should have warned him that he was working ruin. Every intellectually awakened parent who applied one or another of the rival systems in psychology and education that became fashionable during the last thirty years can testify out of his own experience, if he reflects upon it — or at least his children could testify — to the fallacy of over-simplification that is involved in the very conception and application of a system. Life cannot be reduced to a system: the best wisdom, when so reduced to a single set of insistent notes, becomes a cacophony; indeed, the more stubbornly one adheres to a system, the more violence one does to life.

Actual historic institutions, fortunately, have been modified by anomalies, discrepancies, contradictions, compromises: the older they are, the richer this organic compost. All these varied nutrients that remain in the social soil are viewed with high scorn by the believer in systems: like the advocates of old-fashioned chemical fertilizers, he has no notion that what makes the soil usable and nourishing is precisely the organic débris that remains. In most historic institutions, it is their weakness that is their saving strength. Czarism, for example, as practiced in Russia during the nineteenth century, was a hideous form of government: tyrannical, capricious, inwardly unified, severely repressive of anything but its own orthodoxy. But, as Alexander Herzen showed in his *Memoirs*, the system was made less intolerable by two things that had no lawful or logical part in it: bribery and corruption on one hand, which made it possible to get around regulations and to soften punishments; and skepticism from within, on the other, which made many of its officers incapable of carrying out with conviction and therefore with rigor the tasks imposed. In contrast, one may note in passing, the relative " purity " of the

present Soviet Russian regime serves to buttress its inhu-
manity.

This tendency toward laxity, corruption, disorder, is the
only thing that enables a system to escape self-asphyxiation:
for a system is in effect an attempt to make men breathe
carbon dioxide or oxygen alone, without the other compo-
nents of air, with effects that are either temporarily exhilarat-
ing or soporific, but in the end must be lethal: since though
each of these gases is necessary for life, the air that keeps men
alive is a mixture of various gases in due proportion. So it is
not the purity of the orthodox Christian doctrine that has kept
the Eastern and Western churches alive and enabled them to
flourish even in a scientific age, but just the opposite: the
non-systematic elements, seeping in from other cultures and
from contradictory experiences of life; covert heresies that
have given the Christian creed a vital buoyancy that seemingly
tighter bodies of doctrine have lacked.

The fallacy of exclusive systems has become particularly
plain during the last two centuries: never have their errors,
in fact, proved more vicious than in our own time.

Since the seventeenth century we have been living in an
age of system-makers, and what is even worse, system-
appliers. The world has been divided first of all into two
general parties, the conservatives and the radicals, or as Comte
called them, the party of order and the party of progress — as
if both order and change, stability and variation, continuity
and novelty, were not equally fundamental attributes of life.
People sought, conscientiously, to make their lives conform
to a system: a set of limited, partial, exclusive principles.
They sought to live by the romantic system or the utilitarian
system, to be wholly idealist or wholly practical. If they
were rigorously capitalist, in America, they glibly forgot that
the free public education they supported was in fact a communist institution; or if they believed in communism, like the
founders of the Oneida Community, they stubbornly sought

to apply their communism to sexual relations as well as industry.

In short, the system-mongers sought to align a whole community according to some limiting principle, and to organize its entire life in conformity to the system, as if such wholesale limitations could do justice to the condition of man. Actually, by the middle of the nineteenth century, it had become plain that the most self-confident of the systems, capitalism, which had originally come in as a healthy challenge to static privilege and feudal lethargy, would, if unmodified by other social considerations, strangle life: maiming the young and innocent who toiled fourteen hours a day in the new factories, and starving adults wholesale, in obedience to the blind law of market competition, working in a manic-depressive business cycle. As a pure system, capitalism was humanly intolerable; what has happily saved it from violent overthrow has been the absorption of the heresies of socialism — public enterprises and social security — that have given it increasing balance and stability.

Now a system, being a conceptual tool, has a certain pragmatic usefulness: for the formulation of a system leads to intellectual clarification and therefore to a certain clean vigor of decision and action. The pre-scientific age of abstraction, as Comte originally characterized it, was a general period of un-knotting and disentanglement: the numerous threads that formed the warp and woof of the whole social fabric were then isolated and disengaged. When the red threads were united in one skein, the green in another, the blue and purple in still others, their true individual texture and color stood out more clearly than when they were woven together in their original complex historic pattern. In analytic thinking one follows the thread and disregards the total pattern; and the effect of system-making in life was to destroy an appreciation of its complexities and any sense of its overall pattern.

Such a sorting out of systems, with its corresponding divi-

sion into parties, made it somewhat easier, no doubt, to introduce new threads of still different tones or colors on the social
loom: it also encouraged the illusion that a satisfactory social
fabric could be woven together of a single color and fiber.
Unfortunately, the effort to organize a whole community,
or indeed any set of living relations, on the basis of making
every sector of life wholly red, wholly blue, or wholly green
commits in fact a radical error. A community where everyone lived according to the romantic philosophy, for example,
would have no stability, no continuity, no way of economically doing a thousand things that must be repeated every day
of its life: left to spontaneous impulse, many important functions would not be performed at all. By whose spontaneous
desires would garbage be collected or dishes washed? Necessity, social compulsion, solidarity play a part in real life that
romanticism and anarchism take no account of.

Similarly, a community that lived on the radical principle,
divorcing itself from its past and being wholly concerned with
the future, would leave out as much of the richness of historic
existence as John Stuart Mill's father left out of his education:
by cutting off memory, it would even undermine hope. So,
too, a thoroughly Marxian community, where no one had any
life except that provided by the state on terms laid down by
the state, would do away with the possibility of creating autonomous and balanced human beings: thus it would forfeit — as
Soviet Russia has in fact forfeited — the generous core of all
of Marx's own most noble dreams.

In short, to take a single guiding idea, like individualism or
collectivism, stoicism or hedonism, aristocracy or democracy,
and attempt to follow this thread through all of life's occasions, is to miss the significance of the thread itself, whose
function is to add to the complexity and interest of life's total
pattern. Today the fallacy of "either-or" dogs us everywhere: whereas it is in the nature of life to embrace and surmount all its contradictions, not by shearing them away, but

by weaving them into a more inclusive unity. No organism, no society, no personality, can be reduced to a system or be effectually governed by a system. Inner direction or outer direction, detachment or conformity, should never become so exclusive that in practice they make a shift from one to the other impossible.

None of the existing categories of philosophy, none of the present procedures of science or religion, none of the popular doctrines of social action, covers the method and outlook presented here. Not personalism, not humanism, not materialism, not idealism, not existentialism, not naturalism, not Marxian communism, not Emersonian individualism can comprehend the total view that, in the name of life, I have been putting forward in these pages. For the essence of the present philosophy is that many elements necessarily rejected by any single system are essential to develop life's highest creative potential; and that by turns one system or another must be invoked, temporarily, to do justice to life's endlessly varied needs and occasions.

Those who understand the nature of life itself will not, like Engels or Dewey or Whyte, see reality in terms of change alone and dismiss the fixed and the static as otiose; neither will they, like many Greek and Hindu philosophers, regard flux and movement and time as unreal or illusory and seek truth only in the unchangeable. Coming to the practical affairs of life, this philosophy of the whole does not over-value any single system of property or production: just as Aristotle and the framers of the American constitution wisely favored a mixed system of government, so one will favor a mixed economy, not afraid to invoke socialist measures when free enterprise leads to injustice or economic depression, or to favor competition and personal initiative when private monopolies or governmental organizations bog down in torpid security and inflexible bureaucratic routine. This is the philosophy of the open synthesis; and to make sure that it remains open I shall resist the temptation to give it a name. Those who think and act in its spirit may be identified, perhaps, by the absence of labels.

The skepticism of systems is a basic thesis of this book; but it has another name: the affirmation of organic life. If no single principle will produce a harmonious and well-balanced existence, for either the person or the community, then harmony and balance perhaps demand a degree of inclusiveness and completeness sufficient to nourish every kind of nature, to create the fullest variety in unity, to do justice to every occasion. That harmony must include and resolve discords: it must have a place for heresy as well as conformity; for rebellion as well as adjustment — and vice-versa. And that balance must maintain itself against sudden thrusts and impulsions: like the living organism, it must have reserves at its command, capable of being swiftly mobilized, wherever needed to maintain a dynamic equilibrium.